C000186052

DOWNTON AND THE
FIRST WORLD WAR

DOWNTON AND THE FIRST WORLD WAR

Edward Green

Meerstone Publications

Copyright 2002 Edward J Green
All rights reserved

First published by
Meerstone Publications
4 Hamilton Park
Downton
Salisbury
SP5 3QN

A CIP catalogue record of this book
is available from the British Library.

Typeset by
Acorn Bookwork
31 Cherry Orchard Lane
Salisbury
SP2 7LD

Printed by
Bookcraft
First Avenue
Westfield Trading Estate
Midsomer Norton
BA3 4BS

ISBN: 0-9542143-0-7

Front cover: Sergeant William Newman (front centre), Royal Field
Artillery in the trenches, west of the French town of La Bassée,
January 1915.

Back Cover: The dedication of Downton War Memorial, March 1921.

This book is dedicated to the memory of the
people of Downton who served in His Majesty's
Forces during the First World War, or worked
hard at home ensuring adequate food, munitions
and medical supplies were maintained.

This is their story.

Profits from the sale of this book are for the upkeep of
the War Memorial and the general purposes of Downton
Memorial Hall (Registered Charity Number 305507).

Presented

— BY —

The Inhabitants of Downton.

— TO —

A. Newman

As a small Token of Appreciation of the Services

rendered by him, in

"THE GREAT WAR," 1914-1919,

and by this means desires to express their heartfelt Thanks

and Gratitude for the Devotion and Self-Sacrifice which

made possible "The Glorious Victory."

Downton is proud of the noble part played by her Sons in

the Great Struggle for "Freedom, Honour, and Justice," and

in safeguarding the Shores and Homes of our Native Land.

Downton,
  Xmas, 1919.

Citation presented to Downton's servicemen
with gifts, in December 1919 (see p. 172)

Contents

Acknowledgements

The depth of information in this book would not have been possible without the encouragement and contributions of many people.

Firstly, the staff and archivists of various libraries, records offices and educational institutions, who I would like to thank for their courtesy and assistance with my enquiries, specifically:-

The Local Studies Department, Salisbury Library. Wiltshire County Records Office. The Public Record Office, Kew. The British Library. The British Newspaper Library. The Imperial War Museum. Mr John Edwards of the Old Wellingtonians Society. Mr N B Ritchie, Archivist, Wellington College. Mrs Janet Pennington, Archivist, Lancing College. Dr R Custance, Archivist, Winchester College.

My research work and the production of this book has been made easier through the interest shown and help given by the following people, many of whom have local connections:-

Gordon Bishop for sharing the research notes he's gathering about his family history. Bert Blake for additional information on his uncle Edward James Blake who was killed in action in March 1918. David Cockman for the photographs relating to his grandfather Sergeant Harry Noble (pages 89 and 90). Tony Cosens of Sheffield for information on his grandfather Tom Cosens. Vera Finney for items relating to her uncle, Gunner Arthur Jolliffe and the photographs of Jolliffe on pages 121, 226. Lee Flack for the photo of his great grandfather John William Daly of the Merchant Navy, on page 173. John B. Forder for information on Stephen Forder. James T. Fuller for permission to include the photograph on page 41. Adrian Graves of Matching, Essex for additional information on the Graves family tree. Dennis and Margaret Green for family history material. Daphne Greville-Heygate for a copy of her father Major Brian Whitehead's MC citation, and information from the late Mrs Jolliffe. Peter Haydon for additional information on his father, Lance Corporal Jack Haydon and his three uncles who all died as a result of the war. Also for the photograph on page 34. Jean Ireland for pointing out the location of the Belgian refugees' house at Morgan's Vale. Bob and Trudy

Lees for information from farming diaries of Ernest Warren. Sue Light for information on Gypsies and the Great War. Freda Lydford for material collected by Mrs Annie Lydford and particularly for photographs taken by 2nd Lieutenant Frederick Hugh Lydford in 1918. Pat Millington of the Redlynch and District Local History Society for copies of the *Downton Parish Magazines*, 1914-9. Zed and Ilma Malunat of Tasmania for information on Ilma's relations Archibald and Edmund Wrightson. Darron Mills for his artwork. Doreen Newman for the photograph of her uncle Frederick Bailey on page 277, a copy of the citation presented to Downton servicemen in 1919 (page 6) and Battery Sergeant Major William Newman's citation (page 69). Bill Oglethorpe Chairman of the Memorial Hall Committee for information on the Downton British School Charity and for reading and commenting on the draft text of this book. Anthony von Roretz for photography of items. Peter Senior for information on Charles and William Senior and for photographs of his father William (page 263), his uncles Charles and Henry (pages 262 and 135) and his grandfather, Edward Parbery (page 270). Major John Shave for the photographs on pages 44, 110 and 213. Brian Shuckburgh of Hawaii for permission to use the photograph of The Moot on page 177. Philip Smith for the picture on page 272. Steve Vernon for additional information on 2nd Lieutenant Edward St. Laurent Bonvalot and pointing out the photograph of Bonvalot in the *Illustrated War News*. Ken Wilson-Wheeler for his expert assistance in tracing the service history of Gunner Arthur Jolliffe.

Finally, I am particularly indebted to Mrs Linda May Eastman for providing her childhood memories of Downton and its inhabitants in the 1910s and '20s. Also to Sandra Hargreaves for encouragement, help with proof-reading and commenting on the initial draft.

Although the above is a formidable list, I apologise, in case there are any further names that I have inadvertently omitted.

Foreword

My interest in the history of Downton and the Great War has existed since childhood. Great Uncle Ernest is one of the forty-four names of the fallen commemorated at the Memorial Hall and from an early age I knew the story of his bullet damaged pocket watch and some of the circumstances surrounding his death in June 1915. Both my grandparents served in the war (in the King's Own Yorkshire Light Infantry and the Animal Veterinary Corps) and although I am too young to have known either of them I have always been fascinated in hearing of their wartime experiences from other relatives.

It was only recently however, that I decided to find out exactly what had happened to Great Uncle Ern and learn where he is commemorated in Belgium. Through the pages of the *Salisbury and Winchester Journal* I was shocked to read of the somewhat graphic nature of his death. Nevertheless I was intrigued enough to look through later editions of the *Journal* in that year for any information on another relation on the Memorial, George Forder who had died in October 1915.

From the amount of detail given about Downton and the war, I soon realised this would make an interesting local history project and over a period of time systematically read through the Downton news in the *Journal* for the years 1914–19. Although there was often a frustrating shortage of local information and the Downton news was never on the same page every week, I started to gather a vivid picture of life in the village during the war and details of some (but by no means all) of the deaths of Downton servicemen.

Further leads came from the lists of names recorded inside the Memorial Hall, the Roll of Honour in Downton Parish Church and details from the excellent and much visited Commonwealth War Graves Commission web site on the internet. Visits to the Wiltshire County Records Office at Trowbridge, the Public Record Office at Kew and the British Newspaper Library at Colindale, North London substantially added to the information gathered.

I had expected the research to have been fairly straight forward, but as the process continued I was perturbed to discover that three names on the Downton War Memorial were not known to the Commonwealth War Graves Commission. Furthermore other names with Downton connections have been omitted from the War Memorial and the Memorial Hall's commemorative record of those who served.

One valuable source of information I have been unable to fully utilise is a complete set of the *Downton Parish Magazines* for the years 1914–21. These may hold the key to the demise of Private Reuben Batchelor, who was killed in action in November 1914.

If anyone has further information about Downton and the Great War, I would be most interested to hear from them.

Edward Green,
February 2002.

Introduction

The picturesque Wiltshire village of Downton is situated some seven miles south of Salisbury in the valley of the River Avon. Its long history sets it apart from many villages – the Saxon meeting place at The Moot, connections with royalty (Kings John, Richard II and Queen Elizabeth I), the Roman Villa, the eminent Victorian scientists (Wrightson and Fream) researching and teaching at Downton College – are just a few examples of Downton's rich and diverse history, of which many other communities would be deeply envious. One aspect of its history that Downton sadly shares with almost every other village in England can be found about a quarter of the way along its main street, The Borough, namely the War Memorial at the Memorial Hall.

The War Memorial was paid for by the people of Downton as a lasting monument in recognition of the sacrifice of those who had given their lives for their country. It was dedicated by the Earl of Radnor on the afternoon of Easter Sunday, 27th March 1921. Of the forty-four names listed: thirty-nine were soldiers or officers, two were sailors, one was a Royal Marine and two were officers in the Royal Flying Corps. The dead came from a variety of backgrounds. The fallen included professional servicemen, a mathematics teacher, an apprentice blacksmith, a coachman, agricultural labourers, undergraduates, workers at the Downton Tan Yard and a Church of England clergyman.

Some of those recorded on the Memorial were from families who had been living in the Downton area for many generations – in fact in some cases, even before the first Parish Registers were compiled. These include the names Bailey, Eastman, Hobbs, Mitchell, Moody, Musselwhite, Newman and Smith. Others were more recent arrivals in Downton, brought to the area in the early twentieth century by their occupations or the purchase of desirable country properties. Most arrived during the seventeenth and eighteenth centuries.

The alphabetical names on the War Memorial are death's great leveller. For instance the son of the village drowner is inscribed next but one to the nephew of a former Cabinet Minister. Victims of the hostilities are buried as far away as

Denmark, Egypt and Beirut, as well as in the ubiquitous cemeteries at the Western Front. The nature of death ranged from the freak accident to illnesses and deeply poignant deaths. We can barely imagine the sheer terror faced by Privates Elliott and Winton at Chunuk Bair, Gallipoli, defencelessly running for their lives.

Inside the Memorial Hall, the names of the fallen are repeated amongst the 227 names listed on the commemorative boards. This roll of the men of Downton who 'went forth to fight in the Great War,' lists the names alphabetically and includes rank and regiment. With such a large variety of regiments and corps, it is possible to use this information as a basis for further research and to relate the main events of the First World War (or the Great War as it was referred to in the 1920s and '30s), through the experiences and service records of some of the local men who fought.

In addition to military aspects of the war, this book also traces the history of recruitment and life on the local home front – an area often neglected in histories of the Great War. During the years of conflict life in Downton changed dramatically: food shortages, rationing and women working in jobs traditionally taken by men. All these aspects are covered, as are the disastrous floods of January 1915 – by far the worst of the twentieth century.

Downton was deeply involved in the conflict from the very outbreak of the war. Local men were amongst the British Expeditionary Force on the continent in August 1914 and the first Downtonian was fatally wounded just 22 days after war was declared. He had died in captivity 48 hours later. By the time the War Memorial was dedicated in March 1921, another 43 names had been officially added to the grim toll of the war – and there were even more Downton servicemen who perished, whose names were not recorded there.

In an age before mass media the Great War dominated the press and there were brief obituaries every week in the local newspapers. War Office telegrams, bringing news of soldiers' deaths were dreaded by relatives – the sad news rapidly spreading by word of mouth. It is moving to read of the passing of these men and the reader cannot fail to be touched by the tragic loss of life. In the telegrams no circumstances of death were added, notification merely stating 'killed in action' or 'died of wounds.' Families heard stories, but usually had no idea of the real horrors endured in the fighting. Tales have been handed down by word of mouth, through the families – 'We Will Remember Them' glibly stated each year on Remembrance Sunday, yet for the most part these willing brave young men are, unfortunately forgotten.

Certain events particularly stand out in the history of Downton and the Great War. On the home front the proactive achievements of the newly formed Downton Women's Institute helped provide support to soldiers and their families. On the battle front several very moving facts have been discovered during the research. For instance the Vicar's son and Baptist Minister's son were both killed as a result of fatal injuries sustained on the same day. Strange coincidences also. Two of the deceased servicemen (Bob Bundy and Henry Senior) had been baptised on the same day, although not related.

In this book photographs will be found relating to village life, people and places not only during the war itself, but for the a few years either side of the conflict. This is to place the events of the war into the context of Downton in the first 25 years of the twentieth century. The war brought about so many changes to the pattern of English life, some lasting only for the duration, others were permanent. The narrative of the book concludes with a brief look at Downton in the 1920s. To just what sort of village did the fortunate soldiers return?

This book also contains many photographs of Downton's servicemen, their names forgotten for years, faces remembered only by near kin, faded names written in dog-eared photo albums. Stories of many events that were once common knowledge are also now largely forgotten. Those who returned from the war were disinclined to talk of the terrible sights and events, which they had witnessed. There was a great sense of guilt about the comrades they had left behind, and a constant reminder, in the form of widows, orphans and permanently disabled friends. There were few families that did not lose one of their members in the carnage.

Over six million men served in the British Armed Forces; nearly one million of these – three quarters of them from the United Kingdom – sacrificed their lives. Of those killed, approximately half a million were under 30 years of age. One in seven were aged between 20 and 24. This is not a book to glorify war, but to illustrate its devastating impact on a village, with brief details of men's lives and death.

It is only possible to include the events of the war in which men from Downton were engaged, and where possible all the circumstances leading to any deaths have been recorded. It is a well known fact that oral history can be refined and embellished over years of telling. An example of one such interesting story is that of a Downton soldier who was aboard a torpedoed troopship. He was apparently taken prisoner by the enemy and eventually married a German. Unfortunately this and other such stories cannot be included here because it has been impossible to verify their validity. All the stories included, and there are many of interest, have been carefully researched and authenticated.

The 4th Battalion, Wiltshire Regiment leave Bournemouth, March 1916.

Alas regardless of their doom,
The little victims play.

Thomas Gray (1716–1771), *Ode on a Distant Prospect of Eton College*

The Edwardian Summer

The late nineteenth century in Downton had been an era of progress, which seemed likely to continue well into the new century. Stability had been provided by the opening of a number of new facilities in the village, including a new school and the Public Hall. The economic prospects for the area were better than they had been for many decades, not least because

The Borough Cross at the turn of the twentieth century. The cross was restored in 1897 to celebrate the Diamond Jubilee of Queen Victoria. For much of the 1800s the pinnacle of the Cross had been disfigured by an oil lamp.

the opening of the Downton Agricultural College in 1880 had brought a massive amount of welcome trade to the area. All kinds of recreation were popular and Downton boasted several sports clubs, a string band and a brass band. The village's comparative isolation had been eased in the 1860s with the opening of a railway Station at Lode Hill. A degree of security was guaranteed by local Friendly Societies which insured many local workers. This chapter sets the scene by providing an impression of the sort of village in which many of the men who fought in the Great War had spent their childhood and early adulthood. It includes rare photographs of some of the individuals killed in the war, some at work and others obliviously enjoying village life.

The Boer War

At the turn of the twentieth century the thoughts of the people of Downton were with those men fighting in South Africa against the Boers. Unlike the First World War, only a small number of local men took part in the hostilities, nearly all of whom were professional servicemen. Those who did received a limited amount of coverage in the local press. For instance, Downton couple Elias and Sarah Noyce were in the news in March 1900, because all of their four sons were in the Army. Moreover, their five daughters were also married to soldiers. These unusual circumstances interested Queen Victoria who presented Mr and Mrs Noyce with a gift of £5 from the public purse. A grandson of the couple died in the First World War, whilst serving in the Submarine Section of the Royal Navy.

Throughout the Boer War social and cultural life in the village continued virtually unchanged, but the war was frequently mentioned. For instance, at the Downton Cricket Club supper held at the Board School in early January 1900, the subject of the war featured in the after dinner toasts. Over 40 members attended the function to hear the Vicar of Downton, the Rev. Plumptre exclaim that he 'trusted that they would soon win a great victory and establish even higher than now the name of the country of which they were proud to be citizens.' Major Hulse of Breamore responded by stating that:

At present, however, they seemed to be able to think of nothing but this great war. They could meet scarcely any who were not personally affected by it, while there were losses in the district which they all deplored and their deep sympathy went out to those left behind. England had had little wars, but her resources were never taxed as now. Wellington never commanded more than 25,000 or 30,000 English, and they knew the happy results he received. In South Africa there would be probably an army of 120,000 men. Our generals had not had experience in handling such a large body, and until Salisbury Plain was acquired there had been no facilities for practice.

Eventually 250,000 British men took part in the conflict, of which 5,774 were killed and 22,829 were wounded whilst over 20,000 died of disease. To put these figures into the context of the First World War, 20,000 is approximately the number of British men killed on the first day of the Battle of the Somme in July 1916.

Only one man from Downton is known to have been killed in the Boer War. He was Percy Woodford, the youngest son of Mr and Mrs John Woodford. Percy had gone to South Africa in 1901, as part of the 2nd Hampshire Volunteer Company. He was killed in a railway disaster in March 1902. Woodford is commemorated on a brass plaque on the north wall, close to the war memorial, in Downton Parish Church. It reads:

In Memory of
Percy Woodford
aged 25 years
Hants Vol. Ser. Cy.
who was killed at Barberton
South Africa March 1902
Fight the Good Fight

There were a number of false dawns during the conflict, not least in June 1900, when a committee was formed in Downton under the chairmanship of Elias Pitts Squarey to decide how peace should be celebrated. Ideas included a church thanksgiving service, a celebratory tea and the distribution of funds to the poorest in the Parish. Perhaps more controversially it was suggested that trees should be planted all the way along the village green from Pitt House to the Corn Stores. Peace was,

Professor John Wrightson of the Downton Agricultural College, c.1900.

however, to be almost 18 months away and by the end of hostilities on 31st May 1902, the ideas seem to have been shelved.

The Boer War did however have an indirect detrimental affect on Downton as it contributed to the demise of the Agricultural College which closed in August 1906. The war had led to fewer student enrolments and this combined with a revised system of government grants involved the closing or restructuring of private educational establishments. Dr William Fream died at the College in May 1906 and Wrightson, by now aged 66, decided to close the institution and concentrate on his writing and research activities. His eldest son, John Frederick Hulton Wrightson had resigned from the College's staff in 1905. He had served in the British Army during the Boer War and an interesting series of 32 letters written by Wrightson whilst in South Africa were discovered at Charford Manor in the 1990s.

Work

The closure of Downton College had a severe affect on local trade, and many households lost the handy extra income gained from student lodgers, laundry and food preparation. The area's largest employer was Nobes and Hunt Ltd., who owned and ran the operations at the Downton Tan Yard. Leather had been

Workers at the Downton Tan Yard, 1912, seven years before the four storey building in the High Street was constructed.
Back: George Forder, A. Fulford, Arthur Viney, Ernest Smith, Joey Mouland, Arthur Bishop, Ern. Bailey
Middle: Bill Pearman, Jack Harris, Algy Spreadbury, Percy Bailey, Jim Elliott, Lou Hatton, Bert Hatton, ?
Front: Alec Oliphant, Jim Henderson, ? Moody, ? Barker, Bill Barker, ? Randall, George Bailey, John Smith, ? Bush.

manufactured in Downton for hundreds of years and at the turn of the twentieth century a new complex was built next to the churchyard. In 1913 the company became the Southern Tanning Company, but it was still known as the Tan Yard until after the Great War, when the site was further extended.

The photograph of workers at the Tan Yard in 1912 shows three of the men of Downton who were to be killed in the war. George Forder died of wounds received at Gallipoli in 1915, Arthur Viney was killed at the Battle of the Somme in 1916 and Ernest Smith died at Ypres in 1915.

The Indoor Staff of Downton Home Industries, c.1907. Frank and Annie Chalk are front row, 4th and 5th from right. Bill Smith is back row, extreme right.

A new employer of the early 1900s was the Downton Home Industries. This was housed on the East Green in part of a building which had originally been built as the Downton Workhouse and Gaol in about 1730. The stated purpose of the Home Industries was to provide additional income for men and women working in their spare time, but the venture proved so successful that it was able to provide full time employment, particularly for young people and women. The Countess of Radnor opened the new premises in 1902.

At the Exhibition of the Home Arts and Industries held at the Albert Hall in May 1903 Queen Alexandra purchased goods made in Downton. At the same event of May 1905, the woollen materials, hand spun and woven at Downton, were awarded the Gold Cross, which was the highest mark of appreciation possible. The weavers of the winning exhibits were E Godwin, K Newman, and W Plaskett. An unexpected side-effect of the local Home Industries was that it led to a revival in the popularity of the making of Downton Lace, much encouraged by the vicar's wife Mrs Plumptre.

Agriculture of course continued to dominate the local economy, employing many men and women. Throughout this period there were many tempting advertisements in the local papers, enticing farm labourers to emigrate to the Dominions (particularly Canada). For instance in the *Salisbury and Winchester Journal* of 6th June 1908 an advertisement offers 'new free farms in Western Canada' and 'Cheap Land in every province,' but more importantly to the farm labourer, 'Canada needs experienced farm hands.' The Commemorative Boards in the Memorial Hall indicate a few instances of Downton men who emigrated, but came back to fight in the Great War. These included Private Archie Hunt of the Canadian Infantry who emigrated in 1903. The process of emigration accelerated after 1910, when much of British agriculture went into recession.

Leisure

Towards the end of the nineteenth century the local branch of the Temperance Movement was, like other branches in rural England, at its height. At the request of the Earl of Radnor, a household canvass of Downton had been undertaken to ascertain whether there were too many public houses in the village – as there was one pub to every 52 homes. The result of the survey was somewhat ambiguous, but no doubt contributed to the closure of two pubs by the turn of the twentieth century, namely the *Free and Easy* and *The George and Dragon*, both of which were in The Borough.

Despite the closure of two public houses, leisure activities in the village received an enormous boon in 1902 with the formation of the Unionist (Conservative) Club in part of the old Workhouse and Gaol building at the East Green. The club was opened by the Earl of Radnor on the evening of Friday 14th November. He informed those present that he had wanted to open such a club in Downton for some years, but it was only when the old wool stores building became available that he was given the opportunity. The club consisted of a reading room with daily, weekly and illustrated papers and magazines. There was also a games room and further accommodation on the ground floor. In 1902 the club's President was the Earl of Radnor and its Vice Presidents were Earl Nelson, Lord James of Hereford, Mr J. A. Morrison MP, Mr E. P. Squarey, Mr H. Curtis Gallup and Professor Wrightson.

At the club's Annual General Meeting in February 1904, its Secretary Mr Isaac Downer spoke of the unprecedented success of the club, saying that he hoped it would be a 'permanent institution at Downton.' He continued, rather ironically, stating that:

The Club might be the means of doing a great deal of good, and as the young men of today would in twenty or thirty years have the control of this wonderful Empire, and upon them would depend its success or downfall.

At the time of its opening, the club already had 120 members. By February of the following year membership had grown so rapidly that it was decided to extend the premises by constructing two new rooms on the ground floor and a large hall capable of holding 200 people which would be used to house concerts and meetings. A further extension was made to the club in May 1911, when a billiard room was added. This room was officially opened by Lord Nelson and Lord Radnor who played a billiards match against each other. The club survived in Downton for many years, although by 1930 its venue had relocated as the old building was used to house the South Wilts Bacon Factory, which closed in 1970.

Downton's two annual fairs continued into the twentieth century. A cattle fair was held on 23rd April and a fair for sheep and horses on 2nd October. Rents from these fairs had been used to fund the Free School in South Lane, which was founded in 1679. With the advent of Elementary Education in Downton in the 1880s, the Free School closed and the need for the fairs decreased. By 1900 the popularity and interest in the annual fairs had declined considerably. Of much more importance were the annual events of the local Friendly Societies, which were sometimes known as Benefit Societies.

There were at least four different Friendly Societies in Downton at this time: the Wiltshire Friendly Society, the Ancient Order of Foresters, the Girls' Friendly Society and the Wiltshire Conservative Working Men's Benefit Society. The first two of these bodies were the largest and held their annual festivals at Whitsuntide of each year. Both of these societies still exist. The festival of the Wiltshire Society took place on Whit Monday and involved a church service, and a procession of members headed by the Downton or Woodfalls Band. Members usually attended a dinner at the National School followed by a dance and other entertainment in the grounds of The Moot, as the Society was patronised by the Squareys. This was the oldest of the local societies still in existence. It had been founded in 1828.

The Ancient Order of Foresters was by far the largest concern. Its annual festival was held on Whit Tuesday. Again members attended a church service and a parade. Lord Radnor was a prominent member and the Order staged its annual events in Barford Park with lunch in a marquee and sporting activities with prizes. The Foresters even had their own club room in the village. The Downton Branch had been founded in March 1883, with a initial membership of 24. By 1909 that had grown to over 250. World-wide the Foresters at that time had over 900,000 members and over £8m in capital.

The Downton Branch of the Wiltshire Conservative Working Men's Benefit Society was founded in January 1902 with 9 members. By 1909 there were 161 members and the county organisation had capital of almost £87,000.

Culture and Religion

The Downton Brass Band had been founded in the summer of 1889, partly it seems as a breakaway from the Woodfalls Temperance Band but mainly as a new venture for the young men of the village. The then Vicar of Downton, the Rev. Arthur Du Boulay Hill, acted as treasurer and assisted in the purchase of the instruments. Founder members John Smith and Henry Eastman had played in the Woodfalls Band since at least 1880, although they both lived in Downton. Another founder member was George Batchelor, the landlord of the *King's Arms*, three of whose sons are named on the Downton War Memorial. Early press coverage of the band's concerts gave favourable reviews, and even expressed surprise at the high standard of musicianship. For instance the band's performance at a garden party at The Moot in June 1890 was described as giving 'great satisfaction, considering that it has been in existence for such a short period.'

By the early 1900s the band had become an established part of village festivities, accompanying many events. There was also a String Band in the village, but coverage of its events in the local press was much more sporadic. By 1913 it was known as Oswald Coppock's String Band, but it seems to have been disbanded

The Downton Band, c.1907-10.
Back: Jack Bailey, Jim Moody, George Bailey, Charlie Chalk, Ern Bailey, Frank Noble, Fred Blake, Charlie Moody, John Smith
Middle: Sam Senior, Walt Bailey, [?], Frank Bundy, Harry Winton
Front: Sam Durdle (child), Bert Smith, ? Harrington, Ralph Bundy, ? Harrington. One of the Harrington brothers is also pictured on p. 87.

when its members joined up and was not restarted after the cessation of hostilities in 1918.

As with the photograph of the Tan Yard workers, some members pictured in the early photograph of the Downton Band were killed in the war. Ralph Bundy died in the Battle of the Somme in July 1916. Harry Winton was killed in the horrors of the Gallipoli landings. Bert Smith survived the war unscathed, but was permanently disabled whilst working at the No. 12 Veterinary Hospital, Neaufchatel in early 1919.

The remarkable gardens of The Moot were used to stage many cultural events and recreational activities, while it was owned by the Squareys. One Edwardian event in particular stands out, which was a performance of Shakespeare's *A Comedy of Errors* in the amphitheatre in July 1908. It is noteworthy because the company included a young Sybil Thorndike (1882–1976) in the part of Adriana. The actors were from Mr Ben Greet's Company of Pastoral Players, who had just returned to England after a four year tour of the United States. Squarey's interests in local history and archaeology were well known and his history of *The Moot and Its Traditions* (1906), is still a much sought after local book.

A centuries-old tradition in Downton, which still took place in the village at this time, but had died out by the 1920s, was the Mummers' Play. This was performed at Christmas each year, around The Borough Cross, to audiences in the big houses and at the Agricultural College. It was light-hearted play-acting, involving such characters as St. George, Knights, a Doctor, Father Christmas, Beelzebub and King John. There was also of course, a dragon, whose costume was similar in size to the celebrated Hobnob of Salisbury Museum. The plot was straightforward and illustrated the triumph of good over evil. The lines of the play were passed down from father to son, certain families always playing a particular character. Each character would enter the stage, with the phrase 'In come I ...' Some groups of Mummers continue the tradition in a few Wiltshire villages.

Naturally religion was important to the Victorians and Edwardians and in the early 1900s there were four nonconformist places of worship in Downton village, namely the Baptists in South Lane, the Wesleyans at Mill Bridge, the Methodists in the High Street and the Rehoboth Baptists on Lode Hill. There was also the Parish Church of St Laurence. The Vicar at the turn of the century was the Rev. Robert Garland Plumptre, who in a sermon on Sunday 3rd July 1904, spoke of his hopes to construct a second Anglican Church or Mission Room in Downton at Wick.

The Rev. Plumptre retired on grounds of ill health in 1910 and there was immediately a problem over appointing his successor, namely the low stipend paid to the Downton Vicar in comparison with other parishes. The Rev. Lenthall Greville Dickenson, Rector of Brome with Oakley in the Norwich Diocese accepted the appointment as he felt the call. In coming to Downton he had given up £300 a year and a parish of about a quarter of the size of Downton with less than a quarter of the work. He was instituted as Vicar in the autumn of 1910. The Rev. Dickenson and his wife became very involved with the lives of ordinary people in the village and from this compassion and his subsequent selflessness on the Western Front, it is easy to see why he endeared himself to the Parish.

The Choir of Downton Parish Church, 1902.
Back: Joey Mouland, Walter Durdle, B. Senior, George Newman, A. Nicholas, George Charles Stretch, Bowerman, Anson.
Middle: B. Moody, William Newman, P. Nicholas, B. Fulford, Lewis George Stretch, B. Colmer, F. Chalk, William Senior.
Front: W Roles (Organist), R. Durdle, R. Alford, S. Senior, D. Morris, Rev George Garland Plumptre, A. Alford, Frederick Hugh Lydford, A. Mussell, F. Fulford, T. Plaskett (Clerk).
Of the victims of the Great War, this photograph includes Reg Durdle who died in tragic circumstances in 1921. It also has two of the most decorated servicemen in Downton, pictured as choirboys, namely Will Newman who was to be awarded the MM, DCM and Green Diamond and Lewis Stretch who gained the MC in 1918.

Sports

A large variety of sports thrived in pre-war Downton, including football, cricket, cycling and athletics. There was of course plenty of sport at the Agricultural College where ample facilities were sometimes offered to local teams. An annual sports day at the College in April of each year drew a large attendance of members of the public. Professor Wrightson featured prominently in the life of the village and had been a worthy Captain of the Downton Cricket Team, a position later held by H. Curtis Gallup. The Downton Football Club was established in 1895 and by the late Edwardian period it was achieving a high degree of success. A Cycling Club was founded in May 1905.

A popular local sport now virtually forgotten was that of quoiting. This took place in Downton from at least the 1890s and the club played in the Salisbury and District League. In 1903 a new quoiting ground was provided for the village behind the Unionist Club between the two wings of the building. Many local villages had a quoiting team, including a locality as small as Charlton. The President of the Downton Quoiting Club at the turn of the twentieth century was Henry Curtis Gallup of Wick House. The team's captain was Hugh Lydford, who worked as a groom at Wick House.

The Downton Golf Club existed for many years on Barford Down. It had been laid out by Mr Whiteley (Downton's doctor), not long after he came to the village to reside at Hamilton House. Use of the facilities was rather exclusive and there was even a pavilion. Press reports of golf in Downton are sparse, but coverage of a golf match in July 1907 states that the home team convincingly beat Romsey. The list of Downton players is headed by Dr Whiteley and includes Major Francis and Professor Wrightson's son Archie.

Even as early as 1906, there were ominous signs of the war that lay ahead. The Downton Rifle Club was founded in February of that year following an appeal from Lord Roberts to the civilian population of Britain to learn how to use the rifle, 'so that our shores might be effectively defended in case of attempted invasion.' At the club's inaugural meeting fifty local men expressed interest in joining and the new venture was given the full backing of the Vicar, the Rev. Plumptre and Downton Baptist Minister the Rev. E. P. Wright. Colonel Carré was elected Chairman and George H Dunmore Hon. Treasurer. The Rifle Club held its first meeting at the Public Hall on Saturday 17th March when a class of between 40 and 50 men were instructed on how to use the rifle. Afterwards they fired five rounds with good results. More suitable premises were soon found for the club at the old Malt House on the Salisbury Road.

In March Colonel Carré printed a circular appealing for donations for the rifle club and addressed to the people of Downton which pointed out that 'Lord Roberts says it is the duty of every man to learn to shoot the rifle.' The circular further states that 'it is equally the duty of the inhabitants to support those who undertake this responsibility.' September 1906 saw the first rifle match for the Village Cup which took place at the Paradise Chalk Pit off Lode Hill. The competition was won by Mr W Bowerman who was a gardener at The Moot.

Finally there was the recreation for those of greater means, the local hunts, of which two met in the Downton area. Mr H Curtis Gallup was the Master of the Wilton Hunt at the turn of the twentieth century and committee meetings of the Hunters' Improvement Society were regularly held at his home, Wick House. Gallup was the Hon. Secretary of the Hunt until 1906 when he moved from Downton and handed in his resignation to the Earl of Pembroke. The other local hunt was the Downton Foot Beagles which hunted on land near the Agricultural College, the railway and Wick Downs, as well as having regular meets further afield particularly at Bowerchalke and Bodenham Corner.

Politics

From reading through the local papers of this era, the intensity with which the Edwardians participated in political events is quite astonishing. Political demonstrations at elections were common as was reaction to unfavourable election results. The new 1906 Liberal government began to introduce a series of radical social reforms, including state pensions in 1909 and other progressive policies that laid the foundations of the modern welfare state. These were introduced principally by their Chancellor of the Exchequer David Lloyd George. Such radical changes could only have been brought because of the landslide victory achieved by Liberal Leader Sir Henry Campbell-Bannerman over his Conservative and Unionist opponent, the incumbent Prime Minister Arthur Balfour.

One of the more surprising results of the 1906 election was in Downton's constituency of South Wiltshire, where the Liberals took the seat from the Unionists with a convincing majority of almost 10% of the vote. The local press reported that the Liberal Candidate Levi Lapper Morse's victory was in no small part due to the efforts of Howard Collier of Long Close House, Downton. At the declaration of the count however, the crowd took the result badly and shouted down Mr Morse.

In 1909 Lloyd George's 'People's Budget' ran into difficulty, when it was rejected by the House of Lords with its large Conservative majority. Parliament was dissolved and the January 1910 election was fought on the issue of 'Peers vs. the People.' In Downton this election proved controversial from the most unlikely of sources. Writing in the *Parish Almanack* of 1910, the Vicar, the Rev. Plumptre considered the issue of House of Lords Reform and suggested that in order to be a true member of the Church of England, a parishioner must be a supporter of the Conservative and Unionist Party. The vicar's remarks caused an outrage.

Nevertheless the Unionists regained the seat and news of Charles Bathurst's victory at the polls was celebrated with a torch-lit procession from Hill House, through Downton, to Charlton and back. Not to be outdone, the Liberals (often referred to as Radicals) arranged a procession of their own. They may have lost the seat, but their Leader Herbert H Asquith was back in No. 10 and they demonstrated in a fashion that would now seem most bizarre. A coffin was constructed, correct in every detail, bearing the words 'Tariff Reform' outlined in black nails on its sides. Inside was placed an effigy of the Rt. Hon Joseph Chamberlain MP, the former prominent Liberal who had crossed over to the Conservatives mainly because of his opposition to Gladstone's Home Rule Bill for Ireland. Chamberlain was also an ardent supporter of tariff reform, as was the area's new MP, Mr Bathurst.

The coffin was put on top of a trolley and drawn in a procession headed by torch bearers accompanied by people carrying a drum and two or three brass instruments. The procession started at Whiteshoot and marched through Woodfalls, Morgan's Vale and down Lode Hill into Downton. Here the demonstration circled The Borough Cross and proceeded back through the village, passing the Unionist Club en route. The return journey, ended in a field at Woodfalls where the coffin and effigy were cremated and interred.

In the interest of political balance, there was even limited

Downton Railway Station, c.1905.

evidence of the activities of the fledgling Labour Party in Edwardian Downton. Although the Parliamentary Labour Party had only been founded in 1900, a member of the party leadership (and one of the 15 candidates who had stood for the Commons in 1900) visited Downton in April 1907. He was William Ward of West Ham, who came to the village to talk to the Downton Brotherhood. In a procession headed by the Woodfalls Band, the organisation paraded from the Railway Arch to the Public Hall, where Mr Ward gave his speech. He talked about his recently published books *Religion and Labour* and *How Can I help England? Addresses on the Relationship of Social and Political Problems of Today.*

Edwardian Children

Downton children born into that doomed generation of the late 1880s and 1890s were fortunate enough to have several clubs and means of spending their limited leisure time. Firstly there were the more informal local games, one of the best known of which was 'Cross the Bunny.' The young children would form a chain, arms around each others' waists and jump the Bunny. The last one invariably fell in. Mothers would put their muddy, wet children across their knees and chastise them with a sound whack to each word 'I'll gie you jump the Bunny!'

Hamilton House, Barford Lane, Downton, c. 1900. For many years this was the residence of Mr George Whiteley, Downton's long-serving doctor.

There were many more constructive ways of using leisure time, including becoming a member of one of the various clubs aimed at the under-12s. In 1914, the school leaving age for most children was still twelve, providing they passed the labour exam. The age had remained unchanged for over 40 years. Of the local clubs recognisable today, only the Boy Scouts had been founded by this time. The Downton Scouts were formed in 1911 by Major Francis of Hill House, but by far the most popular organisation in Downton at this time was the local branch of the Band of Mercy.

This thriving local organisation was founded in 1903 for the children of both Downton and Redlynch by Mrs Whiteley, the wife of Downton's doctor. It was a junior section of the RSPCA and taught children to care for animals. The Whiteleys provided the Club House with a library, and a nearby cricket field. They also raised money for annual treats, such as outings or picnics on Barford Down. Dr Whiteley had come to Downton in 1885. He was a native of Wakefield, Yorkshire where he was educated at the local Grammar School and then at Edinburgh University. Although referred to as Dr Whiteley, because he was the village doctor, he actually had the title Mr, as he was really a surgeon and physician. The Whiteleys were held in high regard by villagers and in March 1910, to celebrate his 25th anniversary as Downton's doctor, locals collected £174. 6s. 6d. as a special gift. In October 1912 Mrs Whiteley paid for a drinking trough to be placed on the Salisbury Road, for the use of cattle and horses. It was sited north of the junction with Wick Lane and remained there for many years.

Other professionals in the village who helped local children were members of the Agricultural College. The academics and students played a big part in village life, raising money for local good causes. Wrightson taught the boys at Downton Board School sport and who better to give them lessons in gardening than this celebrated Professor?

Gardening at Downton Board School, Gravel Close, c.1898. The School's Headmaster Mr Northover is the man on the right.

Infants at Downton Board School, 1899. Bert Smith is at the end of the back row. His sister Nell is third from the end of the back row. Arthur Bishop is holding the slate. Jack Haydon is on the left of Bishop.

Celebrations

In the 25 years from 1887, there were no less than four Royal celebrations participated in by the people of Downton, the first of which was the Golden Jubilee of Queen Victoria. During the period 1900-14, there were two Coronations – Edward VII in 1902 and George V in 1911. The events of 1902, show how Victorian attitudes towards the *demon drink* were still prevalent. At a meeting held in May 1902, to decide on what form the festivities should take, it was reported that a free barrel of beer had been offered as part of the celebrations. Mr Godwin and Mr Quinton immediately objected and forced a vote on the issue, stating that on previous occasions there had been a certain amount of drunkenness. The motion was easily defeated, but there were a very large number of abstentions. The Vicar said that he would take every precaution to see that there was no drunkenness.

In the event, plans for Edward VII's Coronation celebrations

The celebrations Edward VII's Coronation in 1902 included a Maypole in the grounds of The Moot.

on 22nd June had to be swiftly changed because of the King's appendicitis. The Thanksgiving Service was altered to a Service of Intercession and the parade of decorated carts was postponed until 9th August. Nevertheless, most of the celebrations went ahead anyway, not because of the King's Coronation, but because the Boer War had ended on 31st May and this was a welcome opportunity to celebrate.

As with Victoria's Diamond Jubilee, there was debate on how to spend the money raised as a permanent memorial. In 1902 the ideas ranged from a water cart, the addition of chimes to the Church clock, or a free public library. None of these came to fruition, so by the Coronation of 1911, local people were particularly determined to receive a tangible benefit from the occasion. The Coronation events of that year took place in June and again involved a parade and sports and a tea on Barford Down. This time, following the events, there was a big push by local individuals and clubs for funds to be used to create a permanent recreation ground in the village. In July, Lord

Radnor offered to let 5 acres of land at Wick at an annual rent of £7. 10s., to which the football and cricket clubs offered to pay £4. A committee was formed, but once again nothing came of the scheme, perhaps this was on account of the heavy financial burden required to meet the annual rent.

One Downtonian, Gunner Arthur Jolliffe, took a rather more prominent role in the Coronation Celebrations of George V and Queen Mary, as he accompanied them on their tour of India in 1911. He later died in the war.

The Coming of War

The year 1914 had been one of progress for the people of Downton, for at long last, arrangements were made to provide the village with its first gas street lighting. There had been a protracted argument between two would be companies wanting to supply Downton with gas lighting – petrol gas versus acetylene gas. Each company sought permission to lay supply pipes beneath the village green. The village was way behind the times on this basic facility. Nearby Fordingbridge for instance had been lit by gas since 1867 and by 1914 many towns and cities already had some electric street lighting. Eventually the Parish Council chose the petrol gas option and the Downton Petrol Air Gas Company Limited was established in the early summer of 1914. It operated from premises in Green Lane and its board of directors included Newell Squarey, the son of the late Elias Pitts Squarey of The Moot. It must have been a disastrous investment decision as the company was registered in late June 1914 so close to the outbreak of war. Apart from the supply of gas street lighting to Downton the new company was also contracted for the establishment of a piped water supply for the village. Many urban parts of England had benefited from piped water since the late 1880s. The coming of war severely put back these plans and there was no urgency to revive the scheme after 1918. Indeed Downton did not finally get a piped water supply until the early to mid-1950s.

Even in early January 1914 war with Germany seemed inevitable. The subject was even discussed in Downton on the evening of Friday 9th January at a meeting of the local branch of the Church of England's Men's Society chaired by Downton's Stationmaster, George Stretch. Those present

The Downton Football Team of the final season of peace, 1913-14.
Back: Sid Palmer, Doug West, Bert Randal, Bert Smith, [?], Wally Batten, [?], Ernest Smith
Middle: Rev. W. T. Clayton, Sammy Durdle, [?], Bill Barker, Bert. Newman, Bert Fulford, Rev G. L. Dickenson.
Front: Sid Oliphant.
This rare photograph of Downton Football Team, includes several men who were to fight in the war. Ernest Smith, the team's trainer was killed in June 1915. The Vicar of Downton, the Rev. Greville Lenthall Dickenson, joined up in the early part of the war and was awarded the DSO in 1917.

discussed the proposal 'that war with Germany is inevitable, and that there is urgent need for immediate provision of national conscription.' The motion was proposed by the Curate of Downton Rev. Wilfred Clayton and opposed by Mr H C Spratling. Perhaps surprisingly Colonel Marriott-Smith argued against the motion. The vote of members resulted in a narrow acceptance that war was inevitable, but a very strong rejection of conscription.

While the young men of Downton prepared for harvest and

were enjoying the prospect of summer cricket, swimming in the river and diving at Weir Gaps, an event took place in a distant country, an event that most people hardly even noticed, but which was to have a monumental impact on their lives.

On the 28th June 1914, the heir presumptive of Austria, Archduke Franz Ferdinand, was paying a visit to Sarajevo. It was the Serbian National Day and, during this visit two attempts were made on his life. Unfortunately for the Archduke, his wife, and for the world, the second attempt was successful. The assassinations were followed by weeks of discussions, ultimatums and general threats and counter-threats, but all negotiations failed. On 27th July Austria declared war on Serbia; this led to the mobilisation of troops all over Europe. On 1st August Germany declared war on Russia (who supported the Serbs). Asking the French what their attitude would be to a German war against Russia, France replied that she would act in her best interest.

On 2nd August Germany demanded the right to march through Belgium to enable it to carry out the Schliffen Plan, which assumed France would automatically side with the Russians. Belgium refused. Germany's response was to declare war against France, and the next day invaded Belgium. Britain had been one of the countries in 1839 to agree to guarantee Belgian borders and neutrality. She demanded the immediate withdrawal of German troops from Belgian soil, with the ultimatum that if withdrawal was not completed by Midnight (11.00pm G.M.T.) on 4th August, then a state of war would exist between Britain and Germany. The Germans did not comply.

The population of the civil Parish of Downton was 1,933 in the census year 1911. Over 240 men were to serve in His Majesty's Forces during the forthcoming conflict.

The lamps are going out all over Europe;
we shall not see them lit again in our lifetime.

Sir Edward Grey, 3rd August 1914

August 1914

At 11.00pm on Tuesday 4th August, Britain declared war against Germany in defence of Belgian neutrality. Downton was not entirely stunned as war had been expected and on the Sunday 2nd and Monday 3rd August a few navy and army reservists had left the village after being called up. More followed on the Wednesday and by the end of the week about a dozen men had gone. By the end of the month the first Downton man had been killed in the conflict. At the outbreak of hostilities, the war was greeted with enthusiasm, even idealism. Many young men were keen to join up as a chance to travel and take part in the action before it was all over. Shortly after the declaration of war a group of young men and lads from Downton marched several miles to the nearest recruitment office to enlist. They truly thought it was the 'war to end all wars' and really believed all the propaganda they had seen and heard. Of these early volunteers, several were to be killed in the conflict, including the Battle of the Somme and at Gallipoli.

Linda Smith in 1914.

Troop mobilisation at Amesbury Railway Station, during the First World War. Copyright © J. T. Fuller.

The day war broke out is still remembered by Mrs Linda May Eastman. Born in January 1907, she was 7½ years old in August 1914. She particularly remembers because it was the August Bank Holiday and Linda and her parents John and Rosa Smith made their usual summer visit to relatives Frank and Agnes Deacon at Bulford. Even as a young child, Linda was aware that something was different on that August day. A large number of soldiers were on the move, marching to and from Amesbury railway station.

Panic Buying

The Tuesday morning saw a spate of panic buying with huge quantities of staple foods being bought by housewives. The *Salisbury Journal* reported the mayhem, stating that 'hams were bought so quickly that the supply was soon exhausted and there was also a considerable demand for sugar, tea, cheese and butter.' Although customers were advised to buy in quantities sufficient for current needs, some shops were forced to close, unable to cope with the unprecedented demand. Further chaos was caused on account of the closure of banks until the Friday and many businesses refused to cash cheques.

The huge increase in demand was accompanied by a massive rise in food prices. The price of nearly all foodstuffs increased dramatically during the week. The usual price of flour had been £1. 7s. 0d. per sack, but on the Tuesday local millers increased the price by 11 shillings – an increase of well over 40%. By the end of the week the price had been increased still further to £2. 5s. 0d. which meant the price of flour had risen by two-thirds in less than a week. The price of some foodstuffs (including margarine and sugar) had doubled in the first few days of the war.

The *Salisbury Journal* of 8th August 1914 provides a helpful table of the price increases for the major foodstuffs, to which the author has added a column to show the percentage increase of the prices. A note for the uninitiated – before currency decimalisation in February 1971, a shilling was made up of 12d. (old pence) and there were 240d. or 20s. to the £. A shilling is equivalent to 5p. A pound (lb.) is equal to 0.454kg. The price of bread was presumably measured by the gallon (4.546 litres) as that was the capacity of the dough.

Commodity	Normal Price (per lb.)	New Price (per lb.)	Average Increase
Sugar (lump)	2½d.	5d.	100%
Sugar (castor and granulated)	2d. to 2½d.	4½d.	100%
Butter	1s.	1s. 4d. to 1s. 7d.	46%
Cheese	8d.	10d.	25%
Bacon	1s. 1d. to 1s. 2d.	1s. 4d. to 1s. 6d.	26%
Bread	11d. per gallon	1s.	9%

The Civilian Service Corps

The people of Downton, in common with many communities in Britain quickly formed a Civilian Service Corps. This body of local men is not to be confused with the Home Guard of the Second World War. Its volunteers were not armed to defend the country. Neither did the organisation receive official recognition from government. It did not particularly need to as it was run and organised by local individuals with money and status. Several other local parishes had already established such Corps, including Redlynch, Alderbury, Odstock, Nunton, Coombe Bissett and West Grimstead.

A Corps for the Parishes of Downton and Standlynch-with-Charlton was formed after a meeting in the Public Hall on the evening of Tuesday 11th August. By this time between 20 and 30 men had already left the village to join the armed forces. The Vicar of Downton, the Rev. Lenthall Dickenson chaired the proceedings and explained in a stirring address that Downton was proud of its men who had already gone from the village to do battle in the war. At the close of the meeting in excess of 170 men gave in their names as willing to become members of the Corps.

On the following evening members of the Downton and District Civilian Service Corps paraded in the grounds of Long Close House. This was the home of Mr (later Captain) John Howard Collier until his death in 1921. This property has another important connection with Downton and the First World War, as the inaugural committee meeting of the Downton's Women's Institute took place there in April 1916.

It was resolved that the new Corps should be known as the Downton and District Civilian Service Corps and that Colonel Marriott-Smith of Fairfield House should be the commandant with Major Shortt as second in command. It was further resolved that the commanding officer should elect his own staff. The company was divided into four divisions:-

- No. 1 – Downton, west of Mould's Bridge, to be commanded by Mr J H Collier
- No. 2 – Downton, from Mould's Bridge to Hill House, to be commanded by the Vicar
- No. 3 – Morgan's Vale and Woodfalls division, to be commanded by Mr H P Taunton
- No. 4 – Standlynch-with-Charlton, to be commanded by Mr Hodges

By the end of the first week of the organisation's existence, drill had already been carried out in stretcher bearing. It was hoped that the village would have a 'thoroughly efficient body of men willing to perform any civilian protection work that the authorities might desire them to perform.' Twice weekly drills were

The Public Hall, c. 1910

carried out by the Corps in the early part of the war. As more and more young men joined up, the importance of the Corps diminished and after 1914 the author has been able to find no mention of the Downton Corps in the local media.

A large number of Downton's women had attended a meeting at the Public Hall on 11th August, to decide what appropriate action they could take to assist with the war effort. It was decided to help the Red Cross by making garments and bedding for wounded soldiers and undertaking house-to-house collections for funds. The committee was initially chaired by Mrs Bonvalot with Mrs Dickenson and Miss Squarey acting as joint secretaries.

The First Death

The first Downtonian to be killed in the war lost his life within four weeks of the declaration of hostilities. Private George Henry Hobbs, 1st Battalion, Hampshire Regiment was badly wounded on Wednesday 26th August, in the fighting during the retreat from Mons. He was taken prisoner by the Germans and died two days later. News of the presumed death of Hobbs did not reach Downton until early April 1915, when a letter from a friend of Hobbs who was also a prisoner of war informed the village of the grim news. By that time a further five Downton soldiers, one officer and one sailor had also been killed. Hobbs left a widow and two children.

Private Hobbs has no known grave, but is commemorated on the La Ferte-sous-Jouarre Memorial at Seine-et-Marne, France. The Memorial is situated in a small park close to the River Marne. It commemorates nearly 4,000 officers and men of the British Expeditionary Force who died in August, September and the early part of October 1914.

Volunteers Leave

Twelve of the Downton men who had volunteered for service in the Army left the village on Monday 31st August. Prior to their departure the men attended a short service in the Parish Church and were addressed by the Vicar, the Rev. Lenthall Dickenson, who later presented them with tobacco and pipes on the Vicarage lawn. The Vicar also paid for the men to be taken to Salisbury by car.

Similar services and departures were taking place all over Britain. In neighbouring Charlton-All-Saints about a dozen men had already offered themselves as recruits. Some were disqualified for reasons of age or health, but the remainder left Charlton on Thursday 3rd September. Their departure had also been preceded by a short service in their Parish Church and they too were presented with pipes and tobacco. Colonel Marriott-Smith gave the men words of helpful advice.

From now on the pressure for all young fit men to join the armed forces was intense. The propaganda was ubiquitous, ranging from the subtle, such as phraseology in the local press making reference to the 'young manhood of the village' that 'responded in no uncertain manner to their country's call,' to the blatant recruitment posters. The most well known of these depicted the War Minister Lord Kitchener's stern visage and the accusatory jabbing finger – 'Your Country Needs You!' – that menaced young men into signing up for active service. This image is still familiar to most people even to this day and was one of the most famous – or infamous – campaigns in the history of advertising.

We don't want to lose you,
But we think you ought to go!

Music Hall Recruitment Song

Recruitment

Until 1916 the government depended on volunteers to fill the ranks of the armed forces. The initial rush to join Kitchener's New Army was immense and by the end of September 1914 three quarters of a million men had enlisted. Recruits were keen, as it was widely thought amongst the general public that the fighting would be 'all over by Christmas.' Young men were keen to get their share of the glory. Recruitment continued at the rate of 125,000 per month until June 1915.

In many parts of Britain groups of neighbours and friends enlisted at the same time and served in the same battalion. These groups were known as 'Pals.' The consequences of drafting men from one neighbourhood into the same fighting force were tragic. For instance 2,000 men from Bradford in the West Riding were killed at the Battle of the Somme. They were fighting in three battalions of the West Yorkshire Regiment.

The lists of names in the Roll of Honour in this book show that the men of Downton served in a large number of regiments. There is little evidence of Downton Pals, but clearly some local men did enlist at the same time and to the same unit. Of the names of the dead on the Downton War Memorial, Lance Corporal Winton and Private Elliott were near neighbours on Lode Hill. Both were in the 5th Wiltshire Regiment. Both were killed at Gallipoli in 1915. Later in the war Privates Bailey and Bishop both served in the 8th Service Battalion of the Gloucestershire Regiment. Their service numbers are consecutive (44513, 44514). They were previously in the Hampshire Carabineers, again with consecutive service numbers (2878, 2879). Bailey and Bishop were killed on the same day, 30th May 1918 during the German 'Spring Offensive.' They were both aged 19.

During the early part of the war, local recruitment campaigns were used to raise the volunteers for Kitchener's Army. The first big local recruitment meeting took place in Downton on the evening of Monday 31st August 1914. The Civilian Service Corps marched to the Public Hall, headed by both the Downton and Woodfalls Bands. The Corps' Commandant Colonel Marriott-Smith addressed the meeting which was well attended. Marriott-Smith stated that it was the duty of every man to serve his country in this time of need. That week Colonel Marriott-Smith had received news that his son-in-law Major P. W. B. Henning had been wounded in the fighting.

The *Downton Parish Magazine* of October 1914, provides the following lists of men from the district of Downton. The names in *italics* are of those who were subsequently killed in the war:

Recruits

Walter Bird	Cecil Gunstone	Lewis Norris
George Blake	John Haydon	Ewart Palmer
George Broomsgrove	*George Haydon*	Clement Palmer
Edwin Frank Bundy	William Harrington	Stanley Penny
Bert Downer	Nelson Kingsbury	William Senior
George Futcher	Bert Littlecott	*Ernest Smith*
Ernest Fulford	Douglas Main	*Arthur Viney*
Victor Griffen	*Fred Penn Moody*	*Harry Winton*
Frank Green	Dorin Morris	

The magazine also lists the following names as already in regular service at the start of the war, all of whom were already at the Front, except those marked ⋆. In addition to the men listed, officers Major Marriott-Smith and Commander Wrottesley were also in action. Major Francis of 6th Dragoon Guards had yet to go to the Front.

Percy Bennett	Wiltshire Regiment
Fred Blake	Wiltshire Regiment
James Blake	Wiltshire Regiment
⋆Fred Bundy	Royal Navy
Walter Bundy	Wiltshire Regiment
Walter Burdock	Royal Field Artillery

Edmund Boulter	Wiltshire Regiment
George Boulter	Wiltshire Regiment
*Reg Durdle	Royal Marine Light Infantry
John Elliot	Dragoon Guards
Charles Elliot	Royal Horse Artillery
William Hatton	Royal Marine Light Infantry
*James Henderson	Royal Navy
Gilbert Hibdige	Wiltshire Regiment
George Hobbs	Hampshire Regiment
*Alec Jones	Royal Navy
*Sydney Jones	Royal Navy
**Arthur Keeley*	10th Hussars
Frank King	Wiltshire Regiment
William Lawes	Wiltshire Regiment
Fred Mitchell	Wiltshire Regiment
Harry Mussell	Wiltshire Regiment
Frank Mussell	Wiltshire Regiment
*George Musselwhite	Army Service Corps
William Newman	Royal Field Artillery
William Prayter	Dragoon Guards

Appeals were made for employers to keep open the jobs of volunteers who joined up. The Minutes of Salisbury Rural District Council of 16th October 1914 show the eagerness of

Downton Home Industries and Unionist Club Building, c.1905.

councillors not only to keep open the jobs of roadmen on naval or military service, but also pay their wives the average weekly wages that their husbands had received since October 1913.

The initial success of voluntary recruitment in the area is demonstrated by a report given by John Brown at the AGM of the Downton Unionist Club in March 1915. Brown's position within the Club was 'Acting Assistant Secretary' and in his report it was stated that many of the Committee Members including the President, two of the Vice Presidents and the Chairman had all left Downton to join the armed forces.

Recruitment Drives

Throughout the early months of the war, meetings, rallies, posters and newspaper adverts all publicised the need for volunteers. Men who had enlisted put additional moral pressure on those reluctant to join. Several more local recruitment drives were carried out, the largest of which was a meeting at the Public Hall on the evening of Monday 26th April 1915. The well-attended meeting was arranged by the South Wilts Parliamentary Recruiting Committee and chaired by Councillor Ernest G. Warren of Downton Parish Council. Addresses were given by Messrs. B. Billcliffe, J. McTavish and H. Turney, representing the Committee, as well as Lance Corporal Miller, a Welshman, belonging to the 7th Wiltshire Regiment and Downton residents Commander Wrottesley of the Royal Navy and Captain Gowland of the Royal Engineers, both of whom were home on leave from active service. At the closure of the meeting there was some response to the invitation to serve, the names of the men being taken by a recruiting officer from Salisbury. At the outbreak of the war the Salisbury Recruiting Office was situated in Fish Row, but in 1915 its location was moved to Minster Street at the corner of the Cheese Market (above City and Midland Bank).

The National Register

Although conscription was strongly resisted by the Asquith administration, the compilation of a National Register gave the government a clear picture of the country's manpower

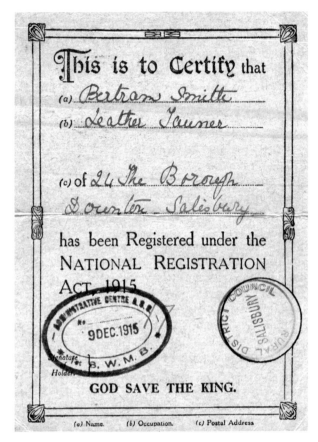

The National Registration Card of Bert Smith
of 24 (now numbered 77) The Borough.

resources. The Register was a census taken on 15th August 1915 of all the inhabitants of Great Britain aged between 15 and 65. It was sanctioned by an Act of Parliament passed in July, to obtain a complete list of men and women with a view to utilising their services if need arose.

Local district councils had the responsibility of compiling the census and in the case of Downton it was the old Salisbury Rural District Council. The Enumerators at Downton for the National Register were Miss Marriott-Smith, K. Warren, D. Warren who had the assistance of Miss D. Coombs, the Rev. Arthur H. Coombs, Mrs Egerton, Mr H. H. B. Harwood, Miss D. Read, Mrs Shortt, Miss Squarey and Mr F. D. Trapnell. At

Standlynch with Charlton-All-Saints the Enumerator was the Headmaster of Downton Council School, John George North-over.

A registration card was given to every person on the National Register. The cards gave the full name, occupation and group number, postal address and signature of the holder, as well as the stamp of the local authority that issued them. During the war they were carried on the person for production, if necessary, to the police or other authority.

The Derby Scheme

The National Register was used as the basis of a subsequent canvass of unenlisted men of military age under Lord Derby's Recruiting Scheme. Under this scheme men 'attested' their readiness to serve when called upon. To publicise the scheme, eligible men were sent a letter from Lord Derby inviting them to attest. Two-and-a-half million men responded positively to the scheme and their details were categorised in 46 groups, starting with Group 1 (18 year old single men). Call up was to be in group order, starting with Group 1.

Surviving papers of the Southern Tanning Company show that the Managing Director of the firm that owned the Downton Tan Yard, Edwin Paine Hunt received a Derby letter under the canvassing scheme in the autumn of 1915. His reply of 2nd November sheds light on some of the wartime activity at the Downton Tan Yard, where workers were producing harness saddlery for the War Office. Hunt's veiled threat begins 'If I joined the Army I should feel it my duty to my family to close up this business as there is no one besides myself who would be capable of carrying it on.' He continues 'The question I ask you to decide is whether I am of most use in the Army or keeping this business going? I am perfectly willing to do whichever you say is best.'

In September 1915 the South Wilts Recruiting Committee approached the Clerk of Downton Parish Council asking for assistance with canvassing under the Derby Scheme and a Mr Butler, the Honorary Secretary of the Committee addressed the Council at their meeting of the 17th of that month. Members of the Council decided to form a Committee to undertake the Canvass with the help of members of the public. On the proposition of Cllr H. Palmer, seconded by Cllr J. Godwin, this suggestion was adopted and Cllr Mrs Warren consented to invite a number of lady helpers to meet the Committee on the following Monday evening to make any necessary arrangements.

Conscription

Canvassing under the Derby Scheme proved a success in Downton. The *Salisbury Journal* of 27th November 1915 reported that there were 'now but few men left in the village who are eligible for service.' Nationally, however, the Derby Scheme was judged a failure. Conscription was the only solution to the problem of recruitment and this was introduced in January 1916 by the Military Service Act. Conscription was a revolutionary move and the first time it had been enforced in Britain. The National Register was now used by the new National Service Ministry to conscript all eligible men. The new law came into effect on 10th February introducing the conscription of all single men and childless widowers between 18 and 40 years of age. Ministers of religion were exempted and provision was made for people engaged on work deemed to be of national importance.

The age level was raised slightly to 41 in May 1916, but the most significant change occurred as a direct result of the German offensive on the Western Front in March 1918. From 15th April, the age was raised from 41 to 50.

At the outbreak of the war all new recruits had been subjected to strict medical examinations. By the time of conscription the rigorous requirements had been relaxed and many potential recruits who had initially failed were invited back. The system of medical categories which had ranged from A1 to C3 was simplified to three broad categories.

Military Tribunals

Under the Derby Scheme, local appeal tribunals were appointed so that men could request a postponement of military service. These continued in existence once conscription had been introduced and now dealt not only with appeals for deferral, but also with conscientious objections to the war. Local Appeal tribunals consisted of between five and twenty-five members (usually five for quickness of decision making). Members were usually local councillors or magistrates. Downton's tribunals fell under the jurisdiction of the old Salisbury Rural District Council. It was quite unusual as it included a woman, Cllr Miss Manning of Tower House, Morgan's Vale.

Unfortunately most local councils (including Salisbury Rural District Council) destroyed their tribunal records, applications and correspondence in the early 1920s, so evidence must be looked for in local newspapers. As the *Salisbury Journal* kept the names of applicants anonymous in its reports of the tribunals, the *Western Gazette* is the best source of information. The *Gazette* provides lengthy reports on the proceedings of each tribunal and gives details not only of the name of the applicant, but also his age, status and medical category.

On a county level the proceedings of the Wiltshire Military Tribunals usually took place at Trowbridge, under the Chairmanship of the Marquis of Bath. Again the committee was comprised of local dignitaries, and also retired military Officers. A typical meeting is that of Friday 27th and Saturday 28th April 1917, recorded in the *Western Gazette* of 4th May:

> *Walter Frank Mouland (32, married A) farm carter of Downton had exemption till July 1st, but a military appeal against this was allowed. Charles Green, engine driver, Downton (18, single A) was refused exemption.*

From the above it can be seen that both men were signified fit for general service in the armed forces. Perhaps they believed their occupations were sound reasons for exemption from national service. The Roll of Honour in Downton Parish Church records Mouland as serving in the forces as a Driver in the Royal Horse Artillery. The Medal index cards at the Public Record Office Kew show that he enlisted in 1917.

Grounds for exemption from military service included conscientious objection, employment in farming, personal circumstances and employment in industry. Examples of attempts at exemption on all of these grounds (except conscientious objection) can be found in the pages of the local press for cases involving people in Downton.

With the obvious importance of farming to the South

Wiltshire economy, a high proportion of cases heard by the Appeal Tribunal concerned agricultural workers. On the introduction of conscription, the Board of Agriculture and Fisheries was anxious for farmers to give up their surplus labour to the army or agree to transfer it to neighbouring farms who had insufficient skilled labour to maintain food production. This increased pressure on farmers was recognised by Salisbury Rural District Council. In March 1916 they appointed Edward Main of New Court Farm Downton to sit on the local tribunal as Farmer's Advocate.

Downton's location on the very edge of Wiltshire meant that some cases were heard in Hampshire, including the following which is just one example of many in rural England that centred around a farmer's son being called up. At a sitting of the Hampshire Appeal Tribunal at Bournemouth on 19th June 1916, a Downton farmer applied for the further exemption for a son aged 20, without whom, he said, 'he could not possibly carry on his farm of 75 acres.' An exemption had previously been granted until 15th June during which time the farmer had made every effort to find a replacement for his son on the farm. He had offered 4d. an hour for a woman farm worker, but without success. The tribunal gave the farmer's son an extension of three months, which was granted without leave to appeal.

At the time of the introduction of conscription many men were declared exempt from call up because of the nature of their occupations. This was particularly the case in the civil service and industries involved in the manufacture of munitions. Such workers identified as essential were given complete exemption from military service, and known as 'badged.' These individuals were listed as being in 'starred' occupations on the National Register.

As more recruits were desperately required, friction occurred between local employers and the Ministry of Munitions when men were 'combed out' of industry and became what was referred to as 'debadged.' On 7th October 1916 the Wiltshire Appeal Tribunal heard the case of three single men employed by the Southern Tanning Company at Downton who had been 'debadged' by the Ministry. A Company representative's argument that the men were essential to guarantee the firm's output was given short shrift by the Chairman of the Tribunal who instantly dismissed the appeal.

Another worker at the Downton Tan Yard, Arthur Bishop

joined the Wiltshire Regiment in 1918 and briefly served in Belgium. Bishop's war service was short-lived however, because he was definitely in a starred occupation and he was recalled to his civilian job in Downton.

Various personal or domestic circumstances were cited as grounds for exemption from military service. On Friday 27th July 1917 the Wiltshire Appeals Tribunal heard the case of Mr J. P. Philpott of Downton who was manager of the gasworks and a bicycle agent. According to a report in the *Western Gazette*, he was 42, single and had the medical category B1. Philpott had been granted exemption from call up until October, but the military objected and forced the appeal. Philpott was responsible for his 74 year old mother. His brother had joined up six weeks previously and his two sisters were married and lived some distance away from Downton. In this instance the Chairman of the Tribunal showed lenience, leaving the previous decision to stand, but adding that if Philpott had been a younger man the decision 'might have been different.'

The Minutes Books of the Downton Parish Council provide an interesting insight into the attempts of the Clerk to the Council to gain exemption from military conscription. The Minutes of 30th August 1916 record:

> *The Clerk stated that, under the Military Services Acts, he had been directed to present himself for a further medical examination – having previously been rejected as being medically unfit – and that in the event of his being passed for service he would wish to appeal to the Local Tribunal for exemption and asked the Council if they would support his appeal.*
>
> *On the proposition of Mr Wookey, seconded by Mrs Warren, it was unanimously agreed to do so; and it was decided to ask the Chairman to represent the Council when the appeal was heard; or, if he should be unable to do so, to ask Mr Harding.*

Attestation and Service Papers

The immensity of the Great War means that there are few British or Commonwealth families without an ancestor who took part in the conflict. As so much has been written in this chapter about the sheer volume of men who joined up in the years 1914-16, some explanation is needed as to the documentation involved in enlisting and how these service papers can now be consulted to obtain further information. Regrettably the building that housed the service records of First World War soldiers and airmen was hit by an incendiary device during a Nazi air raid in 1940. Many hundreds of thousands of records were destroyed and of those that survived many were badly damaged. These, so-called 'burnt documents' were too fragile to be consulted and were only released to the general public in 2000-2 following an extensive programme of copying the documents onto microfilm with a grant provided by the Millennium Commission. They are filed alphabetically in class WO363 at the Public Record Office at Kew.

It is estimated that the surviving records contain the service details of about two million men, but even so these surviving 'burnt document' represent less than 40% of the original total. When researching the records of servicemen from Downton the author was perturbed to find far fewer than this percentage had survived. Many people who visit the Public Record Office in search of their ancestor's service records return home disappointed.

A study of papers relating to Downton Private Bertram Smith, Animal Veterinary Corps, gives an idea of the sort of information available from the attestation papers and service records. These are stored in class WO364, which contains the papers of soldiers who were discharged as disabled and received

Identification disc belonging to Private Bertram Smith, discovered in the garden of his former home *Trevena*, 128 High Street.

Animal Veterinary Corps Cap Badge

Horse-related items made by Private Smith at No. 12 Veterinary Hospital. The watch chain is made from horse hair, the other articles are from shrapnel.

a war pension. Smith's service records amounted to 31 microfilmed pieces of paper, the first of which was Army Form B2512, his Short Service Attestation Form. This was the enlistment form completed by new recruits. This form confirms personal details and the applicant's signature confirming the Oath of Allegiance. The following is amongst the information that can be found on the Attestation Form:

- Regiment or Corps
- Full Name
- Nationality
- Trade or Occupation
- Details of Previous Military Service
- Army Service Number
- Address
- Age (in years and months)
- Marital Status
- Signature
- Date

The Oath is as follows:

I swear by Almighty God, that I will be faithful and bear true Allegiance to His Majesty King George the Fifth, His Heirs and Successors, and that I will, as in duty bound, honestly and faithfully defend His Majesty, His Heirs and Successors, In Person, Crown, and Dignity against all enemies, and will observe and obey all orders of His Majesty, His Heirs and Successors, and of the Generals and Officers set over me. So help me God.

The reverse side of the Attestation Form contains what is referred to as a 'Descriptive Report on Enlistment.' This information is supposed to correspond with information on the Medical History sheet which is applicable to all ranks. There are details of:

- Name
- Height
- Distinctive marks
- Age
- Chest measurements

Beneath this on the form are the name, address and relationship of the applicant's next of kin. Also particulars of marriage and names, dates and places of birth of any children. At the foot of the page there is usually a military history table, showing details of:

- Extra Training Received
- Wounds
- Military Decorations
- Campaigns
- Gallantry Conduct
- Other Injuries in or by the service

There are usually several other documents within the service papers, and from Smith's records it can be discovered that he married his first wife, Elsie Verrell in 1918 and that she was employed in London as the nanny to the step-mother of the late Major Graves. Much other information can be gleaned from service papers and attestation records. For instance they can shed light on the work carried out by the new recruit.

Some of the men who joined up spent their army life in similar occupations to the ones they had carried out as civilians. Sapper William Bundy attested in December 1915. He worked as a steam wagon driver before joining up and in March 1916 qualified as a Field Loco Engine Driver. He spent much of the war working as an engine driver in Bombay and Peshawar in India.

The Hon. Adolphus Edward Paget Graves, (the father of Major Graves), also assumed a similar role to his civilian career. In 1915 he was working as a Railway Transport Officer at Southern Command. Amongst his officer's service papers at Kew is a letter dated 30 June, in which he begs to be posted to France:

Sir,

Having now over six months experience in RTO work at Plymouth, and held many previous railway appointments in civil life, I have

the honour to request you will lay before the Garrison Commander
my application for a transfer to more important overseas work.
   The following is briefly my record:-

a)   *Educated in France and can talk French fluently*
b)   *Trained as a land agent and taught surveying and farming*
c)   *Assistant Superintendent L & NW railway*
d)   *Traffic Manager BNR and afterwards General manager of*
     the Gold Coast Government Railway
e)   *Joined Bird & Co., Calcutta, contractors for railways and*
     docks. Whilst employed with this firm my duties comprised the
     organisation and handling of some 50,000 coolies engaged in
     river and harbour work, earthworks, goods trains and ocean
     steamer traffic (etc.)

Graves cites his previous relevant experience, including work on
the Indian, and Gold Coast Railways from 1887 to 1905. In
1890 (the same year that his son, Evelyn was born), Graves
became a Major and Commanded a Volunteer Battalion. His
letter concludes:

   I am anxious therefore to offer my services overseas where from
my long experience in the East and previous training I think I
could be of more service than at Plymouth viz. either in France,
Turkey, Egypt, Persian Gulf or East Africa.

On 30th September 1915 Graves was appointed Train
Conducting Officer overseas and posted to Havre, leaving
Southampton on 5th October 1915.

The final set of papers amongst the serviceman's records are
usually the discharge papers, documents which, of course
depend on whether they survived the war. Details on the form
include:

- Name
- Address for pay
- Theatre of war
- Medical category
- Military qualifications
- Date issued (date discharged)
- Regiment, rank and number
- Signature
- Year of birth
- Place of rejoining in emergency

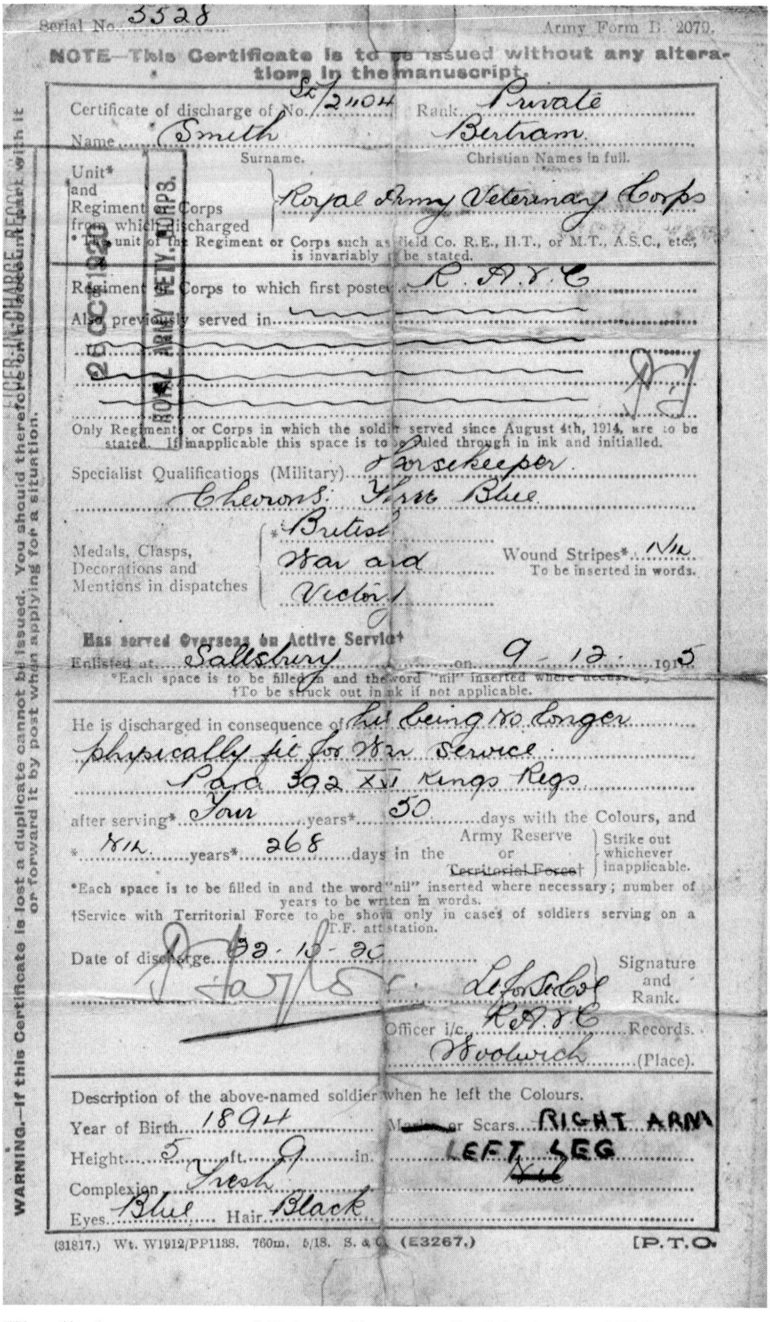

Serial No. 3528 Army Form B. 2079.

NOTE—This Certificate is to be issued without any alterations in the manuscript.

Certificate of discharge of No. SE/21104 Rank Private

Name Smith Bertram

Surname. Christian Names in full.

Unit* and Regiment or Corps from which discharged: Royal Army Veterinary Corps

* The unit of the Regiment or Corps such as Field Co. R.E., H.T., or M.T., A.S.C., etc., is invariably to be stated.

Regiment or Corps to which first posted R.A.V.C

Also previously served in ......

Only Regiments or Corps in which the soldier served since August 4th, 1914, are to be stated. If inapplicable this space is to be ruled through in ink and initialled.

Specialist Qualifications (Military) Horsekeeper

Chevrons: First Blue

Medals, Clasps, Decorations and Mentions in dispatches: British War and Victory

Wound Stripes* Nil. To be inserted in words.

Has served Overseas on Active Service†

Enlisted at Salisbury on 9. 12. 1915

*Each space is to be filled in and the word "nil" inserted where necessary.
†To be struck out in ink if not applicable.

He is discharged in consequence of his being no longer physically fit for War Service. Para 392 XVI Kings Regs

after serving* Four years* 50 days with the Colours, and
* Nil years* 268 days in the Army Reserve or ~~Territorial Force~~† Strike out whichever inapplicable.

*Each space is to be filled in and the word "nil" inserted where necessary; number of years to be written in words.
†Service with Territorial Force to be shown only in cases of soldiers serving on a T.F. attestation.

Date of discharge 22. 10. 20

Signature and Rank. Lt for Col.

Officer i/c R.A.V.C Records.

Woolwich (Place).

Description of the above-named soldier when he left the Colours.

Year of Birth 1894 Marks or Scars RIGHT ARM LEFT LEG

Height 5 ft. 9 in.

Complexion Fresh

Eyes Blue Hair Black

25 OCT 1920 ROYAL ARMY VETY. CORPS

WARNING.—If this Certificate is lost a duplicate cannot be issued. You should therefore on no account part with it or forward it by post when applying for a situation.

(31817.) Wt. W1912/PP1138. 760m. 5/18. S. & Co. (E3267.) [P.T.O.

The discharge papers of Private Bertram Smith, 21104 AVC.

When sorrows come, they come not single spies
but in battalions.

William Shakespeare (1564-1616), *Hamlet*

The Course of the War

The 'war to end all wars' began on 4th August 1914, after Britain
had declared war on Germany. As Britain had no troops on the
continent, after some reluctance to commit men, the British
Expeditionary Force was assembled with Sir John French in
command. The British Army consisted of professional soldiers
with no conscripts. Although they were highly trained, they
lacked numbers in comparison with the German forces. When it
had become obvious that war was imminent, orders had gone out
to all warships on 28th July and the British fleet was prepared.
The Royal Navy was active from the declaration of war.

British troops first arrived in continental Europe on 12th
August; their crossing was guarded by nineteen battleships. The
British Expeditionary Force proceeded towards Mons in
Belgium, which by that time had been virtually overrun by the
German Army. On the morning of 22nd August 1914, the first
shots were exchanged outside the village of Casteau, three miles
north east of Mons. Representatives of almost every British
Regiment were involved in this first battle. The Germans
advanced towards the French troops to the east of the British
line. The French were driven back and called upon the British
for assistance. Sir John French replied that he was unable to
help, as a considerable force of German troops were
approaching the British forces. On 23rd August there was a
prolonged exchange of fire between the opposing sides, with
many deaths and casualties. The British decided to attempt to
hold the Mons Canal against the Germans. The violent Battle of
Mons had begun.

The Retreat from Mons

For an entire day, the British fought to hold the line, but they gradually fell back, beginning the infamous Retreat from Mons. The Wiltshire Regiment was detailed to fight as a rearguard and together with the South Lancashires, held up the enemy for a whole day and half a night, falling back to Caudry. During the next day they repeated this action, falling back to the Aisne and, after the terrible Battle of Le Cateau, held the line as they continued to retreat, exhausted, to the Marne. As the Hampshires retreated from Mons, hotly pursued by the Germans (who took few prisoners), Private George Henry Hobbs was reported missing. After the Battle of Marne, much of the rest of August and September was taken up by entrenching, skirmishing and with some sniping.

The 1st Battalion, Wiltshire Regiment had been heavily involved in close fighting. Downtonians, Privates Walter Bundy and William Lawes were both wounded at the Battle of Aisne and they returned to Downton in early October. Shortly after his return home, Bundy learned of the death of his younger brother Bob, aged 19, who had been fighting by his side when he was wounded on 14th September. Bob had been killed in action six days later. Private Bundy's death coincided with the publication in *The Times*, 21st September of Binyon's famous poem *For the Fallen*.

When the Wiltshires advanced, they dug in but were heavily attacked during the Battle at Neuve Chapelle, west of Lille. The First Battle of Ypres began on 25th October. On that day at Reutel, just north of the Menin Road, a battalion of the Wiltshire Regiment was all but wiped out. The few survivors were taken prisoner. It seems that Private Walter Mouland perished during these engagements. Other Wiltshire Regiment Privates, Harry Mussell, George Boulter, Fred and James Blake were wounded.

An attack at Zillebeke, south of Ypres, was mounted 6th November 1914. Several battalions of Guards were involved, against tremendous odds. During this action so many high ranking officers were killed, and afterwards given graves in Zillebeke Churchyard, that it is known as the *Aristocrats' Cemetery*. As the *Western Gazette* newspaper later reported that Private Reuben Batchelor (3rd Dragoon Guards) had been killed on 6th November 1914, it is highly probable that it was

Company Sergeant Major F. C. Keeley. On the Downton War Memorials the surname Keeley is spelt *Kieley*.

during this time of great slaughter that he disappeared, probably with many 'other ranks.'

In November the Wiltshires moved to Dickebusch and then to reserve positions at Hooge. The battalion returned to the firing line and on 15th November 'D' Company's trenches were overrun, but regained by a tenacious bayonet charge. Company Sergeant Major Frederick Charles Keeley was killed during this fighting at Ypres. He was the son of the late John and Charlotte Keeley of Lode Hill, his father being an Army pensioner who had worked as a gardener in Downton. Keeley's sister, Mrs Downer received a letter from one of the officers at the front saying how sorry they were to lose 'such a brave fine fellow' and adding that had he lived he would have received the DCM.

By the time the First Battle of Ypres ended, 5,000 British and 5,000 German soldiers had been killed in an area of 10 miles north to south and 5 miles east to west. December brought torrential rain, and together with most of Western Europe, the ground rapidly became a quagmire, making many of the trenches untenable. Flooding, in some cases, washed the fire steps away, which made it impossible to fire rifles. The men were in places knee-deep in mud and icy water. Mud clogged rifles, making them useless, movement was difficult and slow, boots were often left in the thick mud, some men even lost their clothing.

1915

Sporadic fighting, trench raids and sniping continued in the early weeks of 1915. On 10th March the British attempted to break through at Neuve Chapelle, aiming to capture the village

Second Lieutenant George
Heremon Wyndham.

of Aubers. The Germans counter-attacked and attacked again on
13th March. Second Lieutenant George Heremon Wyndham,
3rd Battalion, Devonshire Regiment was killed in action on the
Ypres Salient on 24th March. He was the son of Colonel Guy
Wyndham of Charford Manor, Downton. Educated at
Wellington College and Magdalane College, Cambridge,
Wyndham was still an undergraduate when he applied to join
the Regiment on 8th August 1914. His uncle the Rt. Hon.
George Wyndham had been the Unionist (Conservative) MP for
Dover until his untimely death in 1913. He was the Chief Secre-
tary for Ireland in the Conservative Administration 1900-5 and
had been tipped as future party leader to replace Balfour. His
country estate of Clouds at East Knoyle, had passed to his son
Percy (George Heremon's cousin).

Lieutenant Percy Lyulph Wyndham, Coldstream Guards, had
been shot at close range through the head as he was leading his
men out of a wood at Soupir on 24th September 1914. His
grandmother, Madeline Countess of Grosvenor provided a
Memorial Tablet at East Knoyle Church which depicts an
officer kneeling in front of the Angel of the Lord, and lists the
names of her five grandchildren who were killed in the Great
War. Interestingly the individuals are listed in rank order. On
the death of Lieutenant Percy Wyndham, the Clouds Estate
passed to his cousin, Dick, who was George Heremon's younger
brother. He was awarded the MC during the war. A full history

The Wyndham
Memorial at East
Knoyle Church, 2001.

of the Wyndhams and the Clouds Estate is given in the book *Clouds: The Biography of a Country House* by Caroline Dakers, published in 1993.

Edward Priaulx, Lord Glenconner married Pamela Wyndham, sister of George Wyndham MP of Clouds. Their eldest son, Edward Wyndham Tennent was killed in action on The Somme in September 1916. He was one of the war poets. Sergeant Harry Noble of Downton was employed as coachman by this Lord Glenconnor at Lake House near Amesbury.

During this period of sporadic fighting in March 1915, four young men from Downton were wounded whilst serving in the 3rd Wiltshire Regiment. Privates Edwin Frank Bundy, Cecil Gunstone, Fred Moody and Albert Downer who joined the

Corporal Cecil H. Gunstone.   Private E. Frank Bundy.

army shortly after the outbreak of war, had speedily completed their training at Weymouth and volunteered for active service being sent to France before Christmas 1914. All were hospitalised, the worse case being Private Downer who had been wounded in the head. This Private Frank Bundy is not to be confused with Private Henry Frank Bundy, also of the Wiltshire Regiment, who enlisted in the spring of 1915.

Able Seaman William Mitchell was killed on 13th March 1915. His death was not as a result of some naval action, but of a freak accident that could have occurred at any time. Mitchell was among a large audience of sailors being entertained at a show at Parkestone Quay, Suffolk on a Saturday night. A gallery holding fifty members of the audience collapsed, crushing those underneath, including Mitchell who died instantly from a fractured skull. The deceased was 35 years of age and had joined the Royal Navy on leaving Downton Council School. After he had completed his service period, he worked as an agricultural labourer in Downton, before deciding to rejoin the Navy. His last visit to his native village was at Christmas 1914, when he had a strange foreboding he would never return to Downton again. He is buried at Shotley in Suffolk. William Mitchell's brother was mistakenly reported killed during the war on two separate occasions.

A look through the old Downton Parish Registers shows a bewilderingly large number of Newmans. In the early years of the twentieth century there were at least three families of that name in Downton, including a family in South Lane who resided in an old thatched cottage which was burnt down in October 1912 when a young child accidentally threw a fire cracker onto the thatch. The old cottage had been the former meeting place of the Baptists in Downton. The Newman family particularly recorded in this book are the sons of George and Fanny (Ellen) Newman of The Borough. Their picturesque cottage stands opposite the Borough Cross and is now called *Cymbeline* and numbered 51 The Borough. Part of this cottage was once a shop, and the neighbouring Newman's Café is remembered by many local people.

George Newman worked at the Downton Paper Mill. He was also a member of the Downton Fire Brigade, a Parish Councillor and sang in the church choir. He lived into his eighties and was the last surviving Downton bell ringer to have rung the bells at St Laurence's Church during the reign of Queen Victoria. His son, William, had also been in the choir and both father and son appear in the Edwardian choir photograph printed on page 28.

William had been awarded an Exhibition by the Downton British School Charity to finance him at Bishop Wordsworth's School, Salisbury in 1903. He later became a professional soldier, joining the army in 1909. At the outbreak of the war he

Sergeant William Newman (front centre), Royal Field Artillery in the trenches, west of the French town of La Bassée, January 1915.

held the rank of sergeant in the Royal Field Artillery. This remarkable Downtonian was involved in all the major battles of the Western Front and largely escaped injury. Furthermore he received decorations for three separate incidents of gallantry, being awarded the Military Medal, the Distinguished Conduct Medal and the Green Diamond.

Newman took part in the fighting from the time of the retreat from Mons in 1914. He first arrived at the front on 15th August, just eleven days after the declaration of war. Surviving photographs, postcards, correspondence and local newspaper reports provide a vivid indication of his activities during the war. In November 1915 Newman was promoted to the rank of Battery Sergeant-Major. He is described as having had a 'very strenuous time' since he first went to the front. In the fifteen months of the war he had been in the retreat from Mons, the Battle of the Marne, the Battle of Aisne and the fighting around Ypres and at Loos. Throughout all this military action he escaped both sickness and injury. Other members of his battery were not so fortunate. The *Western Gazette* reported that over three-quarters of the men in his battery had been either wounded or killed. In 1917, Newman was awarded the Green Diamond, an Irish Divisional honour.

Sergeant William Newman with members of the Right Section, 30th Battery, Royal Field Artillery in action at Richbourg, 9th March 1915.

"Everywhere and Always Faithful"

The Irish Brigade

56744 B.S. M. W. Newman
C/177th Bde. R.F.A.

I HAVE READ WITH MUCH PLEASURE THE REPORTS OF YOUR REGIMENTAL COMMANDER AND BRIGADE COMMANDER REGARDING YOUR GALLANT CONDUCT AND *constant* DEVOTION TO DUTY IN THE FIELD ON *in July & Aug. 1917* AND HAVE ORDERED YOUR NAME AND DEED TO BE ENTERED IN THE RECORD OF THE IRISH DIVISION.

W.B. Hickie,

Major-General,
Commanding 16th Irish Division,

William Newman's 'Green Diamond' citation.

Another former professional soldier active in the early months of the war was Ernest Smith of the Wiltshire Regiment. The Smiths are an old local family who can trace their ancestry back to the late sixteenth century. Originally yeoman farmers and millers at Standlynch, a branch of the family had moved into the village by the late eighteenth century. Ernest Smith's great, great, great, great grandfather John Smith appears in barrister Alexander Luders's 1785 Parliamentary Enquiry into alleged electoral corruption in the Borough of Downton. At 73 he was the village's eldest resident and was questioned about the boundaries of the old burgage plots. Despite Smith being the most common of surnames there were no other families of that name in Downton until the third quarter of the nineteenth century.

Ernest's father, John Smith, was born in Gravel Close on 1st November 1864. He was a journeyman tanner by trade, but also a barber, street lamp lighter, labourer and a member of the Downton Fire Brigade. He was for some years an active member of the Woodfalls Temperance Band, a founder member of the Downton Band and one of the Downton (Christmas) Mummers. He was also the father of eleven children, not all of whom reached adulthood. John and his wife Rosa planned military careers for their sons as a means of escape from relative rural poverty in Downton, where employment was limited and chances of social advancement slim. Many local families took the same course, which is shown by the number of local professional servicemen killed in the war.

Ernest, Robert and Bertram were three of John and Rosa Smith's sons who served in the Great War. Ernest Smith was born on 28th February 1887 and was their eldest child to survive infant mortality. Ernest had been a professional soldier for many years before the war. He served in the 3rd Battalion of the Coldstream Guards in the Sudan, a few years after the Battle of Omdurman (1898) under Kitchener. This battalion later became the First Camel Corps. Smith sent several interesting picture postcards home to his parents who lived in The Borough. He even owned a camera and some of his surviving photographs were taken on service in Egypt and the Sudan in 1906-8.

Smith was invalided out of the army with dysentery in about 1912 and worked at the Downton Tan Yard, with his father. They are amongst the workers pictured at the Tan Yard on page 21. Ernest was also the coach of the Downton Football Team in the years immediately before the war. He was remembered by his younger siblings, Bertram and Mabel Smith (later Kelly), as being over 6 ft. tall with blond hair and sky blue eyes.

At the outbreak of hostilities in 1914 Smith joined the 1st Battalion Wiltshire Regiment and for the very early part of the war he was an instructor at the Regiment's Camp at Weymouth. He was then given the option of training troops on Salisbury Plain, but instead chose to go out to the Front. It is believed that he was a sniper. Before he left England he advised his younger brother Bert not to join up 'theäse bide where thee bist.'

Sergeant Ernest Smith (front centre) in Belgium, June 1915, a week before he was killed. Several of these men were in the trenches with him when he died. The soldier on the right of the front row is Private Jack Haydon of Downton.

In May 1915 Acting Sergeant Smith was shot at by a German sniper. The bullet hit his pocket watch and this probably saved his life. The pocket watch and bullet were posted home. Now fascinating curiosities, in 1915, stark reminders of the realities of war. Two weeks later Smith was not so fortunate. Sergeant Smith was killed on Hill 60 at Ypres on 8th June 1915. Apparently he had looked out of one of the tunnels and was shot in the head by a German sniper. The parcel containing the pocket watch arrived at Downton some days after Smith's family had received the news of his death. Smith had been engaged to the cook at The Moot.

The War Diaries of the 1st Battalion, Wiltshire Regiment show that Sergeant Smith was the only member of the battalion killed on 8th June. He seems to have been rather unfortunate as

Bullet-damaged pocket
watch belonging to
Ernest Smith

on that day the Wiltshires were relieved by the Honourable Artillery Company and returned to Ypres early the following morning for rest.

Wiltshire Regiment Private Jack Haydon of Downton was standing next to Smith when he was shot. Haydon later reported back to Ernest's family that he had died instantly. In reality Smith took over two hours to die – the nature of his

The entrance to Ypres,
Belgium, 1918.

The Menin Gate, Ieper (formerly Ypres),
Belgium.

KNEE W. A.
LAWRENCE J.
LEA E. H.
LEAL J. L.
NEWTON A. E.
PAGET E.
ROBINSON B.
SAFE F. R.
SHAKESPEARE W. F.
SMITH E.
WILKINS D.
WORRALL J. E.

Sergeant Ernest Smith's name on the Menin Gate.

death was reported in the local paper. There is an even more graphic description of a similar death witnessed by novelist Robert Graves on 9th June. In *Goodbye to All That*, he describes:

> *I saw a group bending over a man lying at the bottom of the trench. He was making a snoring noise mixed with animal groans. At my feet lay the cap he had worn, splashed with his brains. I had never seen human brains before; I somehow regarded them as a poetical figment. One can joke with a badly-wounded man and congratulate him on being out of it. One can disregard a dead man. But even a miner can't make a joke over a man who takes three hours to die, after the top part of his head has been taken off by a bullet fired at twenty yards' range.*

Originally Sergeant Smith had a military grave at Ypres and details of its location were sent to his grieving parents. Regrettably the grave disappeared – it was blown to pieces – during the subsequent 3rd Battle of Ypres (which is also known as Passchendaele). Smith's name appears on Column 1706, Panel 53, M.R. 29 of the Menin Gate at Ieper, Belgium, close to where he was killed in action. The Menin Gate contains the names of 40,242 British servicemen without graves. There are also the names of 6,983 Canadians, 6,198 Australians, 565 South Africans, 421 Indians and six West Indians. At least three other Downtonians are commemorated on this memorial, including two brothers Arthur and Frederick Charles Keeley. Sergeant Arthur Keeley, 10th Hussars, had been killed on 13th May when the Germans had begun a heavy artillery bombardment.

The *Downton Parish Magazine* of July 1915 wrote the following about Smith:

> *It was with deep concern and regret that we received the communication that Corporal Ernest Smith had fallen a victim to the bullet of a German sniper. For some years Corporal Smith served in the Coldstream Guards, at the outbreak of the War he volunteered for service and joined the Wilts. Regiment. He was a straight good fellow, and well liked by all, and he died in the noblest of causes.*

The Newmans and Smiths were typical local families who were to lose at least one son during the war. Another family caught up in the tragic events were the Haydons who of all the families in Downton, appear to have suffered the most devastating affects of the war. William and Emily Haydon moved to Downton from Stowford, Somerset in 1898 and lived in an old thatched cottage at the lower end of The Borough. William worked as a gardener for Professor Wrightson at the Downton Agricultural College. The couple had four sons and one daughter. Three of their sons died as a result of the First World War, their daughter died in early 1923 aged 17.

The son who survived the war – Jack Haydon – suffered terribly during the conflict. Leafing through the pages of the *Salisbury Journal* for the years 1914-17, we read of how Private Jack Haydon was injured on at least four separate occasions, the first of which was in June 1915, shortly after he had witnessed Sergeant Smith's death. Haydon missed the horrors of the start of the Battle of the Somme in July 1916, as he was in hospital at Norwich suffering from shell shock, but by October he had again been wounded. In 1917 he was injured twice – in April and August. Then in the spring of 1918 he was taken prisoner of war by the Germans. The appalling war experiences of Private Haydon were so horrifying as to be almost unimaginable, but Jack Haydon did live into old age. He died in July 1981.

The Vicar goes to the Front

Downton's Vicar, the Rev. Lenthall Dickenson left the Parish at short notice in mid-July 1915, to take up a position as Senior Chaplain to the Forces for the duration of the war. It had originally been intended for him to serve in the Mediterranean, but this posting was altered to the Western Front a couple of days before his departure. The Rev. Dickenson was initially stationed at the Base Hospital at Rouen in France. He wrote about some of his experiences for the *Downton Parish Magazine* of September 1915:

It is now August 20th, five weeks since I arrived in France. The time given me wherein to prepare and proceed to my new work was so short, that it was quite impossible, try how I would, to go round and say goodbye to all of you dear people at home I want, if I can, to give you some account of my present labour and life, there is, however, a difficulty in the way of doing so as frankly and fully as I should like, because we are forbidden by the laws and rules of War Service to give anything approaching a detailed description of the place we are camping in and things that are occurring day by day. I reached this place which is in the neighbourhood of Rouen on Saturday, July 16th, having spent the previous days at General Head Quarters ... There is a large Sanitary Hospital, consisting of thirty-eight wards, all of which are tents. Besides these, there is a large and long wooden building, which we call the 'Hut,' where the most serious cases are placed. In addition to these there are a large number of tents for the officers and the permanent staff. We sleep in tents and feed in tents and associate with one another in tents. This then forms the sphere of work in my new Parish. The wounded arrive continually in large convoys from the Front, in every degree of condition and laid low with every sort of wound, and as we go round daily, from bed to bed, and man to man, the thing that strikes and thrills one most, is the astounding courage of the sufferers, the amazing skill of the Doctors in the matter of recovering and reconstructing, and the touching devotion of the entire nursing staff ...

On Sundays there is always a good attendance at the early celebration, and the same may be said of the other services. One of the most striking sights that I have witnessed was an

Intercession Service on the evening of the Anniversary of the Declaration of War. Some 800 soldiers gathered in the YMCA Hut, and standing (there was no room to kneel) with bowed and bent head, entered most earnestly into a long service of prayer and litany, and some two or three hymns. Nothing could have exceeded the reverence and reality of it all; it was sufficient to shake the sleepiest soul and the hardest heart and the most worldly will. Yes – we have a Living Faith and we rejoice in God our Saviour out here.

The Vicar visited Downton briefly in November 1915 and spoke of his experiences in the hospital and in the trenches of the Western Front. Another instalment of his service as an Army Chaplain is given in the *Parish Magazine* of January 1916:

The last time I wrote to you was from the somewhat comfortable quarters but sad surroundings of a Military Hospital I left that place on October 20th, on my appointment as Chaplian to the 7th Brigade, or rather I should say to half of it, for there are four Regiments in a Brigade and I have two appointed to my charge, viz., the Loyal North Lancs. And the 1st Wilts. I live with the latter by the kind invitation of the Commanding Officer, and I may add that I am exceedingly glad to do so, as all 'the boys' as we somewhat affectionately call them, come from the County I have lived in for several years and many come from villages close to Downton and five from Downton itself ...

The men are in the trenches less than a week and then come out for the same period and return again. The chief thing, other than the offensiveness of the Hun or Boche, (as the foe is called), that brings hardship and much unpleasantness to life is the continuous wet and mud. I had no idea that mud could ever become so deep and cold and miserable an article until these last two months it really beggars description, it has no redeeming point, it often comes over one's knees, and has the evil habit of sticking to one in clods. The second thing that adds to the drabness of life in the trenches is lack of picture papers and cigarettes, these count for a lot in heartening 'the boys.' Thanks however to the very generous kindness of the Mayor and Mayoress of Salisbury and several friends in Downton, these things are coming along splendidly.

The Dardanelles

Less than a week after the Battle of Neuve Chapelle on the Western Front, in the autumn of 1914, an attempt was made by an Anglo-French naval force to break through the Narrows into the Sea of Marmara, intending to then sail across to Constantinople. Kitchener believed that it would not be necessary for troops to go ashore on the Gallipoli peninsula; he expected the Turks to evacuate their garrison there, once the Navy had forced its way through. Six British and four French battleships took part, lines of mines being swept clear before the advancing ships. An unexpected line of twenty mines, however, had been laid parallel to the shore. They wreaked havoc. Three of the battleships were sunk. The others put out of action. The naval enterprise had failed.

Throughout March and April 1915, British forces and supplies were being prepared in the Eastern Mediterranean for landings at Gallipoli. These were eventually made by the forces of Australia and New Zealand who had disembarked in Egypt, diverted when en-route for the Western Front, expecting to accomplish this mission quickly. Among the British soldiers preparing to join the assault was the poet Rupert Brooke, while still on a training exercise on the Aegean Isle of Skyros. He died from blood poisoning after being bitten by a mosquito, he was buried in an olive grove a few hours before his colleagues sailed for Gallipoli.

On 25th April 1915 the Allied landings at Gallipoli took place on five different landing beaches at Cape Helles. As the troops went ashore, they were hit by heavy machine-gun fire. 'S' Beach was hardly defended and the men managed to dig in. At Gallipoli, as on the Western Front, trenches changed hands many times, and after several battles fighting here also became a stalemate. On August 6th a force of Allied ships was assembled and troops landed on a new beach at Suvla Bay. Heavy fighting took place to take and hold the summit of Chunuk Bair, which eventually was held by the New Zea-landers after several attacks and counter attacks. Two batallions sent to relieve the New Zealand forces were from Kitchener's New Army, consisting of those who had joined up shortly after war was declared. These were the 6th Loyal Lancashires and the 5th Wiltshire Regiment and they had never been in action before.

The Loyal Lancashires relieved the New Zealanders at the summit, while the Wiltshires were held in reserve.

At 4.45am on 10th August the Turks were given the signal to attack. The Loyal Lancashires were bayoneted to a man. The Wiltshires, who had been hours without sleep, were at rest in the valley just below, arms and equipment stacked. Defenceless, they could only turn and run, the Turks closely pursuing them. The Battalion was all but wiped out. Private George Elliott of Lode Hill perished during this terrible rout, on 10th August. Private Albert Edward Blandford of Morgan's Vale was also killed. He was the husband of Mrs Annie Amelia Blandford. Three days later Lance Corporal Harry Winton, also of Lode Hill, died of his wounds. It would seem that Private G. Williams was a survivor of this horrendous action. The War Diaries of the 5th Battalion explain how the men were trapped:

... there was a rush of Turks from both sides of the depression which drove the men, unarmed and unequipped down the gulley (Salzli Beit). The bottom of the gulley was commanded by machine guns and so escape was cut off. Three courses were possible: (1). To rush past the machine guns down Salzli Beit – this was tried, but in nearly all cases proved fatal. (2). To climb the northern slope of the ravine under fire and try to escape over the top. (3). Hide in the gulley till night, this was done with more success. (A party of five men was rescued from the gulley having been there 16 days ... They reported numbers of men wounded, who were unable to get away and died of exhaustion and starvation).

Major Henry Reginald Walter Marriott-Smith, Royal Artillery, the son of Colonel Marriott-Smith of Fairfield House was wounded in the Mediterranean Expeditionary Force, on 7th August 1915. The officer had been invalided home from France at Christmas 1914 with frost bite. He was a professional serviceman, born in 1875 who joined the Army as Second Lieutenant at the age of 20 and was promoted to Major in 1912. He served in the Nile Expedition in 1896 being present at the Battle for Khartoum receiving the Egyptian medal with clasp. He was also in the Boer War, where he was mentioned in despatches and received the Queen's medal for gallantry. Despite his long military career, August 1915 was the first occasion in which he had been wounded.

On 28th September Private George Forder died of wounds received at Gallipoli. He was the son of Mrs Fanny Pretty of The Borough and had worked at the Downton Tan Yard before the war. He is pictured on page 21. Forder had previously been a professional soldier with the Wiltshire Regiment, but on the outbreak of war he joined the Dublin Fusiliers.

The Battle of Loos

On 25th September 1915 an allied offensive began on the Western Front, intended to relieve Russia's problems on the Eastern Front. Its objective was to recover the French mining district at Lens, and to capture Lille if the attack succeeded. The front was to be extended from Ypres to Armentières. For the first time, troops of the New British Armies were employed in offensive war on the Western Front and also for the first time, gas was used by the Allies against the Germans. On 26th September at Fosse 8, the British were counter-attacked in a failed attempt to retake the quarries. An attempt to advance on Hulluch was made, but the men were held up by uncut wire, machine gun bullets and gas shells, against which the British troops were not properly protected. The attack was beaten back with severe loss of life. Private Fred Penn Moody was killed during this dreadful battle. He was one of the original 'Downton Volunteers' who had enlisted in the army on hearing the declaration of war in August 1914. He had rapidly completed his training with the Wiltshire Regiment at Weymouth and arrived in France before Christmas. Moody saw much fighting and had been injured on three previous occasions, including one sustained in April when he received a gunshot

Private Fred Penn Moody.

wound to the head and on 17th June when he was wounded in the hand. Private Moody is buried at the Cabaret-Rouge British Cemetery, Souchez, France.

In October 1915, four months after John and Rosa Smith had heard the news of their son Ernest's death, they received another telegram stating that another son, Robert was 'dangerously wounded.' Bob Smith was born in Downton in December 1891. Before the war he worked as footman to Sir Edward Boyle at his country estate in Sussex. Bob was injured in the trenches at the Battle of Loos in September. Initially his right foot was blown off, but as he remained in a muddy shell hole for two days, gangrene spread rapidly. His whole leg had to be amputated in stages, until about an inch remained. The anxiety of John and Rosa Smith must have been intense in December 1915, when their next youngest son, Bertram joined up, enlisting in the Army Veterinary Corps.

Private Robert Smith.

Bob Smith related his war-time experiences to his younger sister 17 year old Mabel, when she visited him at a London hospital on 17th March the following year. The brief resumé reproduced below outlines some of the horrors of the Great War – six months of hospitalisation and extreme pain.

20 Jan1915	Joined the Army (1/19th Battalion London Regiment)
March 1915	went to France
25 Sep 1915	wounded at Loos
16 Oct 1915	left Frepont, France
16 Oct 1915	admitted Northampton General Hospital
26 Jan 1916	left Northampton General Hospital
26 Jan 1916	arrived Higham Ferrers, Northamptonshire
16 Mar 1916	left Higham Ferrers, Northamptonshire
16 Mar 1916	arrived Cambridge Hospital
17 Mar 1916	arrived London Hospital

Nevertheless Bob was successful in subsequent civilian life. Perhaps the only advantage of the war was that it forced society – for the first time – to take a more positive attitude towards people with disabilities. He later ran his own business, but in old age moved back to his native village, being one of the first residents of the Old Peoples' Flats in The Borough, next to the former Police House. His youngest sister Linda Eastman later lived in the same flat (number 19) in the 1980s and '90s. Bob died at a serviceman's home in Portsmouth in October 1972.

On 8th October 1915 a general attack was launched at the Hohenzollern Redoubt. The British Guards more than held their own against six German Battalions. Second Lieutenant Edward St. Laurent Bonvalot of the 2nd Battalion, Coldstream Guards was fatally wounded in action at Loos on that day. His French death certificate records that he died in the early hours of 9th October at the Military Hospital of the Rue Faidherbe. Bonvalot was born at Onslow Square, London in July 1891 and educated at Eton College from September 1903 to the Summer of 1910 first in Mr Tatham's house, and after his retirement in 1909 in Mr Conybeare's. He won the Kings first prize for French in 1908 (perhaps not surprising as his father was French) and rowed in the *Monarch* in the procession of boats on 4th June in his last year. This boat was not necessarily a boat for good oarsmen but had a certain standing and popularity in

2nd Lieutenant Bonvalot.

the school. After Eton, Bonvalot went on to Trinity College, Cambridge, where he gained a 3rd in history.

Bonvalot was one of 5,650 old Etonians who fought in the Great War between 1914-19, of which 1,157 were killed. As only 798 of these served at home, it can be calculated that one in four were killed. Probably the most famous Etonian in the war was the future British Prime Minister Harold Macmillan, who was also injured at the Battle of Loos, on 27th September 1915.

Bonvalot's younger brother Alfred Cecil also served in the Coldstream Guards during the war. He was born at Fernside, Bishops Down, Tunbridge Wells on 16th August 1896 and came to Downton with his family to reside at Wick House in 1912. Interestingly enough, both the service records of the Bonvalot brothers kept at the PRO at Kew contain copies of their birth certificates. Presumably these were required as proof that they were British subjects, in spite of their clearly French ancestry. Like his brother, Cecil was also educated at Eton.

Cecil Bonvalot enlisted on 20th September 1914 and originally joined the 7th Battalion, Wiltshire Regiment. He applied for a commission with the Coldstream Guards on 2nd November of that year and remained with them until his demobilisation on 3rd June 1919 by which time he had been promoted to the rank of Captain. The medical records amongst his service papers show a robust, healthy young man of 5ft 10ins and 11 stone 9 lbs. Later papers record a service life blighted by illness. Illnesses which included farunculosis, a severe attack of boils and atonic dyspepsia. Frustrated, Cecil Bonvalot home on sick leave desperately fought to prove his return to health and eagerness to return to the front line.

In November 1915, Lieutenant Archibald Wrightson was awarded the Military Cross for conspicuous gallantry. Archibald Ingram was the son of Professor Wrightson of Downton Agricultural College and was born in the village in 1882. Archie had emigrated to Canada some time before the war and served as a Lieutenant in the 7th Canadian Infantry Battalion (a British Colombia regiment). His father was present at the investiture by George V in December. Lieutenant Wrightson was wounded in 1916. Archibald Wrightson's brother Edmund also had an interesting First World War career, namely aboard a 'Q' Ship, the *Ilma*.

Other Downton servicemen who received awards in 1915 were Regimental Quartermaster Sergeant Frederick W. Vivian of the 1st Battalion Dorset Regiment and Colonel Marriott-Smith of the Royal Field Artillery. Vivian was awarded the D.C.M. and the (Russian) Cross of the Order of St. George 4th Class. He was a son of Mrs. Vivian of The Borough and had been fighting at the Front since the start of the war. Colonel Marriott-smith of Fairfield House rejoined the army on the outbreak of war and was posted to Secoundergbad, India. He received the DSM.

Mesopotamia, 1915-18

While names of battlefields on mainland Western Europe became well known, several Downton servicemen were involved in fighting elsewhere in the war, including Mesopotamia and Salonica. The war in Mesopotamia involved men from Downton, but fortunately none of them perished, yet the terrible conditions they suffered must have left an indelible mark on each of them – both physically and mentally. In 1915 the campaign in Mesopotamia to protect British oil interests was apparently going well, the British took the town of Kut-el-Amara and marched on to Ctesiphon, intending to take it and march on to capture Baghdad. Regrettably, however, the army's good fortune ended at Ctesiphon. Of the 8,500 British and Indian troops who fought in the battle, more than half were killed or wounded. The British were more than 400 miles from the sea and could expect no reinforcements. The survivors retreated to the garrison at Kut, many more men being killed en-route. The march took thirteen days to complete, the soldiers arriving at Kut on 3rd December 1915.

The garrison at Kut had been prepared to withstand a Turkish attack. There was a bombardment, but soon the Turks were content to wait and starve out the garrison, sniping at the men. There was a British relief expedition mounted, but it was held up by floods, ferocious attacks by the Turkish Army and marauding Arabs. Inside the garrison conditions grew to be almost unbearable. On 7th March soldiers fighting in battles to relieve the beleaguered garrison were reinforced with men who had been evacuated from Gallipoli.

Men of the 1/4th Hampshire Regiment (a territorial battalion) were among the defenders in the garrison. Brigadier-General R. Wapshare, (a well known local name) was commanding the Indian Brigade and another prominent local man held under siege conditions was Captain H. Curtis Gallup of the 56th (Wessex) Brigade, Royal Field Artillery (another territorial force). As conditions worsened, it seemed impossible that the garrison could hold out, but on 10th April 1916, the officer commanding the garrison issued a communiqué:

> *... I ask you to remember the defence of Plevna, which was longer than that even of Ladysmith You will be proud to say one day, 'I was one of the garrison of Kut.'*

On 15th April the first aeroplanes made several air drops. Lieutenant H. P. S. Clogstoun of the Royal Flying Corps, son-in-law of Mrs Carver of The Moot was one of the pilots who dropped provisions into the town, 50 lb. bags being slung on each side of the fuselage and 25 lbs. bags on the undercarriage. Between the 15th and 28th April there were 140 food-dropping flights, and a total of 16,800 lb. was dropped from heights of 5,000 to 8,000 feet. Turkish gunfire prevented supplies being dropped from lower altitudes. Besides food and mail, as well as £10,000 in gold and silver, a 70 lb. millstone was dropped. Although this may appear odd, before the war, Kut was a busy market town with large local supplies of grain. All items were free-dropped, as there was no question of parachutes being available. Some of the drops landed behind the Turkish lines, others in the Tigris.

Clogstoun's brother-in-law Felix Carver was also involved in

Captain H. Curtis Gallup.

the war in the Middle East, serving in the 1/4th Dorset Regiment. Carver was promoted to the rank of Captain in June 1916 whilst he was at Basrah. In August 1918 he was Mentioned in Despatches, by his Commander in Chief Lieutenant General W. R. Carshall, 'as deserving a special mention for distinguished and gallant service and devotion to duty.' He was promoted to the rank of Temporary Major in January 1919 and ended his military service in March 1921 by which time he had been working for the Government's Political Department in Mesopotamia.

Another officer from Downton, in Mesopotamia, was in control of the only Kite Balloon Section of the Royal Naval Air Service stationed there at that time. He was Commander Wrottesley RN, a well-known resident of Wick Lane.

Despite the air drops, the troops inside the garrison started to run out of food. Gradually the pack mules and horses were killed to feed the men and when only the officers' chargers were left, they too were sacrificed, each owner being given the dubious privilege of eating the liver and heart of his own mount.

When it became obvious that the garrison could hold out no longer, on 27th April, three British officers, including Captain T. E. Lawrence offered the Turks £1m in gold if the besieged troops were allowed to leave in peace. The garrison continued to hold out, but the Turks willing to wait. Two days later the garrison surrendered. As they marched out from the town officers were separated from other ranks, some of the sick remained temporarily in hospital, before being forced to join in the death march already being undertaken by their colleagues. The marchers started on 6th May, many men having had their boots stolen during the previous night. On the second day they were forced to march fifteen miles through the atrocious desert heat, with no water or shade being allowed them. Those who dropped behind or fell were beaten. If they did not get up they were left where they fell. P. W. Long, writing in *Other Ranks of Kut*, (1938), recounts that during this dreadful march, many men were killed, nearly all were robbed, and there were several cases of rape. At Ctesiphon, Captain E. O. Moulsey saw men 'dying with green ooze issuing from their lips, their mouths fixed open, in and out of which flies walked.'

On 18th May the marchers reached Baghdad and were 'rested' for three days in a compound with no sanitation or shade. The American Consul in Baghdad paid the Turkish authorities to have 500 men sent to hospital and eventually back to Basra. More than 160 died on that journey. To protect the thousands still being marched northwards to Anatolia, those who reached safety at Basra were forbidden to speak of what they had been through at the hands of the Turks and Arabs. Resuming the horrendous march, at Tekrit these exhausted, emaciated, piteous men were stoned by its inhabitants.

Of the 2,500 British soldiers captured at Kut, 1,750 died on the 600 plus mile march north. Of the 9,300 Indian soldiers captured at Kut, 2,500 died.

The surviving service papers of Captain H. Curtis Gallup contain a confidential statement form from the War Office, dated 21st December 1919. A Standing Committee of Enquiry was attempting to ascertain the circumstances of the fall of Kut on 29th April 1916. Its deliberations cleared Gallup of any blame, stating in a letter of 3rd May of the following year that:

The Secretary of the War Office presents his complements to Lieutenant H. C. Gallup, Royal Field Artillery and begs to state that he is commanded by the Army Council to inform him that his statement regarding the circumstances of his capture by the enemy having been investigated, the council considers no blame attaches to him in the matter.

Progress was made in Mesopotamia as the forces requested to relieve Kut arrived. In 1917 the British Army advanced beyond Baghdad. The Turkish positions were attacked at Gaza, just inside the Palestinian border. British troops, who had been stationed in India were shipped to Egypt. Private Stephen Forder, a member of the ubiquitous Downton family had enlisted in 1914 to the 2/4th Dorset Regiment. Lance Corporal Charles and William Senior both served with the regiments fighting in this area – the Wiltshires and the Dorset Regiment respectively. Both regiments arrived at Suez as part of the 75th Indian Division. On arrival they were transported to Kantara on the east bank of the Canal by rail. This was the base of the Egyptian Expeditionary Force. The 1/4th Wiltshire Regiment entered the trenches south of Turkish-held Gaza three weeks later. Their Brigadier was the Hon. E. Colston, a Wiltshire man. In November 1917 the third battle of Gaza began and the men fought under constant shell fire. On reaching Gaza the evacuation of the Turks was completed, as they were already retreating towards Jerusalem. Wiltshire Regiment Bandsman William H. Harrington, the son of Mr and Mrs George

Bandsman
W. H. Harrington.

Harrington of Wick was wounded in the fighting. The Wiltshires pursued them, but were hampered by lack of water. Later these men were involved in the attack that took Jerusalem.

An interesting story has been recalled by Peter Senior, the nephew of Lance Corporal Charlie Senior. Charlie worked at the Downton Paper Mills before enlisting to join the army, when he lied about his age, as in reality he was only 16. Between leaving school and working at the Mills, Charlie had been employed as a telegraph boy at the Downton Post Office. One winter's day, a telegram was received for a guest staying at Trafalgar House, Standlynch. It stated that a relative was dangerously ill and requested the guest's return to London. Thick snow was on the ground, but in blizzard conditions, the telegram was successfully delivered by Senior. The guest reached London in time, and to show their appreciation the family presented Charlie with an inscribed watch. This precious gift was, unfortunately, lost in desert sands, while Lance Corporal Senior was on war service. Years later, after the Second World War, the watch was returned to Downton by someone who had found it in Egypt. Charlie Senior died in his late 90s in 1996.

Peter Senior's father, William, 1/4th Dorset Regiment survived a sniper attack in Mesopotamia. The man next to him was shot dead, and another bullet passed through William's rucksack and embedded itself in a spade.

The Western Front, 1916

At the beginning of 1916, the Western Front was preoccupied with the mighty Battle of Verdun, being fought by the French against the Germans with great losses on both sides. The British were involved in attack and counter attack, trench raids, and with the ubiquitous sniper. Gas was being used regularly by both the German and British forces.

The first Downton death of 1916 was that of Sergeant Harry William Noble, who died of pneumonia in France. Sergeant Noble's grandson David Cockman has provided the following information about his grandfather, including photographs of Noble and his grave. Harry William Noble was the son of Walter and Rosina Noble and baptised at Downton Parish Church on 12th February 1882. In the early 1900s he served as

Sergeant Harry William Noble. He is also
commemorated on the War Memorial at Lake.

a professional soldier in the Royal Horse Artillery. It was during
this time that he met his future wife, whilst stationed at St.
John's Wood, London. After leaving the army Noble took a job
as a coachman and groom for Lord and Lady Glenconner at
Lake House near Amesbury. The couple lived in a tied cottage
on the estate.

At the outbreak of war in August 1914 Noble was either
recalled to the Royal Horse Artillery, or volunteered for further
service with his old regiment. He was soon sent to France and
did not return. His daughter Rosina (David Cockman's mother)
was born after his departure. Sergeant Noble died in a military
hospital at Rouen on 11th February 1916, aged 36. He is buried
in the military cemetery of St. Sever on the outskirts of Rouen,
along with over 11,000 other British servicemen. Rouen was one
of the main centres for hospital treatment of casualties and most
of the men buried at St. Sever came from hospitals there.

After Sergeant Noble's death, his widow had to leave the tied
cottage at Lake. She moved her three children to Downton
where relatives found a small rented cottage (now demolished)
on Lode Hill, opposite what was then a butcher's shop on the
corner of Slab Lane. Mrs Noble spent the remainder of her life
there and died in the 1970s. As a young widow she had to work
hard to support her three children Bert, Ted and Rosina.

The grave of Sergeant Noble at St. Sever Cemetery, Rouen,
Seine-Maritime, France.

During the day she worked at the Downton Tan Yard. At
evenings and weekends she took in washing and did work for
local middle class families. In particular she worked for the
Ballard family of Hill House.

David Cockman can remember as a boy being shown his
grandfather's army paybook and the official telegram from the
War Office that brought the news of his death. Sadly these
items are now lost, but he does remember his grandmother

The Downton Post Office, The Square, the point of arrival of telegrams in the village during the Great War. This picture dates from c.1905. The postman on the left is Percy Eastman, the elder brother of Leo Eastman who died in 1918.

telling him how the women of Downton would dread the sight of the telegraph boy peddling his bicycle through the village during the First World War.

Another victim of the war died of pneumonia in March 1916. Private William George Haydon was the son of William and Emily Haydon of The Borough. He had enlisted at Bournemouth shortly after the declaration of war and joined the Hampshire Regiment. He had been invalided out because of a leg wound, but underwent an operation and fought his way back to health and rejoined the forces. After his death, the Haydons received a letter from their son's Commanding Officer expressing his regret and sympathy. He wrote:

> *Private Haydon was popular with the men and liked by his company officers. His duties were always carried out well and with willingness.*

In the Great War many chest infections such as bronchitis and pneumonia were caused as a result of gas gangrene. Tuberculosis (or consumption as it was formerly known) had always been rife at the Bottom End of Downton, contributed to by poverty and poor housing conditions, particularly in The Borough, where the low-lying land meant that it was often possible to take up floorboards and see water in the foundations. Ironically the TB caused by these poor housing conditions prevented several local men from joining the armed forces on the grounds of poor health and thus was an odd life-saver. Sergeant Smith's brother William was one of these individuals.

Haydon died at the Boscombe Military Hospital and because of its close proximity to Downton he was the first victim of the Great War to be buried in Downton Churchyard. His grave is marked by a distinctive Commonwealth War Graves Commission headstone. The distinctive design of these stones came about after the war, when it was decided to adopt a uniform pattern of tombstone for all ranks, a plain headstones measuring 2ft. 6in. by 1ft. 3in. Such headstones are inscribed with the soldier's regimental number, rank and name, the date of death, the Cross or other symbol of his faith, the badge of his corps, and a text or other inscription chosen and paid for by his relatives.

After the end of the war over 15,000 men were employed in the work of exhuming and re-interring the bodies and laying out the cemeteries close to where the men died. Not surprisingly it was several years before the task was completed and the Haydon gravestones in Downton Churchyard were not put in place until the late 1920s.

There are seven Commonwealth War Graves Commission headstones in Downton Churchyard, dating from the era of the First World War, including Private Haydon's and that of his younger brother Sergeant Arthur Ellis Haydon MM. The inscriptions on these headstones are reproduced in Appendix III. A further CWGC headstone close to the lych gate in Church Hatch marks the grave of an officer killed in the Second World War, Lieutenant Henry (Harry) E. Phillips, 7th Battalion Wiltshire Regiment Home Guard. Philips was the landlord of the *Three Horse Shoes* and was killed in an accident on Salisbury Plain in April 1942. He had been attending the demonstration of a machine gun with other officers, when the aircraft from which the gun was firing missed the dummies which should have been its target and mowed down the officers. His 20 year old son Cecil Henry Walter Phillips of the 18 Squadron RAF Volunteer Reserve was killed in North Africa on 30th January 1943. He is buried at the Medjez-El-Bab War Cemetery in Tunisia.

Of the forty-four First World War names that appear on the Downton War Memorial seven are officers and all of these are buried in marked graves close to where they died. Of the thirty-seven men 12 are buried abroad, six are buried in graves in England, but the graves of 17 men are unknown and these names are inscribed on various memorials. The final two names are those of two of the Batchelor brothers. It is assumed Private Reuben is buried in France or Belgium and that the final resting place of his younger brother Frederick is in England.

On 25th April 1916, Private William Ghazi Kingsbury was killed on the Ypres Salient, where as well as coping with the

Thought to be Private William Ghazi Kingsbury.

usual skirmishes, the army was in training for the 'push' on the Somme.

The Battle of the Somme

More has been written about the Battle(s) of the Somme, then any other military engagements of the First World War. This was the most devastating of all the battles and the notorious first day – 1st July 1916 – witnessed more deaths and casualties than any previous day's battle in British military history. Britain suffered 57,470 casualties, of which 19,240 were killed. It is therefore not surprising that more soldiers and officers from Downton were killed in this battle than in any other individual action.

The Battle of the Somme was to be fought on a wide front and had been planned as *the* decisive military advance of the war, culminating in a massive infantry assault. Preparations and training for this action had been carried out for months. A heavy artillery bombardment against the Germans took place in the days immediately preceding the battle, and this was intended to weaken the enemy's front line defences. Long ranks of soldiers were to advance slowly over the top and walk across nomansland, reassured that most of the German machine guns had been put out of action. The reality was far from this. The Germans were well prepared and those soldiers who were not immediately shot down became entangled on barbed wire.

Many of those who perished in the slaughter at the Somme were from Kitchener's New Army of volunteers who had enlisted shortly after war was declared in August 1914. Lance Corporal Edwin John Swanborough was killed on the first day of the battle – although news of his death did not reach his bother Charles until the week commencing 17th July 1916. Born at Figheldean he had later lived at Britford before moving to Salisbury Road, Downton. He was 24 and had served in the army for several years, first in the Wiltshires, but had transferred to the Border Regiment some months before his death. Swanborough had been awarded the DCM in January 1916 for carrying an urgent message through heavy shell fire. His last leave had been in April 1916. Swanborough's brother Charles served in the Army Ordnance Corps.

Lance Corporal Edwin John
Swanborough DCM, 1916.

Two officers died of wounds received on the first day of the
Battle of the Somme. Both were Lieutenants and, by tragic
coincidence, one was the son of the Vicar of Downton, the other
the son of the Baptist Minister.

Second Lieutenant Aubrey Greville Newton Dickenson was

2nd Lieutenant Aubrey Greville Newton Dickenson,
2nd Battalion, King's Royal Rifle Corps.

95

born in October 1896, the second son of the Rev. and Mrs Lenthall Greville Dickenson. He was educated at Twyford and Winchester College and passed into Sandhurst in August 1914. In January of the following year he received his commission with the King's Royal Rifle Corps and proceeded to the Front to join the 2nd Battalion in June. He died of his wounds in hospital at Bethune on Saturday 1st July and his remains were interred in the cemetery there the following day. Dickenson had previously been admitted to a field hospital in July 1915 with chicken pox and wounded on 22nd February 1916, remaining on duty at that time.

Dickenson's father, the Vicar of Downton, the Rev. Lenthall Dickenson was also at the Somme in July 1916. The War Diaries of the 1st Battalion, Wiltshire Regiment show that on the night of 30th June/1st July the Battalion had marched from Puchevillers to Varennes 'in the forward area of impending operations.' They spent Saturday 1st July resting after the previous night's march, while preparations were made to join

A copy of the telegram sent to Downton Vicarage relaying news of Lieutenant Dickenson's death in July 1916. [Courtesy PRO, Ref. WO339 4353].

the offensive. On the morning of Sunday 2nd July a full kit inspection of all companies in battle order was made by the Commanding Officer. At 11.30am a church parade was held, the service being taken by the Rev. Dickenson. As Dickenson conducted this service, was he aware that his 19 year old son had been killed in the bloody fighting of the previous day?

Mrs Frances Dickenson received the news of her son's death at the Vicarage on the Sunday afternoon. On Tuesday 4th July a Memorial Holy Communion Service was held at Downton Parish Church for Dickenson. A similar service for Coombs took place at the Baptist Church on 9th July.

The Rev. Arthur and Mrs Coombs of South Lane Baptist Church heard the news of their only son Henry's death on Monday 3rd July. He had died of his wounds at No. 5 Casualty Clearing Station, Albert, France on the previous day. Henry Whitaker Coombs was a 23 year old mathematics teacher at Wellington College, Crowthorne, Berkshire. He had been educated at Keyford School, Frome, Somerset, Manchester Grammar School and Corpus Christi College, Oxford, where he obtained a BA. In late December 1914 he was gazetted Second Lieutenant and joined the Northumberland Fusiliers. By his death, a very promising academic career was brought to an untimely end.

A letter from Mr and Mrs Coombs to the War Office, dated 6th July 1916 survives, in which they ask for more details of

Lieutenant Henry Whitaker Coombs, 18th Battalion, Northumberland Fusiliers.

their son's death. In the reply an informant states that Coombs was 'in a communication trench between supports and front line when he was shot.' A further eye-witness account is given by L. C. Williams of the Lewis Gun School who reports that:

> *On the 1st July about 8 o'clock in the morning we were going along a communications trench near Bacourt Wood and I met stretcher bearers carrying Lieutenant Coombs.*

The *Wellington Year Book* of 1916 contains the following entry relating to the death of Coombs:

> *Lieutenant Henry Whitaker Coombs, Northumberland Fusiliers, died on July 2nd, of wounds received on the previous day. He was educated at Manchester Grammar School and Corpus Christi, Oxford. He came to us as a Master in 1914, and his appearance was so youthful that he was generally known as 'the Boy.' There was something singularly fascinating about the simplicity of his character, and though with us but a short time he was much liked both by members of the School and Common Room. In January 1915, he joined the 18th Northumberland Fusiliers, and only two days before his death, Colonel J. Shakespear (O.W.), when writing to us, spoke of the excellent officer into which Coombs had developed.*

Amongst their surviving service papers are inventories of the effects posted back to their next of kin.

2nd Lieutenant Dickenson	Lieutenant Coombs
4 metal stars	1 gold wrist watch and strap
10 regimental buttons	1 Prayer book
2 shoulder tithes	1 note book
1 letter	1 field service pocket book
1 whistle	1 photo case containing photos
1 lanyard	1 identity disc
1 identity disc	1 field message
1 vulcanite fountain pen	85 centimes in French money
1 credit note case	1s. 11½d.
1 silver cigarette case token (farthing)	

The consequences of the young deaths to the two families were devastating. Within three weeks the Rev. Coombs had decided to leave the village. In a letter dated 26th July, he accepted the position as Minister of Bratton Baptist Church. He writes 'I anticipate the opportunity of regular ministerial work in a village where so many of my happiest times have been passed.' Coombs left Downton for Bratton in early September and remained Pastor there until his retirement in 1923, when he continued to live in Bratton. Lieutenant H. Whitaker Coombs is also commemorated on the Bratton War Memorial.

In the *Downton Parish Magazine* of December 1916, the Rev. Dickenson announced that it was his intention to resign as Vicar from 28th February of the following year. Dickenson who had spent most of previous 19 months working as a Senior Chaplain to the Forces on the Western Front, wrote:

> ... *is there any good ground for hoping that I shall be in such good physical condition, after the strain of war life is over, to be able to take up at once, the thread and the burden of parish work? After much anxious thought I have arrived at the conclusion that, the interests of the parish, the Church and the people, combine together in calling for a resident vicar, in other words for my resignation.*

Dickenson thanked the parishioners for the 'unfailing kindness and friendship' which they had always shown him and his family, and particularly the sympathy expressed at the time of their recent bitter bereavement. He concludes:

> *If because of the war, I cannot remain your Vicar, at any rate I trust that in spite of the war, I may always remain your friend, and as such I hope we may often meet.*

The announcement was received with shock, sorrow and regret in the Parish, as Dickenson was most highly thought of.

Two other Downtonians died in the early days of the Battle of the Somme. Sergeant Arthur Viney, a worker at the Downton Tan Yard was killed on 2nd July. He was the son of the late Charles and Emily Viney. Charles Viney had been the Downton drowner, an occupation which involved controlling the level of water in water meadows. It was a particularly important job in the spring, to encourage early grass growth for grazing. Sergeant Viney's last leave had been in January 1916.

Sergeant Arthur Ernest Viney, 1916.

Private Ralph Bundy of the 2nd Battalion Wiltshire Regiment died of his wounds on 8th July. Before the war Bundy had been a keen member of the Downton Band. News that Private Bundy was officially reported wounded and missing did not reach his parents until late August. A brother, Private Edwin Frank Bundy had also played in the Downton Band before the war and also served in the 2nd Wiltshire Regiment. Another brother, Bernard worked at the Tannery until the day of his death in January 1982, at the age of 86.

In addition to the deaths there were several non-fatal casual-

NOTHING is to be written on this side except the date and signature of the sender. Sentences not required may be erased. If anything else is added the post card will be destroyed.

I am quite well.

I have been admitted into hospital
{ *sick* } *and am going on well.*
{ *wounded* } *and hope to be discharged soon.*

I am being sent down to the base.

I have received your { *letter dated_____*
telegram ,, _____
parcel ,, _____

Letter follows at first opportunity.

I have received no letter from you
{ *lately.*
{ *for a long time.*

Signature only. } *A. E. Viney*

Date January 20 1916

[Postage must be prepaid on any letter or post card addressed to the sender of this card.]

(B12313)—Wt. W 3497/293—1000m.—9/15.   S. & S., Ltd.

Field postcard from Sergeant Viney 20th January 1916.

ties at the Somme. Sergeant Tom King, the son of Mr and Mrs King of Barford Lane and Lance Corporal Albert Downer, were struck down by shell fire, after having engaged in hand-to-hand fighting in a German trench. Their condition was however, not described as serious. Lance Corporal Downer, who had been injured on two previous occasions including being buried alive and suffering from frost bite, was sent to Stourbridge Hospital. Private Edward Moody was shot in the leg and had also been sent back to Britain for treatment at Reading Hospital.

Other Downton men of the Wiltshire Regiment injured at the Somme included Sergeant Edward James Blake, who was wounded for the third time, Lance Corporal William Lawes and Private Percy Hatton who had both been wounded on a previous occasion. Blake was sent to Govan Hospital, Hatton to

Dunston. Private William Mussell of The Borough was very seriously injured.

The catastrophic scale of lives lost at the Battle(s) of the Somme, resulted in changes to how the war was reported in the local media. From the start of the war, The *Western Gazette* had always included a column of photographs depicting their Roll of Honour and photographs of families (particularly brothers) who had enlisted together. The Roll of Honour appeared beneath the caption 'Dulce et Decorum est pro Patria Mori – Died on the Field of Honour' which means 'It is a sweet and seemly thing to die for one's country.' This quotation is now best-known as the title of a Wilfred Owen poem, which he refers to as 'The Old Lie.'

The *Western Gazette* included photographs of dead, wounded and missing, but this practice was quietly dropped in July 1916 after the Somme, being resumed in October of that year but with far less photographs (approximately two per edition) and these were placed within the relevant local news section of the paper. By 1918, presumably because of shortages of raw material, no photographs appeared at all. Local soldiers whose portraits appear in the *Gazette* include: Company Sergeant Major F. C. Keeley, Corporal A. Downer, Private F. R. Batchelor, Private E. F. Bundy, Private A. Downer, Private F. P. Moody, Private W. Mouland, Sergeant W. Beauchamp, Private G. Forder, Private W. J. Hiscock (1915); and Lance Corporal E. J. Swanborough (1916). The *Salisbury and Winchester Journal*, on the other hand, has hardly any photographs at all for the entire duration of the war. The only one of Downton is printed on page 8 of the *Journal*, 16th January 1915 and shows the severe flooding between the Iron Bridge and the Tan Yard.

Of all the deaths of Downton's soldiers and officers in 1916, two of the most touching were of those who had been seriously injured earlier in the war, yet had fought their way back to health despite the severity of their injuries, and re-enlisted in the armed services. Private William George Haydon has already been mentioned; the second case is Second Lieutenant Alfred Ernest Morgan who was killed towards the end of the Battle(s) of the Somme in October 1916. The son of Mr and Mrs Richard Morgan of The Borough, Second Lieutenant Morgan of the Middlesex Regiment was killed in action in France on 29th October. He was 27. Morgan had been born at West Kensington and moved to Fordingbridge when he was 8, where he was educated at the Church of England School. He became an apprentice carpenter, but was keen to join the armed forces and became a member of the Fordingbridge Company of the 7th Battalion Hampshire Regiment (a territorial force). At the age of 20 he joined the Royal Dragoon Guards and proceeded to India and then to South Africa, where he was on service when the war broke out.

His Regiment was sent to France and he saw much of the early fighting at Mons and the Retreat. Morgan was shot through the lungs on 27th October 1914, and his life was in danger. Against the odds, however, he recovered after under-going operations and was eventually declared fit enough to rejoin the armed forces. Once again he proceeded to France, where he was promoted in the field to the rank of a corporal, for meritorious service, and was given a Second-Lieutenancy in the Middlesex Regiment.

Mr and Mrs Morgan received a letter from their son's Captain, in which he stated that both the deceased Officer and his servant were killed instantly by a shell. He added:

> *His death is a great loss to the battalion as he was a most invaluable officer. I had known him for some months and he was always resourceful and cheerful under any circumstances, and his death is very keenly felt by us all. He is buried in a cemetery near the spot where he fell. His grave is marked with a cross with his name and regiment and the Grave's Registration Committee have been informed of its position. Will you allow me to offer my deepest sympathy in your terrible loss and also that of the other officers of the battalion.*

Mr and Mrs Morgan's only surviving son Robert served in France in the Royal Army Medical Corps. He was invalided out in January 1918. The family's business, a barber's shop, at Meadowlands, The Borough, is pictured on the photograph of the 1915 Downton floods on page 146.

Salonica 1915-18

The expedition in Salonica is perhaps the most confusing theatre of the Great War. So many Balkan countries were involved as well as pre and post-revolutionary Russia. As part of

Greece – a neutral country – Salonica was important to the British Empire, as it was a barrier-state across the potential path of the German armies to India and the Far East.

In 1915 the Serbs evacuated their capital Belgrade, the Austrians invaded the neighbouring country Montenegro and Bulgaria (in its ambition to annex Macedonia) attacked Serbia. The Bulgarian army began mobilisation on 1st September. As a consequence of King Constantine's actions, Greece announced that she would not declare war on Bulgaria. Greece was united with Serbia by a treaty of alliance.

British and French forces landed at Salonica during the period 3rd-8th October 1915 at the invitation of M. Venizelos the Greek Premier. King Constantine, unconstitutionally, drove Venizelos from power when the Allies had already begun to land. The King, whose wife Queen Sophia was the Kaiser's sister, was pro-German, as was M. Zaimis the successor to Venizelos, but he backed Greek neutrality.

The Austrians eventually forced the Serbs to retreat across the mountains to find refuge in Albania. The French attempted to link up with the fleeing Serbs. By May 1916 a huge army was ashore at Salonica – more than a quarter of a million men.

Many decades later, it is not possible to know the names of all of Downton's men who were involved in the war in Macedonia, but it was stated that there 'were battalions like one of the

Private Frederick James Chalk (5th from left), Army Service Corps in action in Salonica.

The White Tower at Salonica.

Wiltshires which would march a thousand strong and not a single man fall out.' Nevertheless, it is known that Gunner Burdock, RFA and Corporal Cove, Army Veterinary Corps were both stationed there in 1917. Corporal Fred Chalk was also there in 1916-17 and to him is owed the story and pictures of the Zeppelin.

The wreckage of Zeppelin LZ85 displayed outside the White Tower, May 1916.

105

The airship is the Zeppelin LZ85 which was shot down on 6th May 1916 by HMS *Agamemnon* moored in the harbour. The Zeppelin had carried out attacks on 1st February and 17th March but its last flight had been on 6th May when it was shot down in the marshes. Four officers and 8 men were taken prisoner by the British. The wreckage was exhibited to the populace near the White Tower which was a harbour landmark. The LZ85 had been commanded by Captain Scherrer.

The captured crew said that they were astonished at the way they had been picked out by British anti-aircraft batteries and followed all down the line to Salonica. By the time they got there they were so blinded by the glare of the searchlights converging on them, that they could not see to drop their bombs.

Home Correspondence

During the war all mail was censored, but the troops eagerly looked forward to letters and cards from home. Field postcards were issued as a simple and quick means of keeping in touch. Few letters and cards now survive from local soldiers, but of those the author has found, three show their writers' fondness for Downton. Battery Sergeant William Newman, writing in 1916, wistfully reflects on courting in Moot Lane, then a beautiful country lane with steep banks on either side, filled with wild flowers and topped by tall horse chestnut trees. There were then no houses at all between Moot Farm and the railway bridge, so the area was very secluded.

On another occasion, in a postcard dated 16th October 1915, Newman, surely the most hardened of the local soldiers puts on a brave, if anxious face about the future:

We are having rather a lively time at present but have still good hopes of pulling through quite safe ... If we have a bit of luck and are still living we might be home for Xmas 1917.

Lance Corporal Reginald Durdle, on a postcard to Frank Chalk, dated 27th November 1916, wrote:

I am in the pink. Do you remember the old home song, Downton, Downton, Home Like Downton? I am so longing to get back to the old place. I have had enough of this show.

Romantic postcard overwritten with 'Moot Lane.'

The grim humour of the Western Front.

The song to which Durdle is referring was the *Downton Home Song*, which had been written by John Northover the Headmaster of Downton Board School to celebrate the Diamond Jubilee of Queen Victoria in 1897. It was performed regularly in the village, to the tune of *Dulce Domun*, the Winchester College Song. The *Downton Home Song* consisted of five verses and two choruses. It began as follows:

> Comrades, let us lift together
> Heart and voice in chorus;
> Sing we our melody,
> Welcome to our holiday
> Thoughts of home sweet home before us.
>
> Downton, Downton, homelike Downton,
> Downton, Downton, homelike Downton,
> Memory sweet that ne'er will leave us,
> Home that ever will receive us.

1917

The Vicar of Downton, the Rev. Lenthall Greville Dickenson preached his farewell sermon at St Laurence's Church at the Sunday evening service of 18th February 1917. He left Downton the following day, returning to his duties as Senior Chaplain to the British Forces in France. On the Saturday evening the Vicar had been presented with gifts from grateful parishioners in a ceremony at the Lecture Hall of the Unionist Club. These included a cabinet of the Queen Anne period, a Chippendale arm chair and an antique brass plate warmer.

The Rev. Dickenson was greatly missed by the people of Downton who remembered that he had given up so much to come to the Parish in 1910. The family had hoped to stay in the Downton area but their attempts to arrange to rent *Willersley Cottage*, Morgan's Vale fell through and they had to seek accommodation in Salisbury. At the end of the war they were living at the Old Rectory at Durrington. A brass plaque on the inside of the entrance door on the south side of Downton Church commemorates the Rev. Dickenson. By the time the Rev. Dickenson had left the Parish his replacement had already been appointed, namely the Rev. George Salmon, a curate from Horsham, West Sussex.

Senior Chaplain to the Forces, 3rd
Class (equivalent rank Major)
Lenthall Greville Dickenson DSO
and Mrs Dickenson, c.1919.

As Senior Chaplain to the Forces, Dickenson had a successful career in the war. His army records show that he served abroad from 12th July 1915 to 1st September 1917. Despite this long period on the Western Front, he was not wounded and his only injury was a broken little toe on his right foot. Nor did he stay away from the Front line trenches. Peter Haydon recalls his father Jack talking about meeting the Rev. Dickenson walking along the trenches and asking if any of the soldiers came from Downton. In June 1917, the Rev. Dickenson received the DSO. The Rev. Dickenson left the armed forces at Larkhill for the diocese of Winchester in early December 1919. He changed his name to Trotman-Dickenson during the following year. He relinquished his position as Senior Chaplain to the Forces in September 1921, but was appointed Honorary Chaplain to the Forces in October of that year.

Dickenson's eldest son Captain Edward Newton Dickenson was awarded the Military Cross during the war. He had enlisted at Darlington on 24th September 1914, the day before his 29th birthday. He was born at Burnley, Lancashire and educated at Winchester College, later working as a teacher. Captain Dickenson was also mentioned in despatches.

The War in the Air

Two of the names recorded on the Downton War Memorial are of officers in the Royal Flying Corps, both of whom were killed in action in 1917. Major Evelyn Paget Graves is the highest ranking officer recorded on the Memorial. His father the Hon. Adolphus Edward Paget Graves also served as a Major during the Great War. Graves was born at Nagpur, Maharashtra, India on 5th June 1890. His family history is interesting, as his great, great grandfather, Thomas, 1st Baron Graves was the Admiral who surrendered the British Fleet during the American War of Independence. He was also the sixth cousin once removed of the novelist and war poet Robert Graves. The family's connection with Downton was that they lived at Headlands House.

The Hon. Adolphus Graves was the nephew of Lord Graves and, as we have seen, spent much of his professional life working in transport logistics in parts of the British Empire,

Headlands House, c.1900.

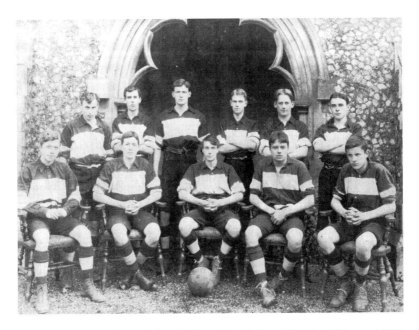

Graves (third, back row) in the Lancing College Football Team, 1907. The player on the extreme right of the front row, Allan Oswald Miles, was later a Second Lieutenant in the 13th Battalion, Gloucestershire Regiment and killed on 30th June 1916.

particularly in India and the Gold Coast. His son Evelyn Paget was educated at The Wick, Brighton, where he was Head Boy, followed by Lancing College, West Sussex, which he attended from January 1905 to July 1908. Here he was head of his House (The Olds), and also a member of Hopewells Football XI.

On leaving Lancing in 1908, Graves completed his education at Freiburg in Germany, returning to England to join the Royal Military Academy in 1909. He passed out of Woolwich into the Royal Artillery in December of the following year and served four years in India with the 25th Battery Royal Field Artillery. He started flying lessons in July 1914 and, having gained his wings on 3rd October 1914, he joined the Royal Flying Corps in the same month.

In February 1915 Graves had a severe accident when his machine (a Gnome Martinsyde) came down from 700 feet at Netheravon, and he suffered a broken right arm and a compound fracture to his left leg, which left him permanently lame. He described the fall, as 'not really disagreeable,' but that he just felt as if he was 'going to walk out of one room into another.' Following his recovery, several months later, he was appointed Staff Captain and Brigade Major to General Higgins, the Chief of the Air Service. After returning to active flying in December 1915, he was a Flight Commander in 20 Squadron, before being sent back to England on promotion to take command of a Training Squadron at Hounslow. In November 1916 he had another accident when he slightly injured his right leg. Nevertheless, he rapidly recovered and returned to France to take command of the famous 60 Squadron in December 1916 at the age of 26. His predecessor had been another disabled officer, Smith-Barry who had crashed his plane near Amiens in the retreat from Mons.

Squadron Commander Graves's successor, Group Captain A. J. L. Scott wrote a book on the history of 60 Squadron, published in 1920. Members of the squadron were awarded one Victoria Cross and 5 Distinguished Service Orders. Pilots of 60 Squadron included Harold Balfour, Albert Ball, A.D. Bell-Irving, Billy Bishop, K. L. Caldwell, J. B. McCudden, W. E. Molesworth, C. F. A. Portal and R. R. Smith-Barry. Scott's book also gives a vivid account of the demise of Major Graves:

Hameau, the correct name of the station being Filescamp Farm. Here, with the aid of the local Royal Engineers and thanks to Graves's tireless efforts, an almost ideal little station was created in the orchard adjoining the great grey walls of M. Tetus's demesne. This was a very old and pictur-esque house, half farm and half château, and was removed some two miles from a main road or railway line, a circum-stance which prevented the aerodrome being bombed at night for a very long time, as it was hard to see from the air. An admirable mess, with a large brick fireplace, corrugated-iron hangars, together with Nissen huts for the officers and N.C.O.s and good accommodation for the men, were all built by the sappers. At this station in M. Tetus's orchard the squadron found a quiet retreat when not actually engaged with the enemy. It is, perhaps, appropriate here to observe that every pilot at this time did, on the average, three patrols in two days over the line, and seldom returned to the aerodrome without a brush of some kind with the Boche. The contrast between our quarters and those occupied by the infantry and gunners in the line was striking. We had cream at every meal, and a hot bath-made by digging an oblong hole in the turf and lining it with a waterproof sheet-whenever we felt inclined.

With the beginning of March 1917, the Boche became very active in the air. The D3 V-strut Albatros appeared in numbers on the 3rd Army front, and about the same time a squadron of red-painted machines of this type, known to the R.F.C. as 'the Circus,' did a good deal of damage to British machines and annoyed us very much. One aeroplane in particular, called the 'Pink Lady' on account of an absurd story that it was flown by a woman – the machine itself was coloured bright red – was often seen between Arras and Albert. It is thought that the pilot was Freiherr von Richthofen the elder. This machine it was that, venturing well over our side of the line on March 6, 1917, crashed an F.E. and went on and engaged and shot down Evelyn Graves, whose machine caught fire. When picked up, he was found to have been shot through the head, so that he was spared the pain of death by burning.

Major Evelyn Paget Graves

Thus a potentially brilliant career had reached a particularly grim end. Presumably the bullet wound came from Graves's own service revolver.

To find a member of the RFC on a village War Memorial is quite unusual, to find such a high-ranking officer as Graves is even more unusual, but one who was allegedly shot down by the Red Baron is a definite rarity. Several books have been written about the 'Red Baron' von Richthofen, and it must be pointed out that despite Scott's commentary, it seems likely that Graves was actually shot down by OffizierStellvertreter (German Warrant Officer) Wilhelm Cymera. This is pointed out in a German book *Abschusse Feindlicher Flugzeuge und Ballone* and also suggested by Norman Franks in *Above The Lines* (1993) and Trevor Henshaw in *The Sky their Battlefield* (1995). Henshaw places the location of Major Graves's crash-site as being approximately 1,500 yards west of the village of Wailly. He was shot down at approximately 1.50pm.

The *Lancing Magazine* of April 1917 contains a lengthy obituary of this prominent Old Boy, part of which states:

> *He was killed on a day made quite remarkable by the intensity of the aerial activity, and not without great sacrifices. He was in a famous squadron. Other Old Lancing Boys too young to know him at school had met him out in France, and brought back the report of his extraordinary charm. We have lost a man of great gentleness combined with energy, a man of spirited affection and devoted to duty, a man wonderfully humble and generous and satisfactory as a soldier and a friend.*

There is no mention of Graves's death in the local press and information contained amongst his service papers gives a confused picture of the events of 6th March 1917. Twenty year old Lieutenant Philip Solomon Joyce went missing earlier that day and it seems that whoever wrote the telegrams confused the incidents surrounding Joyce's disappearance and the death of Graves. Graves was reported missing, and his assumed death is not first reported in the national press (*The Times*) until 13th March. He is buried at Avesnes-le-Comte Communal Cemetery. Neither Joyce's aircraft or his body was ever found and he is commemorated on the Arras Flying Services Memorial.

As with Lieutenants Coombs and Dickenson, the service papers of Major Graves include the inventory of items (dated

24th June 1917) sent to his next of kin, in this case his father, Major the Hon. Adolphus Edward Paget Graves. The list includes five items (1 watch (broken), 1 pilot's badge, 1 collar badge, 1 gold ring, 1 collar stud) and is particularly harrowing, considering the circumstances of his death.

The second Royal Flying Corps Officer on the Downton War Memorial is Lieutenant Arthur Amyot Steward of the Royal Field Artillery, who was killed in action on 6th October 1917. He was the son of Canon Steward, a former Principal of Salisbury Training College and later Rector of Boyton, Wiltshire. Like Lieutenants Wyndham and Coombs, Steward was also educated at Wellington College. His university education was postponed by the Boer War, during which he held a commission in the Norfolk Militia and saw nearly two years service. In 1904 he went up to Magdelen College, Oxford. His career between graduation and 1911 is not known, but in that year he attended Wells Theological College and was subsequently ordained by the Archbishop of York and first appointed a curate in Hull. At the outbreak of the war he was on the staff of St. Mary's Johannesburg and worked amongst the local miners. He returned to England and offered his services as a combatant officer, and was given a commission in 1915 in the RFA, proceeding to the Front in April 1916.

His most recent appointment had been a transfer to the Royal Flying Corps, in which he served as an observation officer. His duties included ascending high above the trenches in a basket

Lieutenant Arthur Amyot Steward.

115

attached to a balloon, taking observations of enemy positions. Such a role involved a high degree of danger, and it is strange to imagine a Church of England clergyman in such a position. It is extremely ironic that, although killed in action, his death occurred not whilst in a balloon, but resting in his dug-out, when it was hit by an enemy shell. Steward was 35 and left an estate valued at £3,606. 2s. 2d. His possessions sent home to his widow at The Moot included three unopened letters.

The Western Front, 1917

On 9th April, attacks were made simultaneously on Vimy Ridge, by the Canadian Force, and by the British on Arras. Both offensives proved to be successful, taking the first and second German lines. The success of this fighting was due in no small part to the 'Rolling' or 'Creeping' barrage, which was the brainchild of Brigade Major Alan Brooke. On that night, it began, unexpectedly, to snow, the attack resuming the next day. On 11th April, British men and horses advanced in a blizzard. They were, however, halted by wire and pushed back by machine gun fire. Private Ernest Batchelor was killed during this day. The Battle of Arras ended on 17th April.

Nomansland, The Salient, Ypres, 1918.

116

Thought to be Private Fred Newman, Gloucester Regiment.

The Allies decided to push forward again, choosing the Ypres area as the main battle front. In this 3rd Ypres battle, advances were made but the fighting was hampered once again by mud, sometimes so deep that men actually drowned in it. In October a renewed attack was made, its objective to take Passchendaele Ridge. On 28th September Gunner Percy Moody died at the Casualty Clearing Station. Private Fred Newman was killed in action on 22nd October. He was the son of Mr and Mrs George Newman of The Borough and brother of Warrant Officer William Newman who was awarded the DCM in 1917. Private Newman had been killed whilst serving in the Gloucester Regiment. He had left his native village before the war, to live at Lyme Regis where he joined up.

Another man from the Downton area was killed in action at Passchendaele. He was Private Charles William Reynolds of the Machine Gun Corps. His widow, Elsie gave birth to their son Gordon shortly after her husband's death. They had been married for two years. Private Reynolds is commemorated in St. Mary's Church, Redlynch. He was the son-in-law of the former Downton Police Sergeant George Hatton who retired in about 1904. George Hatton's three sons, Charles, Percy and William are all included on the commemorative boards in the Memorial

Hall. Mrs Reynolds lived in Waterside for many years and her son Gordon is included on the Downton War Memorial for the Second World War.

1917's Worst Casualties

Throughout the year of 1917, the local press reported some particularly nasty injuries sustained by local servicemen, which resulted in their discharge from the services. Lance Corporal Frank Mussell, Wiltshire Regiment, returned to Downton in early March 1917. He had been shot in the head, while in action in Mesopotamia and this had resulted in the loss of his sight. Despite his severe injuries, Mussel was described as exhibiting 'a wonderfully bright bearing ... and is looking forward to the completion of arrangements for his reception into a home for the disabled for the purpose of being taught a trade.' Lance Corporal Mussell's brother Harry, had also been invalided out of the Wiltshires, suffering from rheumatism. Another brother, William was shot through a lung during action on the Western Front, but recovered and continued to serve with the Regiment in France.

Another severe casualty of March 1917 was Sapper Charles Newman, the son of George Newman of The Borough. Newman was invalided out of the Royal Engineers with cerebrospinal meningitis or 'spotted fever,' a condition which left him deaf in both ears. He was only 18 and had been in the forces for just a few weeks.

Private Percy Hatton, the son of Mr and Mrs George Hatton of The Borough, returned to Downton from hospital in late April 1917, awaiting his discharge from the Army, owing to an injury. Private Hatton had joined the Wiltshire Regiment as a volunteer in October 1915, when just over 18 years old. He was wounded twice, once in the shoulder by shrapnel, and on the other occasion in the right thigh by a bullet. This second injury caused a shortening of the limb and his discharge from the army, some months before his 20th birthday.

Other casualties of 1917 included:

- Private J. Mussell, Wiltshire Regiment, who had been shot in the head.

Former Private Charles Newman and Battery Sergeant Major William Newman. Note Charlie is wearing a silver 'invalided out' badge on his right lapel. This silver badge was issued by the British War Office during the Great War to members of the forces invalided from war service.

- Private Victor Gwyer, Wiltshire Regiment, injured at Mesopotania.
- Gunner Bert Littlecott, RHA, wounded, in action on the Western Front.
- Corporal Clement Palmer, RGA, gas posisoning.
- Private Ernest Aylett, 6th Dragoon Guards, received severe shrapnel wounds in the shoulder and legs.

'Q' Ships

The loss of British naval and merchant vessels from the beginning of the war by the U-Boat menace was unrelenting, and had become particularly acute during 1917, when food supplies were becoming dangerously low. One way in which U-Boats were successfully destroyed was by the use of so-called 'Q' Ships, which were also known as Mystery Ships or Hush Ships. These were decoy vessels, intended to look like innocent fishing or trading ships. In reality they contained Royal Naval personnel and were equipped with the latest anti-submarine weapons.

A prominent Downtonian was the Captain of one of these ships. He was Lieutenant Commander Edmund Gilchrist (Eddie) Wrightson, the son of the well-known Professor. His early career had been in the Merchant Navy, where he had traded along the coast of China. During the war he commanded the 'Q' Ship *Ilma* (formerly the *Merops*), which hunted and sank two German U-Boats off the coast of France near Bell Isle Bay on 21st and 22nd November 1917. For this feat he was awarded the DSO.

The whole ship's company of twenty-eight men shared in an official reward system. Edmund received £52. 7s. 1d., his second in command, an M. Murchison was paid £31. 8s. 4d. The ship's skipper, F. Havies received £25. 2s. 8d. and the rest of the crew got between £10. 9s. 5d. and £16. 15s. 1d. each, depending on rank.

Gunner Arthur Jolliffe

Despite the fact that Major Graves was the highest ranking officer of those from Downton killed in the First World War, information on him was not, initially, easy to find. For instance there was no obituary in the local press and his surviving service records were vague and of course included that misleading telegram.

Similarly, Arthur T. Jolliffe was one of the most difficult names to discover any information about. As with the other 43 listed on the Memorial, the task of finding details of his death began by consulting the records of the Commonwealth War Graves Commission. Their records did not include an 'A. Jolliffe' as having died on active service for the period 1914-21, so the research of Arthur Jolliffe became a particular challenge, as has the continued attempt to get his name officially recognised.

Unlike the so-called 'burnt documents' of soldiers' records of the Great War, all Royal Marine service and attestation records survive, and are preserved at Kew. Jolliffe's papers are to be found amongst the records of the Royal Marine Artillery. He joined the service in March 1906 and served continuously until

Gunner Arthur Thomas Jolliffe, onboard the *Natal*. The date '21st December' is written on the back of this photograph. It was probably taken in 1912, when the ship carried the coffin of the U.S. Ambassador Whitelaw Reid.

the day of his death. His character record throughout this period was described as very good.

He had an extremely interesting service life, which included at least two duties on escort vessels. The Coronation of King George V in 1911 was closely followed by an important Royal Tour of India. The King and Queen sailed on HMS *Medina*, which had been specially commissioned for a few months, to replace the Royal Yacht *Victoria and Albert*, which was too small to accommodate the enormous entourage. HMS *Medina* was in fact a luxury liner, and Gunner Jolliffe was on board as part of the escort to the Royal party. King George V and Queen Mary attended the Delhi Durbar, for which event Jolliffe received the Coronation Durbar medal. HMS *Medina* arrived back in England on 4th February 1912. Following a Church service on board, their Majesties presented all members of the ship with a memento of their voyage to India. Gunner Jolliffe was personally presented with a music programme of a concert that had been held during the visit.

Later in 1912, Gunner Jolliffe had another important duty to undertake. The American Ambassador to Great Britain, Whitelaw Reid died in office in December and following a Memorial Service at Westminster Abbey, the Ambassador's coffin was taken to Portsmouth to be taken back to his native country for burial in New York. The coffin was carried on board the armed cruiser the *Natal*.

During the First World War Jolliffe was stationed at Stanger Head Battery in the Orkney Islands. He was married to Julia May Witt in March 1916, and a clock presented to him in that year is now in the possession of his niece, Vera Finney. It carries the following inscriptions on a brass plaque:

Presented to
Gunner A T Jolliffe RMA
from the NCOs & Men of Stanger Head Battery
whilst on Active Service 1915 & 1916

A telegram among his service records reveals that he died of cardiac failure on board the Hospital Ship *Garth Castle*, in August 1917. He clearly died on active service as the records contain the initials 'D.D.' which stands for 'Discharged Dead.' This is further confirmed by his Death Certificate, from the Index of Marine Deaths. He was buried at Fordingbridge

Cemetery on 12th August 1917. Although the initials RMA appear after his name on the memorial inscription, his grave is civilian. He is also commemorated on the Fordingbridge War Memorial, presumably because his wife's family came from the town. Mrs Jolliffe, who lived in Long Close for many years, died in March 1979, aged 96.

Jolliffe is one of the three 'lost' names on the Downton War Memorial who are not commemorated by the Commonwealth War Graves Commission. The author is one of several researchers trying to get men such as Jolliffe officially recognised as having died in the service of their country. It had been hoped that by the time this book was printed Gunner Jolliffe's name would have been officially added to the CWGC's Roll of Honour and steps put in place to give him a distinctive CWGC headstone. Correspondence with the CWGC – despite being backed up with evidence that Jolliffe died in the war – has so far received deeply disappointing replies. Jolliffe died after a long and steadfast career for his country. His memory deserves better treatment.

2nd Lieutenants

By 1918, 'promotions in the field' were occurring on a regular basis and there are a few examples of men from Downton who were promoted to the rank of Second Lieutenant. These included Sam Durdle, Reg Light, Lewis Stretch and Fred Lydford. Sergeant Instructor Ambrose S. (Sam) Durdle was the son Walter Durdle of High Street, and the younger brother of Reg. He was gazetted to a Second Lieutenancy in the 6th Battalion, Rifle Brigade in the spring of 1917. He had only joined the Wiltshire Regiment less than two years before, but had rapidly passed through various positions to become a Sergeant Instructor.

Unfortunately, Durdle's service records do not survive, but those of other Downton Second Lieutenants do. The records of Second Lieutenant Reginald Francis Light, Royal West Surrey Regiment, show that he received his temporary commission in October 1917, but say little about his new role. There are however some particularly interesting papers relating to injuries he received at St. Quentin on 17th September 1918. Lieutenant Light was blown up by a gas shell and the resulting injuries included being blinded for a period of six hours, plus several recurrent side-effects in the months that followed.

Lance Corporal Frederick Hugh Lydford had enlisted in December 1915 and was given a second lieutenancy in June 1918, presumably so that he could assume a senior position at Prisoner of War Camp No. 177 at La Clytte in Belgium. During his active service, Lydford took a series of photographs of life in the camp and at the Western Front. This unique series of 125 photographs is preserved in an album and some of these have been reproduced in this book. Lydford was killed in a road accident in 1927, but his son, Gordon is well remembered in Downton, being a Church Warden for many years and a keen football player. He died in July 1996 aged 75.

Colleagues of 2nd Lieutenant Lydford try on their gas masks at Crookham Cadet Training School, 1918.

2nd Lieutenant Lydford with German war souvenirs at Messines Ridge, 1918.

2nd Lieutenant Lydford, 1918.

Miniature helmets made from shells by German Prisoners of War, 1918.

Cork screw made from munitions fragments and shrapnel.

The Officer's Mess at 177 Prisoner of War Camp, 1918.

Prisoners of War undertaking salvage work at La Clytte, 1918.

German prisoners en route to 177 Prisoner of War Camp, 1918.

The entrance to 177 Prisoner of War Camp, La Clytte, Belgium, 1918.

The Prisoners' Compound at 177 Prisoner of War Camp, 1918.

2nd Lieutenant Lydford in the ruins at Dickebusch, Belgium, 1918.

Looking towards the German Front Line, 1918.

The Cathedral at Ypres, 1918.   The Cloth Hall at Ypres, 1918.

Hospital, Menin Gate, 1918.

Destroyed German Gun at   War Graves at Ypres, 1918.
Salient, 1918.

Ruined Gas Works at Ypres, 1918.

Ruined Water Tower at Ypres, 1918.

Ruins of Church at La Clytte, 1918.

Shell damaged train at Mons, 1918.

Ypres in ruins, 1918.

Ouderdom in ruins, 1918.

Children in the dugouts of the devastated
area of Messines Ridge, Flanders, 1918.

1918 – The German Spring Offensive

On 21st March 1918, a great German offensive was launched. It
was intended as an all out effort to bring victory for German
forces on the Western Front. The first objectives were to drive
the British from the Somme and the French from the Aisne,
and then to threaten Paris. The battle started with a five hour
bombardment. Gas shells were utilised to weaken the ability for
counter-attack. Aircraft were employed by both sides. In spite
of fighting tenaciously, the strength of the German onslaught
was too much for the 5th Army. In the battle for Manchester

Hill, one British regiment fought to the last round and the last man.

Sergeant Edward James Blake, 1st Wiltshire Regiment was killed on the same day the German offensive was launched. The War Diary of the Wiltshires states that:

> *A complete reserve infantry brigade was encamped around the railhead at Achiet-Le-Grand. One of the first shells hit the medical hut of the First Wiltshires, killing nine men but subsequent shelling killed only one other man in the rest of the Brigade.*

The Service Sheet of Sergeant Blake records his activities in the armed forces from January 1915 to July of the following year:

26 Jan 1915	Sailed from Southampton
27 Jan 1915	Disembarked Harve
1 Feb 1915	Joined Battalion
12 Feb 1915	Influenza – admitted to 7 Field Ambulance
22 Jun 1915	Wounded in action, gunshot wound, left forearm
23 Jun 1915	Admitted to 2 Canadian General Hospital, Boulogne
29 Jun 1915	To England
15 Dec 1915	Embarked
17 Dec 1915	Rejoined Battalion
6 Jul 1916	Wounded in Action, gunshot wound right hand and shock
7 Jul 1916	Admitted to 77 Field Ambulance
9 Jul 1916	To England on *Asturias* and admitted to 18 General Hospital

Corporal William Alfred Gunstone was also killed on 21st March 1918 and on the following day, Private Frederick James Bennett died of his wounds. Gunstone's family home was at The Headlands, Downton. In addition to the three deaths in March, several Downton soldiers from the Wiltshire Regiment were taken prisoner by advancing Germans at this time. These included Lance Corporal Jack Haydon and Privates Edwin Frank Bundy, Albert Patience, William Taylor and Sidney Ridout. For many weeks these soldiers were reported as missing, presumed dead. Remembering his war-time experiences, years later, Private Ridout commented on how he and his

E. Frank Bundy, from an old photograph of Downton Band, c.1925.

colleagues had been taken by surprise at the Germans' rapid advancement. He recalled looking out of the trench and there was not a soul in sight, but suddenly the whole field of his vision was full of Germans advancing from the horizon. He said the 'ground was black with them like ants.' Sadly, Sidney Ridout's twin boys served in the Second World War and were operating a gun together, when one of them was killed, the other severely injured.

Private Frank Bundy, 2nd Wiltshire Regiment was amongst those taken prisoner in March 1918. His unusual encounter with a German officer was reported widely in the local papers on his return to Downton in January 1919. This is how the *Salisbury Journal* reported the story:

Private Bundy has a somewhat interesting experience while lying wounded on a stretcher by the roadside after he had been captured by the Germans. A German chauffeur having driven up in a car and dropped some German officers noticed Bundy and the name of his regiment and asked him whether he really came from Wiltshire. Bundy replied in the affirmative and the German, whose name was Max, then mentioned that he was at one time in the service of a Wiltshire peer as butler. On Bundy mentioning that he actually knew his lordship and came from Downton, the German gave him coffee – he regretted he could not offer eatables – and made arrangements for his early removal from his unpleasant position. Bundy feels that had it not been for the German's kindly act, and the speedy attention to his wounds that it secured, his sufferings would have been very much greater and his life probably endangered. Max is stated to have had 'a history' while in England.

German troops entered Soissons on 22nd March and by 30th May they had advanced as far as the River Marne, near Château-Thierry. Once again the Germans threatened Paris, forcing the French back towards Soissons; at their centre they were half-way between the Aisne the Marne. The British retreated too, in order to keep contact with the French.

During the night of 28th to 29th May, the British 19th Division arrived in omnibuses, to fill the gap between the two Allies. The shelling was intense and the fighting ferocious. Privates Fred Bailey and Charles Bishop of the Gloucester Regiment perished during this action. Bishop was reported missing in May, but confirmation of his death did not reach Downton until September. In October 1918, Private Bailey was still officially missing and his death was not confirmed until the end of the war.

Temporary Second Lieutenant Lewis George Stretch, Machine Gun Corps was awarded the MC for conspicuous gallantry in June 1918. Stretch was the eldest son of the former Downton stationmaster and had been educated at Bishop Wordsworth's School, Salisbury. He received his commission in early October 1917. His citation was officially recorded as follows:

For conspicuous gallantry and devotion to duty while in command of two machine gun positions, one of which was surrounded and bombed by the enemy. He, leading his team, rushed the enemy with bombs and revolvers, and broke through them and forced them back under our artillery fire. Later, he visited his other gun and found the team missing, and though he himself was again surrounded, he evaded capture and killed several of the enemy with revolver and rifle fire.

After a series of attacks and counter-attacks, during the summer, the Allies began to advance and drive the Germans back. At this

Sergeant Harry Senior.

time Private Albert George Kimberley Musselwhite died on 19th September. Another Downtonian, Sergeant Harry Senior died on 25th September, when he was instantly killed by an enemy shell.

The first four days of October 1918 saw the Allied Armies advancing on all sectors of the Western Front. Signaller Bert Sheppard, Shropshire Light Infantry was a fatality on the first day of that month. He was killed in action and had served for seven months in France. This fighting saw a 30 mile section of the Hindenburg Line completely over-run.

In the last days of the war, before the Armistice, the Vicar of Downton, the Rev. George Salmon left the village to take up a position as Chaplain to the Forces. Writing in the *Parish Magazine*, Salmon stated that he was not leaving because he was tired of the Parish, but 'because I think it my duty to do what I can to help the soldiers.' Salmon had put forward his name several months previously, but was only accepted for war service in October 1918. Salmon returned to Downton in

November 1919. During the time he was away, Parish responsibilities were carried out by two Curates-in-Charge, the Rev. Tomlin and the Rev. Bryant.

The Rev. J. W. S. Tomlin had some traumatic war-time experiences. At the outbreak of the conflict he had been the Principal of Warminster Missionary College, but as most of the students joined up he was forced to close the college and apply for an Army Chaplaincy. He served with two battalions of the Worcester Regiment from March 1916 to May of the following year. During that time he was in three sections of the Western Front – at Neuve Chapelle, on the Somme, in front of Mouquet Farm and by Chaulnes. He was at Chaulnes when the Germans retreated and he followed them with his division over devastated country until almost within sight of St. Quentin. On Easter Day 1917 he took his last service in France in a roofless church and shortly afterwards was invalided home and discharged. By November 1918, six of his former students at Warminster College had been killed, as had the Vice-Principal of the College.

During October and early November 1918, it was obvious that the war was drawing to a finale. Negotiations were made for the cessation of hostilities on all fronts. On the battleship *Agamemnon* off the island of Mudros Turkish and British negotiators worked out the details of a Turkish Armistice. This ended the British campaign in Mesopotamia on 30th October. The war in Palestine and Syria also ended. Fighting continued on the Western Front where, on 4th November, Wilfred Owen was killed during an assault on the Sambre Canal. As the Allies advanced, the Canadians entered Mons on 10th November. The final Armistice was signed the following day.

They have no lot with our labour in the day time,
They sleep beyond England's foam.

Laurence Binyon (1869-1943), *For the Fallen*

The Home Front

The stresses and hardships of war concentrated the minds and energies of the British population in a way that no previous conflict had done before. Numerous local and national initiatives were founded to support the war effort. They would change the face of England forever in many ways. Perhaps the most significant change at home was the readiness of women to move into occupations which had previously been regarded as 'male territory.' Local newspaper reports and surviving Minute Books provide an illuminating insight into the daily lives of those remaining in Downton. We read of the hospitality shown by local people towards Belgian refugees, the numerous fund raising efforts and the sterling work carried out by the newly formed Women's Institute. Each aspect is well documented and makes fascinating reading. As if the people of Downton did not have enough to contend with as a result of the war, severe flooding which took place in January 1915 stretched their resilience even further. Again their response to the crisis was impressive. Almost every aspect of domestic and village life was radically changed by the war. British Summer Time was introduced in 1916 to save fuel and increase opportunity for that other valuable commodity of labour. Even weddings were much changed and the bridegroom frequently had to make do with an 'acting best man.'

Belgian Refugees

The German invasion of Belgium was followed by stories of German atrocities, which evoked considerable sympathy for the many thousands of refugees who fled to Britain. Two such families were provided with early accommodation in the local area, in the High Street Downton and at *Eden Villa*, The Ridge, Morgan's Vale. The Belgian refugees in Downton lived in Church House, the bow windowed property (now number 14 High Street) which is immediately opposite *The King's Arms*. The property had been left to St Laurence's Church by Elizabeth Baily Hooper, to be used as the 'residence for a female Lay Reader of the Church of England for the benefit of Downton.' She had died in July 1914, aged 79. It was previously called *The Laurels*, but following Miss Hooper's bequest it became known as *Church House* and belonged to the Parish Church until 1955. A Church Army Sister had lived there for some years.

The property, described as having five bedrooms, two reception rooms and a large garden, was rapidly furnished for use by refugees and was ready for occupation by mid-October. A family had moved into the house by the first week of November

Thought to be a photograph of two of the Belgian refugee children who lived at Church House, High Street from October 1914 to the summer of 1916.

138

1914. The *Salisbury Journal* quaintly reported that their 'wants are being looked after by a committee of ladies and the parochial clergy.' The ladies included Mrs Aylett, Mrs Bonvalot, Mrs Carver, Mrs Coombs and Mrs Warren.

The Deflour family, Belgian refugees accommodated in the High Street are vividly remembered by Linda Eastman. She was about the same age as one of the Belgian children, a disabled girl, who would sit in her long basket wheelchair in the bay window of *Church House*. She made bracelets and rings for the local children, with tiny beads. Linda and the girl were friends with the daughter of Mr Barker of Tannery House and the three girls would take boat trips up the river.

In Downton there is a more tangible reminder of the Belgians' stay in the district. Early on the morning of Monday 1st February 1915 one of the refugees living at The Ridge, Morgan's Vale died of a seizure. He was 65 year old Mr Adolphus Christianus Ferdinand Demolder who, together with his family, had fled Ostend after the outbreak of the war.

The family were Flemish and Mr Demolder's funeral service took place in the Parish Churchyard on Wednesday morning of that week in accordance with the rites of the Roman Catholic Church. Although the service did not take place inside the Church itself, this was probably the first time a Roman Catholic service had been held on Anglican Church property in Downton since the Reformation. The local residents were deeply sympathetic to the widow and family of the deceased. The papers sympathised too, and Mr Demolder was not described as a refugee, but as having been 'the guest of the people of Morgan's

Mr Demolder's gravestone in Downton Churchyard.

Vale and Woodfalls.' The house used to accommodate the Demolders at Morgan's Vale still stands, although its name has since been changed from *Eden Villa* to *Rosebank*. It is situated next door to Morgan's Vale and Woodfalls Village Hall.

The tangible reminder is the headstone on Mr Demolder's grave, which was presumably paid for by local people. It is in the form of a cross and has a Flemish inscription. This is one of the most unusual gravestones in Downton Churchyard and quite a rarity in Britain. The inscription reads:

Ter
Zalice Gedachtenis
Van
A. Demolder
Overleden 1 Februari 1915
in den ouder dom van 65 jare

Local sympathy for the Belgian people continued throughout the war, with regular Church collections. In August 1915 an appeal leaflet was distributed throughout Downton asking for funds. It begins:

> *On behalf of seven million Belgians who have dared to stay in their native land, we appeal to our fellow countrymen throughout the British Empire. A great emergency has arisen; an emergency which involves our national honour.*

Both families of Belgian refugees left the Downton area in the summer of 1916. They moved to Le Havre which was both a base of the British Expeditionary Force in France and the seat of the Belgian government from October 1914 to November 1918. Surplus items of furniture from the house in the High Street were sold at the Public Hall on the evening of Wednesday 12th August, raising between £50 and £60 which was donated to the Red Cross Working Party.

Wiltshire historian Ivor Slocombe has written about several domestic aspects of the First World War, including Belgian refugees. In *Local History News*, Winter 1999, Slocombe reveals that Agatha Christie's famous detective Hercule Poirot was inspired by a group of Belgian refugees who lived in a nearby house. The character of Poirot was first introduced in Christie's *The Mysterious Affair at Styles*, in which the detective solves a murder mystery during a visit to Styles House. Poirot had been visiting the house, because its owner 'had kindly extended hospitality to seven of my country people who are, alas, refugees from their native land.'

Floods

January 1915 was a particularly bleak month for the people of Downton. The war had not been 'all over by Christmas' 1914, indeed it was painfully clear that the war would continue for some considerable time. Villagers also had more immediate problems of their own to deal with when severe flooding occurred in the New Year. The entire length of The Borough was flooded – from The Headlands to the Mill Bridge – a scale of local flood catastrophe that had not occurred within the living memory of the people of Downton in 1915, nor since. These were the worst floods in Downton since at least the time of the Napoleonic Wars. The February edition of the *Downton Parish Magazine* reported that 125 houses had been in deep water for a period of fourteen days. The *Salisbury Journal* of 9th January 1915 stated that 'a low lying area of over half-a-mile in length

The January 1915 Floods outside the White Horse. Bert Eastman is on the right of the boat in the foreground. Doug West is second from left.

The flooded East Green of The Borough, looking toward the Corn Stores and the Iron Bridge. The old man in the centre of the picture is Mr Witt. Theo Plaskett is second from right.

on the road to the station, it is one great expanse of water, with the flooded homes mostly occupied by working class families on either side of the street.'

The local community was quick to respond to the crisis. The Rev. Lenthall Dickenson, the Vicar of Downton appealed for funds and a total of £67. 6s. 11d. had been raised within four weeks. The Downton Floods Distress Committee was formed under the Chairmanship of Mr Northover the Headmaster of Downton Council School. The Council School itself and an empty cottage in Waterside were used as temporary accommodation and as bases for the distribution of supplies of food and coal. Mr Macan, the land agent of the Longford Estate (which owned most of the flooded properties) supplied villagers with punts. The Southern Tanning Company was particularly generous at providing flood relief.

The floods were recalled by Bert Giles of Church Lane, Charlton-All-Saints, in an article in the *Salisbury Journal* of 17th November 1977. Giles was a carpenter with the Downton firm Wort and Way. He and Bert Tanner had the job of constructing wooden walkways over the most badly flooded

Beyond the Iron Bridge, the flooded Bunny on the right of the picture adds considerably to the huge amount of water at this part of the village. Note the plank walkway for pedestrians. The building with the tall gable and bow window was the last venue of the Downton Unionist Club, which was wound up in 1958.

areas. 'Trouble was, they were constructed on a Saturday and washed away by the flood on the Sunday.' This was by the second Bunny in The Borough and the above photograph shows the ferocity of the flooding there.

Linda May Eastman, then a child aged 8 has vivid memories of the two weeks of flooding. She was living at the family home of 24 (now 77) The Borough in 1915. There was great excitement amongst the local children and she can remember racing between The Borough and the back garden to see whether the water in The Borough or the water from the carrier in the Catherine Meadows would flood the house first. Looking back, she realises it must have been a time of intense anxiety for her parents John and Rosa Smith. Being confined to the upstairs of a small house with a large family must have been extremely difficult. She smiles as she recalls the 'toilet arrangements' used by the flooded households that were even more primitive than usual!

Although some photographs survive of the floods of 1883 (particularly of students from the Downton Agricultural College taking boat trips along The Borough), this flood was the first in Downton to have been widely captured on camera. It coincided with the golden age of the picture postcard (1904-18), when a large variety of local events and scenes were photographed and sold. There are at very least twenty different postcards of the January 1915 floods.

Elsewhere in South Wiltshire the flooding was equally severe. In Salisbury the Fisherton Street part of the city was particularly badly affected, also the Cathedral Close and the Cathedral itself, where the waters reached a depth of 5½ inches. The floods were not without loss of life, a Canadian soldier was drowned at Amesbury.

Astonishingly, the Minutes of the general meetings of Downton Parish Council following the floods make no reference to them at all. Members of the old Salisbury Rural District Council did take action to alleviate difficulties caused by the floods. They were particularly concerned about the risks to public health from polluted wells and water supplies. At their meeting on 8th January they directed the District's Medical

Newman's Shop, The Borough, opposite The Cross. Fanny Newman is standing in the doorway. Her son Will was in the trenches on the Western Front when this picture was taken (as shown by this book's front cover illustration). Another son, Fred was killed in October 1917. A third son, Charlie lost his hearing in the conflict.

Part of Newman's Shop and other old thatched cottages in The Borough. The cottage immediately to the right of the submerged fencing was the home of Fanny Pretty, the mother of another of Downton's war dead, George Forder, who died of his wounds in October 1915. Mrs Pretty had an important role in early twentieth century Downton as she laid out the village's dead. She died in 1922. Annie Marsh is standing second from left in the boat. She married Frank Chalk in August 1919 and died in 1982, aged 86.

Officer of Health to have notices printed warning inhabitants to boil all milk and drinking water. The Council also instructed the Inspector of Nuisances to arrange for disinfectants to be supplied to the occupants affected by the flooding. At their meeting on 5th February, the District Council arranged for the Downton Petrol Air Gas Company to fix a hydrant, tap and water meter outside the Downton Gas House. Piped water was supplied until 26th March, with an average daily quantity of 445 gallons (2,023 litres) being consumed.

In spite of the severity of these floods in Downton, two amusing incidents stand out. A well known local story about the 1915 floods tells of a householder who kept pigs, but when the sty was flooded out he moved 'the gentlemen that pay the rent' to one of the upstairs rooms of his flooded house. Having checked copies of the *Salisbury Journal* for January 1915 this story is actually recorded, but sadly the man's name is not

The January 1915 floods looking towards the Mill Bridge. Water pours into several properties including the former *George and Dragon* pub off the right of the picture. The odd single storey building in the centre of the picture was Edsall's Forge. Beyond that are the buildings and sheds of the Downton Tan Yard. The tallest brick buildings which dated from the turn of the twentieth century were demolished in November 2000.

mentioned. If he lived in one of the old cottages in The Borough with narrow, twisting stairs, how did he manage to get several pigs upstairs? The second incident can be found in the Minute Book of the Downton Parish Council's Public Hall and Lighting Sub-Committee dated 29th January 1915. It records that a gas light opposite the *Three Horse Shoes* in The Borough was broken when a boat crashed into the lamp post.

The misery of the floods in Downton did not end in January 1915. In mid-February of that year Downton was flooded again. This time the area of flood was much smaller – from Mould's Bridge (then still sometimes referred to by its old name of Kingston Bridge) to the Iron Bridge.

Entertaining the Troops

It was not uncommon for troops to be billeted in rural areas. For instance long before the war, in 1892 the 69th Field

Artillery of the Royal Artillery 'passed through Downton on the march' from Portsmouth to Oakhampton on Dartmoor, where their annual practice took place. The 97 men (and 80 horses) were billeted in Downton for the night of 21st July and a smoking concert was arranged for them in the National School.

There is little evidence of billeted troops in Downton during the Great War. The only example covered in the local press is from early in the war, when, on the night of Monday 8th March 1915 nearly 300 Royal Engineers were billeted in the village. The *Salisbury Jou*rnal records that these men were 'heartily welcomed by the inhabitants.' The Rev. Lenthall Dickenson Vicar of Downton and his assistant the Rev. E. Iden Hart hired the Public Hall, fitted it out as a reading and recreation room. A concert was held there in the evening and a shooting match arranged with the Rifle Club. The Committee of the Unionist Club threw open what the paper described as 'their commodious premises' to the soldiers for games. The *Journal* concludes that 'the men left early the next morning, having spent a thoroughly enjoyable visit to the village.'

Air Raid Precautions

On the night of Saturday 16th November 1940 at 10.30pm, German aircraft dropped two landmines in the Downton area, one of which fell on soft ground at New Court Meadows, causing superficial damage to several properties in The Borough. Local air raid activity in the Second World War is well known, but it may not be realised that air raid precautions were also taken during the First World War.

Between 24th December 1914 and 17th June 1918 there were 51 airship raids and 57 aeroplane raids over the British mainland, killing 1,414 people. These deaths were in addition to those killed in bombardment from the sea. Although none of the bombing raids took place as far west as Downton, air raid precautions were observed by villagers and enforced by the Lighting Committee of the Parish Council.

The Lighting Committee reported to the Parish Council on 22nd March 1916 that the lighting of all street lamps in Downton had ceased in order to comply with the Government's new 'Order as to Light' requirements dated 8th February. The

Chief Officer of Police gave the Council the option of lighting four lamps in the village because of fears for road safety, but these lamps had to be properly shaded on top and have the top two-thirds of their glass painted black. In 1917 the remaining gas lights were removed and placed in storage until 1919. The four permitted lamps were situated at:

- The junction of The Borough with the Salisbury Road
- Mould's Bridge (then a narrow humpback bridge, noted as a traffic hazard prior to the war)
- The Mill Bridge
- Moot Lane Corner (old cottages caused a sharp blind bend in the road where the High Street meets Lode Hill)

In February 1916 the village's Public Hall Committee was also instructed to comply with the new regulations and all the Hall's windows were covered with brown paper. There is evidence that the blackout precautions were not taken particularly seriously. In July of that year the Committee agreed to a request from Mr Edwardes Jowle to remove the brown paper from the large windows at the front of the building prior to his evening concert. Jowle had complained that it would otherwise have been 'excessively stuffy' in the Hall.

As gas was now only required to light four street lamps in the village, the Clerk of the Parish Council wrote to the Downton Petrol Air Gas Company requesting that its gas bill be cut in recognition of this massive drop in supply. The Company quickly responded and a letter dated 27th March stated that they could not see their way to make any reductions.

Working Parties and Fund Raising

Local women were quick to establish a number of fund raising committees in Downton, the most enduring and successful of which was the Red Cross Working Party, which collected money to spend on materials used by members to make hospital items for wounded soldiers. The annual report presented to members at the Unionist Club in March 1917 states that in 1915 the working party had made 380 bandages and 688 garments. As well as parcels sent to troops at the front, beneficiaries included:

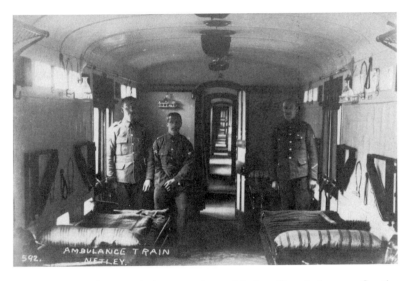

The interior of an ambulance train at Netley Hospital, near South-ampton, c.1914.

- Red Cross Hospital, Southampton Docks
- Red Cross Hospital, Netley
- Red Cross Depot, Salisbury
- Salisbury Infirmary

The Red Cross Working Party was wound up in April 1919 when a report of the organisation's success was given. Between its establishment in 1914 and its final meeting in February 1919 a total of 6,691 garments had been made for hospitals tending wounded troops. Funds received from collections, jumble sales and other activities amounted to £452. 10s. 0d., of which £322 had been spent on the purchase of materials. The remaining balance of £130. 10s. 0d. was distributed thus:

- £50 to the Salisbury Infirmary as a token of gratitude for the care extended to the wounded from Downton
- £60 to the Downton War Memorial Appeal Fund
- £10 – Baptist Church War Memorial Fund
- £10 – Parish Church War Memorial Fund

The remaining 10 shillings was donated to the Boys' Return Gift Club.

Closely related to the activities of the numerous working parties were the varied fund raising events that took place during the war years. Fund raising played a much larger part in village life than today, because basic local facilities such as hospitals and district nursing relied heavily on charitable donations. Fund raising objectives in Downton during the Great War can be divided into three categories. Firstly there were the funds raised for the Red Cross and for local hospitals treating sick and wounded soldiers. Then there were the funds raised for Downton soldiers, sailors and officers, both serving in the war and those who had been taken prisoners of war. This money was used to buy them comforts. Finally, local villagers reacted to the news of events abroad during the war. In 1914-15 funds were raised for the oppressed Belgians; later on in the war Serbian people were also the beneficiaries. Such compassionate fund raising was not a new phenomenon in Downton, despite much local hardship. For example in the early weeks of 1897 the workers of the Downton Tan Yard arranged a house to house collection to raise money for famine relief in India.

The comfort of Downton's servicemen serving away from home was a strong feature of the fund raising events, right from the start of the war in August 1914, when money was raised to buy tobacco. The run up to the first Christmas of the war saw a variety of such events in the village. On Thursday 17th December a concert was held in the Public Hall to raise funds to purchase additional troop recreation tents on Salisbury Plain. The event organised by the Vicar and his wife with music provided by the South of England Temperance Band under their conductor John Green. The previous evening had seen an encouraging attendance at a whist drive in the lecture hall of the Unionist Club, which had raised money for cigarettes for soldiers. All Downton's servicemen and officers were sent Christmas gifts each year for the duration of the war.

In addition to the local initiatives, there were several nation-wide schemes aimed at sending comfort to the troops. The most well known of these is Princess Mary's Christmas gift box, 1914. This was an embossed brass tin, measuring 130mm x85mm x30mm, which contained a pipe, tobacco, cigarettes, a lighter and a Christmas card. The lid of the tin is inscribed with the phrase 'Imperium Britannicum' above a profile of Princess Mary with the words 'Christmas 1914' beneath. At the sides

In 1918, Trafalgar Square was transformed into a model battlefield to stir the imagination of those at home and help increase the purchase of War Bonds.

and corners of the lid are the names of the Allies – 'Belgium, France, Servia [Serbia], Montenegro, Russia and Japan.'

The Downton War Savings Association was formed in June 1916 for the Parish. At its inaugural meeting a total of 14s. 6d. was collected, just a shilling short of the amount required to purchase a certificate. By late-January of the following year the Association had raised £229. Further success occurred the following month when village organisations started withdrawing funds from their bank accounts and investing the money in the Association. These included the Downton Women's Institute and the Downton and District Horticultural Society which invested £30 in the initiative.

By February 1917 a Wiltshire Prisoners of War Fund had been established towards which many Downtonians subscribed and monthly collections were taken. Several local soldiers were taken prisoner in the spring of 1918. A local Wiltshire Regiment Prisoner of War Fund was co-ordinated by the old Salisbury Rural District Council. In its two years of existence people from Downton contributed £174. 0s. 9d. to the fund.

The most successful individual fund raising event of the war in Downton appears to have been an auction and jumble sale

151

held at the Public Hall on Wednesday 7th July 1915. The auction included clothing, china, furniture, poultry, rabbits, doves, a sheep, cakes, flowers, vegetables and eggs which were auctioned by Mr Wallis of Woolley and Wallis. Over £124 was raised for the Duchess of Westminster's Hospital in France. The event was organised by Mrs Wyndham of Charford Manor whose son 2nd Lieutenant George Heremon Wyndham had been killed in action in March 1915.

Downton Women's Institute

The importance of women to the local war effort cannot be over-stated. From the very start of the conflict local women worked hard for the war effort in munitions and crop production as well as carrying out numerous fund raising activities. Some local women including Miss Squarey and Miss Phyllis Taunton left Downton to work where they thought their labour could best be offered. Miss Taunton worked at a YMCA hut in Verrdrouse, France. In February 1918 a special ceremony took place at the Public Hall when over 40 members of the Women's Land Army were presented with armlets and stripes for long service.

A valuable source of information about the part Downton's women played in the war is the Minute Book of the Downton's Women's Institute, which is preserved at the Wiltshire County Records Office. The Institute was the second women's organisation formed in Downton; a Mothers' Union had been formed in Downton almost three decades earlier in January 1887. Downton Women's Institute was founded in April 1916 – the first W.I. in Wiltshire, the sixteenth in the British Isles. The impact of the Women's Institute in the Downton of the First World War was massive. A huge variety of new schemes and forward-thinking ideas were initiated. Within just two and a half years of its formation the Institute was described in the local press as a 'real force in the life of the village.' It is little wonder that by the end of the war the Institute could boast a membership of almost 100. Comparison of the wartime Minute Books of the proactive Downton Women's Institute and passive Downton Parish Council is startling.

The Institute's first public meeting took place in the Public Hall at 2.30pm on Friday 14th April 1916. That afternoon's

Munitions workers, January 1917 including Bessie
Senior (left). Note the triangular 'On War Service' badges.

proceedings included music by Miss D. Coombs, an address by
Mrs Larkham of Salisbury on garments made from old stock-
ings and an Exhibit from the Red Cross Working Party of
German relics from France, shown by Mrs Marriott-Smith. A
large number of women turned up at the Hall and after the
meeting thirty-seven names were taken of women who wanted
to join. At a Committee Meeting held immediately afterwards it
was decided to hold all future meetings at 2.00pm on the first
Thursday of the month in a room in the Unionist Club. A
committee was established, but little did some of the women on
this first committee realise how tragically the war was to affect

their lives. Mrs Carver had been elected President, Mrs Dickenson Vice-President, and the committee also included Mrs Coombs and Mrs Steward. All of these women were to lose loved ones in the months ahead.

At the Institute's next meeting held at the Unionist Club on 4th May there were talks on both the Daylight Saving Bill and the war time experiences of Mrs Carver's son, Ralph, who had just arrived back from Egypt. The Minutes record that Carver 'gave a graphic description of the rescue of officers and crew of the *Taro* which was sunk by a German submarine off Port Sallum. All on board being made prisoners and taken into the desert where they and their guards were near starvation when rescued by a fleet of armoured cars under the Duke of Westminster in February last.' Unfortunately the Minutes provide no more details of Carver's experiences, but it does give an indication of the horrors of the war being talked about in the village. Such news from the front doubtless strengthened the resolve of the folk of Downton to contribute to the war effort.

The Institute was incredibly proactive and by the end of May had introduced a scheme for the co-operative selling of vegetables in Downton, which benefited both small producers and local consumers. Amongst the other initiatives set up by the Institute was the collection of waste paper for salvage and the widespread collection of wild flowers and herbs for the war effort. The plants, which were required for medicinal purposes, included comfrey, foxglove, dill, fennel, even dandelions, and particularly the dead nettle. Once collected the plants were dried and sent to local depots.

In 1917 the Institute turned its attention to the shortages of certain food stuffs. Once again a co-operative scheme for the buying and selling of locally grown food was set up. The Downton Institute went further, by renting a large field in Barford Lane and growing potatoes for sale to Downton's households at a reduced market price. The subject of shortages and food production is given more attention later.

One of the food products that was in shortest supply was sugar and the Minutes of the Downton Institute give a strong clue as to the association of jam making with Women's Institutes, typified by the phrase 'Jam and Jerusalem.' The Minutes of a Committee Meeting held at The Moot on 2nd February 1917 record a resolution passed by the Institute and Downton and many other branches throughout the country which was addressed to the government's Food Controller:

In view of the probable further restriction in the consumption of sugar, and in order to prevent the loss of valuable food stuff the Downton Women's Institute urges the government to ensure that cottagers with fruit gardens, small fruit growers and cottagers who will pick wild fruit for home consumption should be allowed sufficient sugar to enable them to preserve their home grown and locally picked supply of fruit.

In July of the following year at another Committee Meeting at The Moot, the subject of 'Communal Jam Making' was discussed as some 28 lbs. (12.7 kg) of sugar had been given to the Institute for that purpose. Mrs Marriott-Smith 'kindly offered the use of her kitchen and fire' at Fairfield House. The jam that was produced was distributed on a co-operative basis.

The enthusiasm for jam making was merely a small part of the many and varied activities carried out by the Institute. Members also reacted to events as war progressed. A notable example is another resolution passed at Downton in July 1918 and forwarded to Mrs Page at the American Embassy:

The members of the Downton W.I. at the meeting held on Independence Day 1918 wish to record their deep gratitude to the women of America for the sacrifice they are making on behalf of the great cause of this country and they pledge themselves to make the best possible use of the food sent to England.

Apart from the immediate practicalities of assisting Downton during the war, Women's Institute members showed a great keenness to shape a better Downton for the returning service-men. Sixty-five members attended a meeting at The Moot on 2nd May 1918, when a competition was held for the best suggestions as to how the Institute could help the village. The most popular ideas were for a children's playground, public baths, a boot club for children (as a preventative health measure), a crèche for the children of Institute members and the urgent need for a large number of state aided houses in Downton.

Institute members were assigned to carry out enquires about how these improvements could be brought about and report back to the meeting of 3rd June. Not all the suggestions came to fruition. For instance, Mrs Warren reported that Mr Barker of the Tan Yard had 'promised to give a piece of land for a swimming bath with arrangements for hot baths along side after the war, but nothing could be done at present owing to the labour shortage.' The Institute was not successful in finding a field suitable for a playground. A field in South Lane was suggested, but a local butcher was unwilling to give up his tenancy of the land. A crèche however had been set up during Institute Meetings and Mrs Carver had written to the Ministry of Reconstruction on the subject of providing more badly needed state-aided housing. The idea of a Boot Club had been very well received and by December 1918 over £41 had been subscribed to the club.

The work of the Women's Institute in Downton assisted the village in so many ways during the war; a small but important contribution was helping to maintain morale. From the start of the war a bell at Downton Parish Church had been tolled daily at noon as a constant reminder of the needs of Downton's soldiers, sailors and officers serving abroad. By the summer of 1917 this practice had stopped, but on the suggestion of Mrs Carver it was revived when members living near the Church were encouraged to volunteer as ringers. A Roll of Honour detailing the names of the men of Downton who were serving in the forces had been displayed in the Church Porch since the early months of the war. The Institute suggested it needed bringing up to date and in April 1918 the Committee arranged a house-to-house canvass to record the names of all Downtonians serving abroad. The result was neatly copied onto two large sheets and this Roll of Honour is still displayed in Downton Church, next to the War Memorial.

The Institute still made time to hold a limited number of social activities, which were much welcome brief diversions from the hardships of war-time. One such event was organised by Mrs Brand in February 1917 who wanted some kind of 'cheering entertainment to relieve the tedium of the present war time conditions.' The event took place in the Public Hall on the evening of Monday 19th February, but 'in consequence of war conditions and food restrictions, no refreshments were provided.' It nevertheless raised over £8 for the Lord Roberts' Workshops for permanently disabled soldiers and sailors. A collection made in the Parish Church some 15 months previously had raised a similar amount.

The Hall was crowded and Miss Squarey gave a speech about the charity for which the money had been raised. Miss Ruth Legassicke Squarey was a formidable character of late nineteenth and early twentieth century Downton. The daughter of Elias Pitts Squarey of The Moot, she was a local artist and accomplished violinist. Soon after the outbreak of the war she left Downton for London to work as a forewoman in a factory which employed disabled ex-servicemen under the Lord

The redoubtable Miss Squarey.

157

Roberts' Scheme. At the fund raising event she commented that one of the outstanding features of her experiences at the factory was 'the wonderfully brave outlook that the disabled men had on their future lives.' After the Great War Miss Squarey lived at Headlands House, the property which had formerly belonged to Major the Hon. Adolphus Graves. By the early 1950s she was Downton's oldest resident and unveiled the restored Borough Cross (which had been damaged by the New Court landmine in November 1940) as part of the events to celebrate the Coronation of Elizabeth II in 1953. Miss Squarey died on 16th November 1959 aged 96.

Another occasion during the war when Miss Squarey showed much resolve was in an argument with the Parish Council's Public Hall and Lighting Committee in December 1917. The Downton Women's Institute wanted to start serving mid-day cooked meals to local school children and to use the Public Hall for this facility. Miss Squarey asked for details of hire costs and was disturbed to find the fees were 1s. 6d. per day, plus the Institute had to provide its own fuel to heat the Hall, cook the meals and hire the caretaker. Miss Squarey dug her heels in, and wrote back with what she considered would be acceptable to the Women's Institute, who were, after all, helping the village out by providing this service during the war. The W.I. were prepared to pay 2s. 6d. per week and did not require the caretaker. The Committee accepted. Miss Squarey had won through and the scheme provided desperately needed hot meals for local children. By December of the following year over 5,000 meals had been served.

A similar attempt at excessively charging the Women's Institute had occurred in February 1917, when the Downton Unionist Club increased the hire charges of its Club Room from 1s. 6d. to 4s. (an increase of almost 167%). The Institute refused to pay the massively over-inflated amount and voted with its feet, by transferring meetings to the Gravel Close Institute instead.

Food Production

In the early twentieth century the British economy was heavily dependent on overseas trade and therefore particularly vulnerable to a large-scale war in Western Europe. Most raw materials including wool and timber were imported from aboard, as was two-thirds of all food consumed. This included most of the wheat, butter, meat, almost all the sugar, all the tea and a large proportion of fruit. Shipping was directly attacked by the Germans from the start, first by surface raiders and then by their ruthless submarine campaign. Shipping losses were substantial, but labour and raw material shortages caused severe delay in the building of replacements. In 1917 the enemy came within an estimated six weeks of starving Britain out.

Once again local women were at the forefront of the push to increase crop production. One of the first schemes undertaken by the newly formed Downton Women's Institute involved the sale of surplus crops. It was started by the Institute's first President Mrs Frances Dickenson who was the wife of the Vicar. From May 1916 anyone in Downton wishing to sell their excess garden produce could take it to The Moot on Wednesday evenings where it would be bought at the market price. This price had been ascertained earlier in the day by telephone from Salisbury. The scheme was a success and reflected the expansion of the allotment movement throughout the country.

Despite the enormous enthusiasm of local growers, the success of the allotment movement was not guaranteed. Crops were of course prone to natural disasters, the worst of which occurred in the late summer of 1918. Local fruit crops were blighted by a massive infestation of wasps, which was particularly severe in the Downton area.

By early 1917 the government initiated a big push for more home production of crops and produce. A Dairy School for the Women's Land Army was established on part of the Longford Estate; its basic aim was to teach town girls how to milk cows. Several talks were given to local groups on aspects of food production. For instance, in January of that year an address on Productive Poultry and Egg Production was given to members of the Downton Women's Institute. Local businesses cashed in on the push for crop production too. Throughout the war the local press was full of advertisements tailored towards the hostilities. Just one brief example is an advert for garden tools by Woodrow & Co., Castle Street, Salisbury which appeared in the *Salisbury Journal* in February 1917. It is headed 'Be Patriotic – and Grow Your own Food.'

The Downton Horticultural Society had been founded in 1905. During the First World War the society changed its name to the Downton War Time Horticultural Society as part of local efforts to encourage the growth of vegetables and fruit. The society secured additional allotments for the use of villagers on Lode Hill and in the late summer of 1917 mounted an exhibition at the Public Hall, to encourage local householders to grow more garden crops. The show was opened by the Society's President Mrs Bonvalot. An entrance fee was charged, which together with funds raised from the sale of produce was donated to the Red Cross Working Party.

In the spring of 1918, the Committee of the Downton Women's Institute held an emergency meeting at Fairfield House, to consider the proposal to rent a large piece of cultivated land from a local farmer on which to grow potatoes for local members. The measure coincided with the government's 'Potato Push' an attempt to grow an extra half a million tons of the crop. It was decided to rent land in Barford Lane from Mr Wookey of Barford Farm, which he offered at a rental of £8 ploughed and manured. The cost was too high for committee funds, so a large proportion of the rent was lent by Mrs Carver of The Moot.

As with most of the work undertaken by the Women's Institute in Downton during the war, the work was carried out on a co-operative basis. Those who worked on the land should have first option to purchase crops at cost price. Members who had contributed to the scheme in other ways would then be allowed to buy, followed by other W.I. members in both cases at cost price. Finally all remaining crops were to be offered on open sale to anyone in the Downton area.

The venture proved an enormous success. The acre of land was planted with 11½ cwt (584 kg) of seed potatoes from which a crop weighing over 11 tons (11.18 tonnes) was harvested in September 1918. Of these 5 tons were sold to Institute members and in the village, 3 tons were sold to Lynwood's Greengrocers in Salisbury, 3 tons were stored for winter seeding, 1 cwt (50.80 kg) given to the harvest thanksgiving. Profits amounted to between £15 and £20.

Purchases of other commodities were undertaken on the same co-operative principle by the Women's Institute in Downton. A scheme for the purchase of coal was initiated by them in July 1918. Orders were taken from local householders during the summer and because of the large quantity purchased, the W.I. was able to secure a price of 33s. 6d. per ton which was 8s. 6d.

less than the market price – a saving of over 20%, plus free delivery.

In February 1918, Mrs Carver negotiated the supply of milk with Mr Wookey of Barford Farm. This was to solve a milk shortage at the Lode Hill end of the village and Wookey agreed to supply up to 30 gallons (136.38 litres) of milk per day at 1s. 9d. a gallon.

The push for further food production continued after the war. In December 1918, a meeting at the Council School led to the formation of a Boys' Rabbit Club. The Club received the support of the County War Agricultural Committee and the idea was to market 400 dozen rabbits weekly at 1s. 6d. per lb. The meat produced was to be made available to locals on advantageous terms. A similar scheme had been looked into by members of the Women's Institute in April of that year, but the idea had to be abandoned as it was too labour intensive.

In early July 1919 Institute members turned their attention to helping farmers and market gardeners in Belgium and France, whose land had been devastated by retreating troops. A fund raising event in the grounds of The Moot raised over £30, which was donated to the Royal Horticultural Society's War Relief Fund.

Although the Women's Institute's idea of supplying good quality foods at a fair price originates from the First World War, similar ideals were revived in Downton in 1981 with the establishment of the weekly Women's Institute market. This still takes place in Downton every Friday morning at the Memorial Hall.

Rationing

Fear of food shortages amongst the general population led to panic buying and hoarding, which in turn – via the rudimentary economic process of demand and supply – pushed up prices. Unlike the Second World War, when a national system of rationing was introduced at the start of the conflict, rationing during the First World War took place on a more ad hoc basis, with several local discrepancies. The Imperial War Museum provides the following list of rationed items, based on data in a book *British Food Control* by William Henry Beveridge published in 1928.

Sugar – National rationing existed from 31 December 1917 to 29 November 1920.

Butter – National rationing existed from 14 July 1918 to 30 May 1920.

Lard – National rationing existed from 14 July to 16 December 1918.

Margarine – National rationing existed from 14 July 1918 to 16 February 1919.

Butcher's Meat (uncooked) – National rationing existed under Meat Scheme from 7 April 1918 and under General Scheme from 14 July 1918 until 15 December 1919.

Bacon and Ham – National rationing existed under Meat Scheme from 7 April and General Scheme from 14 July until 28 July 1918.

Jam – National rationing existed from 2 November 1918 to 15 April 1919.

Tea – This was not rationed nationally but its distribution was controlled by national registration of customers based on 2oz. per head from 14 July to 2 December 1918.

The subject of rationing and food supply were very close to the heart of Downton's MP, the Rt. Hon. Charles Bathurst. A Conservative first elected in January 1910, Bathurst served as a Minister in the Lloyd George Coalition government. He was Parliamentary Secretary to the Minister of Food, December 1916 to July 1917 and Chairman of the Royal Committee on Sugar Supply from August 1917. Bathurst's background was in agriculture. Before the war he had been an ardent supporter of tariff reform.

Amongst the unexpected side effects of the food shortages was that it strengthened the position of the Temperance Movement for the prohibition of alcohol. It was argued that at a time of shortage, barley was being wasted in the manufacture of beer. A national campaign for prohibition continued for the duration of the war and during demobilisation. Restrictions to pub opening hours were introduced during the war to discourage absenteeism from work. In Downton also, the Temperance lobby remained strong. In April 1916 the Dorset and Southern Temperance Association held their quarterly meeting in the village.

Owing to the massive labour shortage at home, enemy prisoners of war were used to work on local farms. Information on these prisoners is scarce, but because of a tragic accident at

Food Shortages – comic postcard from December 1917.

Barford Park Farm in December 1917 some details of a
prisoner who worked there are recorded in the local press. On
Monday 3rd December Joseph Jurock – an 'Austrian Pole' –
sustained severe abdominal injuries after being run over by a
wagon. Dr Whiteley was quickly on the scene and Jurock was
taken by car to Salisbury Infirmary, where he died three days
later of blood poisoning following an operation. Jurock was

The Rt. Hon Charles Bathurst MP.

only 19 years old and had been working at the Farm owned by Mr Wookey.

In the light of the severe food shortages and rationing towards the end of the war, it is not surprising that any new grocery store opening in 1917-8 would have experienced a difficult few months trading. This was the case of the Downton Co-op which opened its doors for the first time towards the end of the war. Nevertheless, in August 1918 it was reported that the 'expecta-tions' of the Co-operative Society's new Downton Branch 'had been fully realised. The difficulties experienced in obtaining supplies had retarded the full development of the branch, but notwithstanding these the progress made had been substantial.'

Those ends in war the best contentment bring,
Whose peace is made up with a pardoning.

Robert Herrick (1591–1674), *Epigrams*

Peace Celebrations

The signing of the Armistice on the eleventh hour of the eleventh day of the eleventh month, 1918 makes this date amongst the most well known landmarks in world history. The news of the cessation of hostilities reached Downton shortly after the signing took place. The news of this extraordinary Monday morning was (according to the *Salisbury Journal*), 'celebrated with a quiet dignity and soberness.' The bells of the Parish Church were rung and flags and bunting displayed in the streets. At two o'clock the children of Downton came to the Church for a service of thanksgiving.

1918 Armistice Celebrations

On the Tuesday evening a united thanksgiving service was held in Downton Church, which was filled by a congregation numbering about 500. The Rev. J. W. S. Tomlin, Curate-in-Charge took the service. He was assisted by Downton Baptist Minister, the Rev. Alfred Harris who read the lesson and offered prayer. The Rev. Tomlin delivered an address, in which he 'voiced the universal feeling of gratitude to Almighty God for the greatness of the victory.' The choir, grouped at the altar rails sung a solemn *Te Deum*. Another special service took place at the Church the following day. This time the address was given by Colonel Marriott-Smith of Fairfield House.

The afternoon of Wednesday 20th November saw the first of

Downton's formal Armistice celebrations, specifically aimed at children. A half-day holiday had been secured for the children who were each provided with chocolate and a flag. A procession led by the Downton Band marched through the village to the East Green where fancy dress and a variety of sporting competitions took place, including the sack race, egg and spoon race, potato race and wheel barrow race. The weather, although foggy was fine and everything passed off successfully.

At 8.00pm a large crowd gathered in the meadow to the south-east of Mould's Bridge, where an effigy of the Kaiser was burned on a large bonfire, to the cheers of spectators. The Downton Band, under their conductor Ernest Bailey played patriotic songs. Later a whist drive and dance were held in the Parish Hall. Proceeds of between £10 and £11 were given to the Soldiers' Return Fund.

December 1918 General Election

Three days after the signing of the Armistice, the Prime Minister Lloyd George announced his intention to hold a General Election and this took place during the following month. This was the first election since 1910, but more importantly it was the first general election at which women could vote. Six million women over the age of 30 were given the vote as a result of the 1918 Representation of the People Act, which was passed in June. Another Act gave women the right to stand for election to the House of Commons.

The decisive part played by women on the home front during the First World War had brought about these major changes in the law. Yet it is a little known fact that minor political rights had already been achieved for women several years before 1918. The Forster Education Act 1870 permitted women ratepayers to vote for and become members of local School Boards. The County Councils Act of 1888 gave them the right to vote in County and County Borough elections. After much debate, an Act of 1907 permitted women to become members of County and Borough Councils and even hold office as Mayor. To the Suffragette Movement which was at its height in the years immediately before the war, the extension of their franchise from local to national elections was the next natural step forward, yet to their frustration the move was resisted.

166

In Downton many of the women voters took a keen interest in their new rights. For instance, at a Women's Institute Meeting in the Vicarage garden on 5th September 1918 Mrs Steward of Codford gave a speech on 'Women's Use of the Vote.'

During the war all local elections had been postponed. Under a circular from the Local Government Board, dated 23rd December 1914, local councils had their attention drawn to the provisions of the Local Authorities (Disqualification Relief) Act stating that Council members serving with H.M. Forces were not to be disqualified from office for non-attendance of meetings. Vacancies were filled by co-option. At Downton, one of these vacant seats on the Parish Council was taken up by Mrs Warren of Wick Farm who was Downton's first woman councillor. She accepted her seat in September 1915.

As well as the enfranchisement of women over 30, the December 1918 General Election saw the introduction of extensive boundary changes. Downton and Wilton now became part of the Salisbury constituency. Captain Bathurst the previous MP for the area had been elevated to the peerage on 15th October 1918 when he was created Baron Bledisloe. His successor Hugh Morrison was elected unopposed in November for Wilton, and then took the new Salisbury seat in the December election, defeating Alfred Ernest Brown who had served in the war as a Lieutenant in the Somerset Light Infantry and been awarded the MC and Italian Silver Star for Valour. Morrison was to remain the area's MP until 1932, with the brief intermission of 1923-4 when he lost Salisbury to a Liberal candidate, another holder of the MC, Major Hugh Lawrence Fletcher Moulton.

Influenza

November 1918 witnessed the start of a mass 'flu epidemic which was to continue well into the following year. The *Salisbury Journal* records that 54 people with 'flu were admitted to Salisbury Infirmary in a single day. At the height of the epidemic the local firm of undertakers Downer and Bailey were carrying out two funerals a day. The consequences for many local families were devastating. In early January 1919 Private S. F. Chalk of the 2nd Devonshire Regiment returned to Downton as a widower. His wife had recently died from 'flu and double pneumonia whilst he was a prisoner in Germany.

The fear of catching 'flu was also intense. In March 1919, a local farmer fearing he had caught the illness took his own life with a shot gun. The gun was the instrument used for three local suicides on three separate occasions. By grim coincidence the gun had been sold by the first deceased man's family to the second man and then to the third who lived at Standlynch. After the third suicide, relatives of the deceased threw the gun over the weirs (known locally as *the Waterfalls*) at Standlynch.

The Return of the Troops

The first servicemen returned to Downton from the continent in early December 1918. These included Private Sidney Ridout of the Wiltshire Regiment who returned to his home in The Borough on Tuesday 3rd December. He had been taken prisoner in March of that year during the German Spring Offensive. Another prisoner who returned during the same week was Mr J. G. Rogers of Lodge Drove. Rogers of the Mercantile Marines was unfortunate enough to have been in Germany in August 1914 and was interned at the outbreak of war.

The following week saw the return of Captain H. Curtis Gallup, the former resident of Wick House. Gallup (who had been taken prisoner at the fall of Kut in 1916) arrived in England from Turkey and returned to Downton on the evening of Wednesday 11th December. He was welcomed by his many friends and the Church bells rang out to mark his freedom.

Towards the end of 1918 all servicemen about to return from the front were sent a postcard from a village committee. The postcard, typically patriotic depicts John Bull with the message 'with Best Wishes from Downton, Xmas 1918' and 'a dinner awaits your return.' It also shows views of the River Avon from the Mill Bridge and Borough Cross.

The Christmas holidays 1918 were quiet and included the playing of carols by the Downton Band on Boxing Day. Private Walter Bundy, Wiltshire Regiment rejoined the band after returning from hospital. A New Year's Eve Dance in the Public Hall raised over £5 for the Servicemen's Return Fund.

Several ex-prisoners of war and servicemen returned to Downton in the New Year of 1919. These included Wiltshire

Postcard sent to Downton's servicemen, Christmas 1918.

Regiment soldiers Sergeant William Lawes, Lance Corporal Jack Haydon, Private Edwin Frank Bundy and Private William Taylor, all of whom had been taken prisoner in the German March 1918 Offensive.

Many events took place in 1919 at which the returned servicemen were provided with entertainment and a meal. These included the following:

- Monday 10th February – Between thirty and forty released prisoners of war together with discharged and demobilised soldiers were entertained to an evening tea at The Moot by Mrs Carver.

- Thursday 13th March – Between fifty and sixty servicemen were entertained at the *White Horse*, through the kindness of Mr R. J. Read of New Court.

- Wednesday 9th April – Approximately 130 returned soldiers and sailors were provided with a dinner in the Public Hall, courtesy of the Southern Tanning Company.

At the event at The Moot, the following resolution from the Downton Women's Institute was read to those present:

We, as members of the Downton W.I. wish to record our deep gratitude to the sailors and soldiers of this village for their faithful service to King and Country. We recognise also that by steadfastness of our men and their comrades, our food supply has never failed and the safety of our homes has been assured. We pray that all blessings may attend them on their return to civil life.

1919 Peace Celebrations

Peace celebrations throughout South Wiltshire were held on Saturday 19th July. At Downton the Church bells were rung in the early morning and at 10.30am a procession headed from the railway arch on Lode Hill to the Parish Church for a united service. The Downton Band headed the procession which consisted of servicemen and ex-servicemen. The Church service was conducted by Downton's Curate-in-Charge, the Rev. A. S. Bryant, and the Rev. A. Harris of Downton Baptist Church. In a simple ceremony a wreath was placed on the Roll of Honour in the Church porch.

Following the service the procession resumed and made its way to The Headlands and then back to the Public Hall where 164 servicemen and ex-servicemen were given a cooked meal. A mass village tea was provided in the afternoon at the Public Hall, the Council School, the Wesleyan Chapel and the National School. Although a large number of villagers took part, it was far short of the 1,300 catered for. The remaining food was distributed throughout the village by motor lorry provided by Mr Henry Barker of the Southern Tanning Company. In the evening a concert was staged at the Public Hall by the Downton Band and dancing took place late into the night.

The reason for the lower than expected attendance, was the wet weather, which forced many of the events to be postponed to the following Saturday. These activities included a parade of the Downton Fire Engine and decorated vehicles through the village to The Moot. Sports events and a fancy dress competition took place in a field off Moot Lane and prizes were given to the winners. Local children were provided with tea and presented commemorative peace mugs. Pensioners were also given gifts and cigarettes were handed out to soldiers and former soldiers. In the evening a bonfire and fireworks display was staged on Barford Down. The means for the peace celebrations came largely from a generous donation of £125 made by the Southern Tanning Company.

On 19th December 1919 a special ceremony took place at the Public Hall. All returned Soldiers, Sailors and Officers were presented with cigarette cases on behalf of the inhabitants of Downton by Colonel Wilfred Ashley MP. Nearly 200 men received these gifts; the funds for their purchase had been raised to send Christmas presents to the troops for Christmas 1918, but not needed because of the signing of the Armistice. The Downton Band provided musical entertainment, but entertainment of a different kind was given by Downton's new doctor, Major Brian Whitehead MC who demonstrated some conjuring tricks. Salisbury-born Dr Whitehead was the son of a former Mayor of the City. He graduated from Cambridge and undertook his training at St. Bartholomew's Hospital, London after which he joined the Army in 1914. Whitehead served in the Royal Army Medical Corps and although his service records do not survive, the medal index at the Public Record Office shows that he entered the war on 21st November 1915 and his Theatre of War was France. In 1918 Major Whitehead was awarded the MC. His citation reads as follows:

For conspicuous courage and devotion to duty on 17th April 1918 at Westoutre when this village was being heavily shelled by the enemy, he went about in the open attending wounded. Afterwards he proceeded through a heavy barrage of artillery fire to the main dressing station where he rendered much

The ruins of Westoutre Church, 1918, from the photographs of 2nd Lieutenant F. H. Lydford, Somerset Light Infantry.

171

Ruins of a cottage at Westoutre, 1918.

The ruined interior of
Westoutre Church, 1918.

*valuable service under heavy shellfire in rescuing and getting
wounded out of danger.*

Local servicemen were also presented with a citation to show the
gratitude of the people of Downton. Recipients included Mr
John William Daly, a merchant seaman on a supply route
during the war. Daly was born in London in 1882 and lived at
Green Cottage, The Borough. His family was originally from a
small fishing village in Ireland called Ballyshannon. The citation
reads:

*Presented by the Inhabitants of Downton to
Mr Daly
As a small Token of Appreciation of the Services
rendered by him in 'The Great War,' 1914-19, and
by this means desire to express their heartfelt
Thanks and Gratitude for the Devotion and
Self-Sacrifice which made possible 'The GloriousVictory.'*

*Downton is proud of the noble part played by her
sons in the Great Struggle for 'Freedom, Honour
and Justice,' and in safeguarding the Shores and
Homes of our Native Land.*

Downton, Xmas 1919.

Mr John William Daly of the Merchant Navy.

The Comrades Club

The first mass organisation of former Great War servicemen was called the Comrades of the Great War. Its inaugural meeting took place on 10th October 1917. Within two years of its formation there were 1,693 branches in Britain and Ireland, consisting of over 600,000 members. The largest branch was at Manchester with a membership of 15,000. There were 27 branches in

Wiltshire of which three (Salisbury, Swindon and Trowbridge) were over a thousand strong.

Downton's branch of the Comrades was founded following a meeting on the evening of Wednesday 15th January 1919. All discharged and demobilised men residing in the district of Downton were eligible for membership. The first committee was under the Chairmanship of Major Francis with Mr P. W. Morgan as Secretary and Mr E. Aylett as Treasurer. It also included the Curate-in-Charge of Downton Parish, the Rev. J. W. S. Tomlin. At the time of its first AGM in the January of the following year, the Downton branch had over 200 members.

The Comrades' organisation had both a social and a limited political role. A club room was provided for members above the *Three Horse Shoes* Inn in The Borough. The room described as 'exceptionally pleasant and comfortable' was opened by Colonel the Rt. Hon. Wilfred Ashley MP on Monday 13th October 1919. Colonel Ashley had served as a Major in the 3rd Hampshire Regiment during the Boer War and was Chairman of the Anti-Socialist Union. The room included a billiard table and Colonel Ashley presented the club with pictures of King George V and Queen Mary.

The Borough c.1910, showing the *Three Horse Shoes* Inn, where the Comrades held their meetings in an upstairs room. Armistice Celebrations took place on this part of the village green in November 1918.

Presentation of War Honours

Many of the recognised honours earned by officers and men during the Great War were not awarded until after the cessation of hostilities. At least two of these ceremonies of decoration took place in Downton during 1919. Both events were for the presentation of the Distinguished Conduct Medal and each were treated as special occasions involving celebrations participated in by a large number of villagers.

Sergeant Drummer William Charles Bundy of the Wiltshire Regiment had returned to Downton on crutches at Christmas 1918. His hospitalisation was directly due to the gallant act for which he was awarded the DCM. William Bundy was the son of Mrs Elliott of The Borough. To many in Downton he was known by his nickname of 'Churby' Bundy. He had been wounded in the war on at least one previous occasion in the summer of 1916, when he was badly gassed.

Bundy's award ceremony took place on the evening of Monday 28th April 1919 at the Public Hall. The event began with a procession through the village of members of the Downton branch of the Comrades of the Great War. The parade was headed by ex-Sergeant Bundy and the Downton Band of which Bundy had been a member before enlisting in

William Charles Bundy, from a photograph of Downton Band, c.1931.

175

the forces. Bundy had continued his musicianship during the conflict and had been awarded the Regiment's Silver Bugle.

Major Owen Francis presided and introduced Colonel Sir Arthur Holbrook KBE who was to perform the presentation. The Colonel spoke of the pleasure it gave him to be present and stated that every town and village should recognise bravery on the field of battle because it was 'the fighting instinct of the people that had made the Empire great.' He congratulated Sergeant Bundy on his gallantry, and said his name 'ought to be a household word in the village for generations to come.' The *Salisbury Journal* recorded the gallantry that led to the award of the DCM as follows:

> *On the morning of September 13th 1918, Sergeant Bundy with his regiment the 1st Wiltshires went into the firing line to relieve the Leicester Regiment. The latter, who had lost heavily the previous day, were holding the line, a partially dug trench with about 120 men, and so intense was the shell fire that it was found impossible to carry out relief properly. Sergeant Bundy, taking a view of the ground in front of his platoon, and observing one officer and three men too badly wounded to 'get in' went to their aid, and crawling from shell hole to shell hole, brought all four in safely. While getting the last man into the trench he received a shrapnel wound in his right knee.*

The second Downtonian to be presented with the DCM in 1919 has already been mentioned several times in this book, Battery Sergeant Major William Newman of the Royal Field Artillery. The formal presentation ceremony took place in the grounds of The Moot on the evening of Monday 18th August 1919. Newman was presented with both the Distinguished Conduct Medal and the Military Medal by Brigadier General the Earl of Radnor. This is the recommendation that secured Newman his DCM:

> *On 17th August 1917, at Ypres, this warrant officer was in the gun line when the Battery was being heavily shelled. One gun received a direct hit just as the Battery had finished firing. Battery Sergeant-Major Newman at once went forward to get the detachment who, although not wounded, had been stunned away from the gun. This he succeeded in*

The grounds of The Moot where Newman's presentation ceremony took place.

doing in spite of being under heavy shell-fire at the time,
thereby saving almost certain casualties. He has been largely
responsible for getting ammunition up to the gun line, and has
shown a great coolness and ingenuity in avoiding shelled
areas, and it is mainly owing to his zeal and determination
that the ammunition supply has been maintained.

Resumption of Peace-time Leisure

Gradually some of the regular pre-war leisure activities enjoyed
by Downtonians prior to August 1914 began to function once
again. These included the Downton Choral Society and the
Downton Football Club. The *Western Gazette* of 24th October
1919 reported that the Club had made an excellent start to the
1919-20 season, in the third division of the Salisbury and
District League. On Saturday 18th October Downton had
defeated the L & SW Railways Team in a 'fine game' by 7-2.

177

Battery Sergeant Major William Newman, October 1921. His medals are (from left to right): the Distinguished Conduct Medal, the Military Medal, the 1914-15 Star, the British War Medal and the Victory Medal. The final three medals were known as 'Pip, Squeak and Wilfred' after three characters in a popular newspaper cartoon.

The scorers were Biddlecombe (3), Plaskett (3) and Philpott (1), described by the *Gazette* as 'a really brilliant shot.' In their previous match Downton had enjoyed victory in another high scoring game, defeating a team from the RAF 12-0. Hardly any football matches had taken place during the war, the only example found being friendly match played between Downton and Bishop Wordsworth's School, Salisbury in February 1918. The match was played in a meadow lent by Mr Holman.

The Downton Football Team of 1919–20.
Back Row: Bert Randal, Sammy Durdle, Sid Oliphant.
Middle Row: B. Oliphant, Bill Barker, Mr Pearman, Mr Dommett, Bert Masters (captain), Bert Newman, Percy Bailey, Mr Oliphant, Bert 'Pec' Fulford (trainer).
Front Row: Sid Rowden, William 'Buff' Blake, Harold Plaskett, Billy Oliphant, Bert Jacobs, Frank Chalk.

The October Downton Fair had continued throughout the war, although there is only one report of it in the local press. This was the fair of October 1917, which took place on the first Tuesday of the month. It was described as an 'old established fair,' mainly concerned with sheep. Old farming diaries written by Ernest G. Warren of Wick Farm now in the possession of Mr and Mrs R. Lees of Gravel Close show that Warren frequently visited this fair, but there is no mention of the April fair. It is unclear whether this event was postponed for the duration of the war. Both fairs were abandoned in the 1920s.

The Continued Toll of the War

The cessation of hostilities on 11th November 1918 did not, of course, put an end to the miserable catalogue of deaths. The Downton War Memorial records the names of at least six servicemen who died after the Armistice was signed. The first of these deaths occurred on 29th November, only eighteen days later, when Prince Leopold Eastman died in hospital at Alexandria. Prince Leopold was the son of Henry and Mary Eastman and the younger brother of Bert Eastman who for many years ran his basket making business from the thatched cottage next to the Iron Bridge. Bert died in January 1956 aged 80. Leo Eastman was also a basket and wicker chair manufacturer and lived in a cottage in Waterside. He left a widow and young daughter.

Of all the names on the War Memorial 'Prince L Eastman' is strikingly unusual. The family story was that Leo Eastman received that most distinctive name because he was born on the same day that Queen Victoria's son visited Downton. This was on Wednesday 21st December 1881, when the Prince's carriage came through Downton on his way to a Civic Dinner in Salisbury. The Prince had been staying at West Park near Rockbourne for a few days. Disappointingly however, Leo's birth certificate shows that he was in fact born in February 1885, over three years after the Royal visit and indeed, some eleven months after the Prince's untimely death from haemophilia. Nevertheless the birth certificate does solve part of the riddle as it records his mother's maiden name as Prince.

Eastman is a surname that will be always associated with Downton, because of the family's connection with George Eastman of Kodak camera fame. The link started in 1638 when Roger and Sarah Eastman sailed from Southampton to Massachusetts Bay on the ship *Confidence*. Roger was the son of Nicholas Eastman of Charlton. Roger's wife Sarah had the maiden name of Smith and came from the same Standlynch family already mentioned in this book. Therefore, from a little ancestral research it can be deduced that Private Leo Eastman and Sergeant Ernest Smith were both the 9th cousins twice removed of the famous American George Eastman. A further more recent connection between the two families occurred on Boxing Day 1929, when Ernest Smith's youngest sister, Linda May married Leo Eastman's nephew, Gilbert.

Another soldier with Downton connections died in November 1918, although his name is not recorded on the War Memorial. Lance Corporal Reginald Augustus Stretch of the 2nd Wiltshire Regiment was the son of George Charles Stretch who had been the Stationmaster at Downton from January 1905 until the summer of 1914. Lance Corporal Stretch died in Hospital at Etaples, France on the 19th, from terrible injuries sustained a week before the Armistice, when he was wounded by a 5.9 shell. Stretch was educated at Downton Council School in Gravel Close and had worked for the London and South Western Railway Company. The 23 year old is buried in the Etaples Military Cemetery. His elder brother, Second Lieutenant Lewis Stretch MC was with him during the last four days of his suffering.

After leaving Downton in 1914 George Charles Stretch became Stationmaster at Lyndhurst Road Railway Station in the New Forest. The Station is some distance from the town of Lyndhurst and in 1995 it was renamed 'Ashurst (New Forest).' Therefore Stretch is not recorded on the Lyndhurst War Memorial, but in the Parish Church of Ashurst and Colbury where a brass plaque commemorates those who died in the Great War.

The New Year of 1919 continued to bring bad news to Downton. Private Albert Edward Patience, 2nd Wiltshire Regiment, died on 8th January whilst on his way home from Germany. Patience had been taken prisoner of war in the spring of 1918. He is buried in Denmark at the Western Cemetery, Copenhagen. His family home was in The Borough, close to the *Three Horse Shoes* Inn.

Geoffrey Thomas Hunt died on 23rd February at Salisbury

Etaples Military Cemetery in the 1920s, before the grave markers were replaced with the distinctive permanent CWGC headstones.

Infirmary. Hunt had only returned to Downton from France about two weeks before his death and contracted an illness a few days after his homecoming. He was the youngest son of Amos and Emily Hunt of The Borough and had served in France for three years. He is buried in Downton Churchyard. The funeral service was conducted by the former Vicar of Downton, the Rev. Major Lenthall Dickenson SCF, DSO. The coffin, covered in the Union Flag, was followed by about thirty Downton soldiers. Hunt's brother, Corporal Archie Hunt had emigrated from Downton to Canada in 1903, but had visited his old home, whilst on leave from the front, serving in the Canadian Army contingent.

Military Medallist, former Sergeant Arthur Ellis Haydon died at the home of his parents in The Borough on 31st March. Haydon had joined the army at the outbreak of the war in 1914 and was sent to the Western Front in the late summer of the following year. Haydon married Rose Spreadborough during his final leave from the fighting in January 1918. In March, shortly after his return to the front, he was taken prisoner and remained in German hands until the signing of the Armistice. Haydon, who had been wounded on three separate occasions during the war, died of pulmonary tuberculosis. The funeral was of a military character and included a firing party being formed by the Northumberland Fusiliers from Durrington, although Haydon's Regiment had been the King's Royal Rifle Corps. Haydon's widow gave birth to their daughter Violet in November 1919.

Of the servicemen who returned to Downton from the front, perhaps the most expected death was that of former Lance Corporal Percy John Aylett of The Borough. The son of one of Downton's butchers, Aylett enlisted with the Territorials, on

Sergeant A.E.Haydon, who was awarded the Military Medal for destroyning an enemy machine gun base.

30th May 1912 at the age of 16. He was posted overseas in the early days of the war and had been a casualty long before his 18th birthday. He was discharged sick on 23rd October 1918, being described as 'suffering from [shell] shock and complications.' He died on 4th September 1919, aged 22.

Chronologically, the final name to appear on the War Memorial is that of Able Seaman Reginald James Nicklen of HMS *Caradoc*. A native of Downton, Nicklen drowned in an accident off the Russian coast on 22nd September 1919. The 19 year old had joined the Navy in 1916 and at the time of his death was taking part in post-Armistice operations in South Russia. The records of the Commonwealth War Graves Commission confusingly state that Nicklen's parents resided at Newhouse, Redlynch. Mr Nicklen worked there later on when the records were compiled, but the family had resided at The Headlands, Downton until 1918. Nicklen's younger sister Mrs E. Wort died in 2001, aged 91.

Memorial Plaques

Very shortly after the cessation of hostilities, all nearest relatives of deceased officers and men were sent a letter from the War Office, asking them to confirm details of the deceased's next of kin so that a plaque and scroll could be issued. These letters appear to have been sent out with undue haste. The one sent to Mrs Bonvalot at Wick House for instance is dated 15th November 1918, a mere four days after the signing of the Armistice.

The decision to commemorate the fallen in such a fashion had been made by the government in 1917 and hundreds of plaque designs were entered in a competition eventually won by Mr E Carter Preston. A 'Memorial Plaque Factory' was opened at Acton, West London, but production had to be expanded to the Woolwich Arsenal on account of the huge number of plaques required.

The plaques are of bronze and about the same size as a modern CD. Around the edge are the words 'he [or she] died for freedom and honour.' Each plaque was posted along with a brief complement slip (120mm × 190mm) bearing the signature of George V. Another item posted separately was an illuminated scroll measuring 280mm × 180mm. The name of the

HE whom this scroll commemorates was numbered among those who, at the call of King and Country, left all that was dear to them, endured hardness, faced danger, and finally passed out of the sight of men by the path of duty and self-sacrifice, giving up their own lives that others might live in freedom. Let those who come after see to it that his name be not forgotten.

Cpl. Ernest Smith
Wiltshire Regt.

A Commemorative Scroll.

commemorated individual is hand-written beneath the inscription, along with his rank, regiment, corps or ship. Red ink was used for members of the Army and blue ink for the Royal Navy. Names recorded on the plaques themselves give no indication of rank, regiment or indeed nationality. Due to the perishable nature of paper, far more bronze plaques now survive than scolls.

There is something deeply macabre about commemorating the fallen in such a way and deeply sobering to think that over a million such plaques were issued.

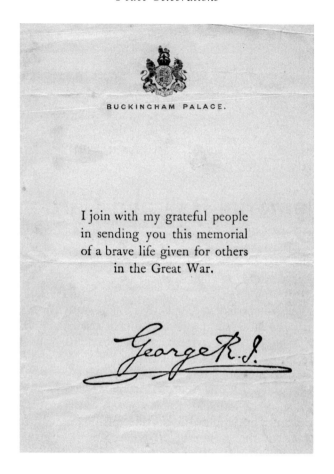

Complement slip posted with Plaque.

Tranquil You Lie Your Knightly Virtue Proved,
Your Memory Hallowed in the Land You Loved.

Sir J S Arkwright (1872-1954), *O Valiant Hearts*

Memorial Hall and Gardens

Almost every village in Britain and France has a War Memorial; the exact number for the UK is not known, but is estimated at 54,000. War Memorials vary greatly in appearance and function, but are usually situated at a focal point of the village. The most common type is in the form of a cross, such as the one commemorating the war dead of Morgan's Vale and Woodfalls. Other local examples include Charlton-All-Saints' Memorial where the names are inscribed in the gable of the lych gate at the entrance to the churchyard. Redlynch's War Memorial is a roadside shrine, but the most unusual local example must be at Nomansland in the New Forest, where the War Memorial is built over a well.

It is not only the form of the War Memorial that varies greatly, but also the way that the names of the fallen are recorded. The most helpful type of memorial for the local and family historian is one that records name, rank, regiment and date of death. Downton's Memorial records Christian name and surname; Redlynch, Charlton and Morgan's Vale merely record initial and surname. The forty-four names on the Downton War Memorial are listed in approximate alphabetical order. The names of the fallen are duplicated on the boards inside the Memorial Hall which also list rank and regiment, but these were compiled over two years after the War Memorial was dedicated and are not free from inaccuracy.

Downton's War Memorial

Discussions about how Downton would permanently commemorate its war dead initially took place at a meeting in the Public Hall on 11th December 1918. A large number of suggestions for an appropriate Memorial were put forward. These included the erection of a cenotaph close to the Borough Cross, the addition of two bells to the Church peal, a chiming Church clock, and the foundation of a new Cottage Hospital for Downton (the old Cottage Hospital which was situated at the corner of Slab Lane and Lode Hill had closed in the 1870s). None of these ideas came to fruition, although in November 1946, two bells were added to the Church peal as part of the commemoration for those who fell in the Second World War.

The Downton War Memorial Committee was established and on 1st January 1919 the Committee opened an account for the receipt of subscriptions and donations for the War Memorial project. The small amount of money remaining from the 1911 Coronation Celebrations was contributed to the funds which were also to be used for Downton's Peace Celebrations. A total of £1,503. 17s. 3d. was raised during the Memorial Fund's existence.

Downton Memorial Hall c.1925. The building remained little changed until 2001 when a side extension was added providing a new foyer, toilets, kitchen and disabled access.

The British School

By January 1919 it had been decided to place the War Memorial at the front of the Public Hall and if possible purchase the building for the village. The Hall has an interesting history prior to 1919. From the late nineteenth century it was used for social events and public meetings, but it was originally built in 1840 as the Downton British School for boys. British Schools were so called, because they were founded by the *British and Foreign School Society*, a non-conformist organisation that insisted on non-denominational religious teaching. The Church of England established a rival society – the *National Society for Promoting the Education of the Poor in the Principles of the Established Church* – in 1847 and this body built Downton National School (now the Church Hall) in Barford Lane in 1849. The Downton British Girls School was established at the Bournemouth Road end of the Borough in 1846. The building (which now houses Headlands Garage) had briefly been used as a Nonconformist Chapel and narrowly escaped destruction in January 1897 when neighbouring cottages were destroyed in a disastrous fire.

In June 1887 Downton celebrated Queen Victoria's Golden Jubilee. A free dinner was provided for the inhabitants of Downton, Charlton and Standlynch at Barford Park. The Woodfalls Band played (the Downton Band was not founded until 1889) and many sporting events took place. Funds for the day's activities had been provided via subscriptions administered by a Committee under the chairmanship of Elias Pitts Squarey of The Moot. Money raised was also used to provide Downton with a Reading Room and carry out improvements to the British School to make it suitable for the purpose of holding meetings and entertainment in the evenings and out of school hours. These improvements costing £85. 17s. 6d. involved the removal of the gallery and fixed desks. A platform was placed at the far end of the Hall and new removable desks purchased, so that the building could be used for non-school activities. Additional money for the project was raised by Miss Squarey who gave a concert and by Professor Wrightson and the students of the Downton Agricultural College.

The British School failed its inspection by the HM Inspector of Schools in the summer of 1893 on account of its basic facilities being deemed 'unsuitable for modern requirements' and between £1,200 and £1,500 was desperately required to build a new school in the village and carry out alterations to the National Schools in Downton and Redlynch. A meeting of ratepayers voted for the formation of a School Board by the narrowest of margins and the election of the Board took place in October. The event attracted much controversy as Lord Radnor failed to gain a seat on the Board. Schools Boards had existed in many urban areas for over twenty years and, for the first time in Downton, responsibility for the provision of education was now taken away from charities or religious organisations and put into the hands of the state. By February of 1894 the School Board had taken over the running of the British Schools in Downton and set about deciding on a suitable site for the new school. The Paddock in Gravel Close was chosen and on 12th July the Education Department had approved plans for a new school to cater for 160 boys, 75 girls and 75 infants.

The British School's last Headmaster (and the Board School's first Headmaster) was John George Northover who came to Downton from the Wallops in 1889. Northover was also for many years the organist and choirmaster and bell ringer at Charlton-All-Saints Church, as well as being the conductor of the Downton Band. During the war Northover was the enumerator for Standlynch-with-Charlton when the National Register was compiled in 1915. It must have been particularly poignant for him to receive the sad news of the deaths and injuries of many of his former pupils.

The new Board School officially opened on Wednesday 12th February 1896 and children attended classes there from the Monday of the following week. The old British School was now redundant and on 10th February 1897 a meeting was held at which it was decided to secure the property as a village hall. The building was renamed the Public Hall, placed in the hands of the Charity Commissioners and tenanted by the Parish Council from 1899 on a 21 year lease at £10 per annum rental. This income was largely used to finance the Downton British School Charity, which also (following the closure of the Free School), received funds from the two annual Downton fairs. The charity awarded Exhibitions (the payment of fees) to Downton pupils who were successful enough to attend Bishop Wordsworth's School in Salisbury. In 1912 for instance, Exhibitions were awarded to Ivy Aylett, Walter Harold Plaskett and George Pressley.

A huge variety of entertainment and activities took place in the Public Hall over the years. It was the first place in Downton where films were shown. The *Salisbury Journal* of 20th May 1899 gives details of this, as part of a lecture by Mr J Bennett-Stanford the (Boer) War Correspondent for *Western Morning News*. During the First World War the building was used extensively for events related to the war effort, which ironically included recruitment drives.

The Memorial Hall

By February 1919 negotiations were underway between the Hall's Trustees and the War Memorial Committee. In June of that year Mr Pye-Smith a Trustee of the Hall had an interview with an official from the Board of Education and it was agreed to offer the building on a 999 years' lease at a fixed rental of ten guineas per annum. The money (as before) was to be used for educational purposes.

Plans for the alteration of the building were approved in March 1920 and the new portico designed by Mr Bernard Masters was constructed by Messrs. Wort and Way at an approximate cost of between £600 and £650. The Downton firm of builders Downer and Bailey carried out the other alterations to the Hall plus the extension to the rear of the building to the plans of Mr Michael Harding.

Downton War Memorial was dedicated at a service held on the afternoon of Easter Sunday 27th March 1921. The short service opened with singing of the hymn 'For All the Saints who from their Labours Rest' accompanied by the Downton Band conducted by Ern Bailey. The Earl of Radnor unveiled the Memorial Tablet and gave a speech of dedication. The *Salisbury Journal* of the following Friday described the Memorial as follows:

The new frontage is built of stone, and forms a colonnaded entrance to the old hall. It is rectangular in plan, and comprises an entablature projecting from the front of the hall, and supported by four stone columns. The frontage has been faced with stone, which material has also been utilised in the paving of the floor of the portico. In the centre of the stone facing has been placed a tablet which contains the names of the fallen.

A parade of the Ancient Order of Foresters headed by the Downton Band pictured outside the Public Hall in 1919 or 1920. Double-bass player John Smith is immediately behind the man carrying the leading banner. Edwin Frank Bundy (moustache and trilby) is in the centre of the picture behind the trombone player. William Charles 'Churby' Bundy is the furthest to the right of the picture of all those carrying instruments. He is wearing a bowler hat and note the DCM medal on his waistcoat. Immediately in front of him is another cornet player Bert 'Pec' Fulford.

The tablet bears the Inscription: 'Lest we Forget. To the memory of the men of Downton who fell in the Great War 1914-1919.'

A large number of villagers attended the service, including relatives of the fallen, plus the former Baptist Minister and Vicar of Downton who had lost sons at the Somme. Before the two minutes silence, the 'Last Post' was sounded by three ex-Wiltshire Regiment soldiers: Sergeant William Bundy DCM and Privates Walter Bundy and George Whatley. This was followed by the Reveille and the service concluded with the hymn 'Now Thank We All Our God' and the National Anthem.

The Dedication of Downton War Memorial, Easter Sunday 1921.

A copy of the order of service for the dedication of the Downton War Memorial survives in the Downton Women's Institute 1956 Scrapbook, which is preserved at the Wiltshire County Records Office.

The day of the Memorial's dedication had been a particularly sad one for the people of Downton. Immediately before the dedication service, the funeral took place of one of the village's wartime servicemen. Frank Haydon had served in the Royal Garrison Artillery in Malta and France and was demobilised in 1920. He died on 23rd March at Harnwood, Salisbury, aged 22. Much sympathy was felt for Mr and Mrs Haydon who had now lost three of their four sons since 1916. The Haydon's only daughter Kathleen Emily died of tuberculosis on 4th January 1923 aged 17. Frank's gravestone is civilian, but his two brothers have distinctive Commonwealth War Graves Commission headstones.

The tragic personal legacy of the war continued the following month. On Sunday 1st May, Bert Eastman discovered the body of a young man floating in the river near his home. It was Corporal Reginald Henry Durdle of the Royal Marine Light Infantry who had been missing for a fortnight. Reg was the son

Three Haydon graves in Downton Churchyard – the two CWGC graves are of Arthur Ellis Haydon MM and William George Haydon. Behind is the civilian grave of Frank Haydon. The sister and parents of the three Haydon brothers are buried close by. Mrs Emily Haydon died in September 1935. Her husband, William Ellis died in 1949.

Corporal Reginald Henry Durdle, Royal Marine Light Infantry, who served on HMS *Prince of Wales* in the Mediterranean during the war.

of Walter Andrew Durdle a shoemaker who lived at a pictur-
esque thatched cottage in the High Street (now numbered 19
and called *Harebell Cottage*). Walter Durdle had also been the
Sexton at the Parish Church for many years and was the last
Engineer of the old Downton Fire Brigade. Reg Durdle was the
cousin of the four Haydon brothers.

Reginald Durdle joined the Royal Marine Light Infantry on
20th March 1911. His service records kept at the Public Record
Office, Kew describe him as 5ft. 6½ins. and of a 'fresh
complexion.' They also repeatedly state his character record as
'very good.' His intelligence and humour is borne out in some
surviving postcards he penned whilst on active service, which he
usually signed as 'Regimo.' Before joining the Marines, Durdle
was a carpet weaver in the factory otherwise known as Downton
Home Industries, which occupied part of the old Union
Workhouse and Gaol Building on the corner of Green Lane. An
inquest was held in another part of this building – the Downton
Unionist Club on 2nd May 1921. A verdict of suicide was
recorded.

The Downton Mace

The dedication of the War Memorial in the Spring of 1921
coincided with an important event in the recent civic history of
Downton. In April the Parish Council received a letter from
Lord Radnor offering to present the Council with the ancient
Mace of the Borough of Downton. The history of the Downton
Mace was described by the late Roy Woodford, writing in the
March 1966 edition of *Downton Parish Magazine*.

*The Mace was made in London by Gabriel Sleath in 1714.
Around its head are four cartouches bearing a forester's horn,
a chevron of the Eyre family, an arrow pointing downwards,
and the Arms of the Duncombe family. The Royal Arms are
in relief on the head under the arches. The Duncombe and
Eyre families represented the Borough in Parliament from
1707 till 1714*

*At the abolition of the Borough, the Mayor, named Hobbs,
refused to hand over the mace to the Lord of the Manor as
requested at the Manor Court, unless the Steward produced
the Record of the Borough. This was not complied with on the*

grounds that it was dilapidated and indecipherable. Hobbs left Downton with the mace and resided at Shirley in a house which he called Mace Cottage. The mace was later discovered in a Southampton pawn shop by Mr Manning, a miller who lived at the Parsonage Manor, and it was purchased by Lord Radnor.

Lord Radnor's offer was of course accepted by the Parish Council and a letter was sent to him expressing 'the Council's appreciation of his Lordship's public-spirited action in thus offering to pass on to the Council a gift of historic interest and value to the Parish of Downton.'

The formal presentation of the Mace to the village of Downton took place at the Memorial Hall on the evening of Tuesday 9th December 1921. The ceremony was made in conjunction with the formal opening of the renovated and extended Memorial Hall, which had been carried out under the direction of the War Memorial Committee. A new stage, new seating and heating appliances had been supplied and the building was fitted with a damp proof course and completely redecorated.

At the ceremony Lord Radnor explained the history of the Mace and paid tribute to the work of the Parish Council. The inscription 'Presented to the Borough of Downton by the Earl of Radnor and Viscount Folkstone 1921' was added to the Mace.

The Mace was placed on display in the Memorial Hall and remained there until 1970, when it was removed to Salisbury Museum. At the time it had been hoped to make a replica Mace to be kept in the village.

Other War Memorials

The Memorial Hall is not the only Memorial in the village to Downton's First World War Dead. There are also War Memorials in the Parish Church and the Baptist Church, both of which were dedicated in 1920.

The War Memorial in Downton Baptist Church was formally unveiled and dedicated at an evening service on Friday 28th May 1920. The tablet is of Sicilian marble, 3ft. 6in. square with half circular corners and fluted edges. It reads 'To the Glory of

God and in Memory of the Men of Downton who fell in the Great War 1914-1919.' It contains the names of forty-four officers and men, and the words chosen for War Memorials by Mr Rudyard Kipling 'Their name liveth for evermore.'

There are also two individual memorial tablets in the Baptist Church. Oscar Taunton's Memorial is of white marble with a grey marble border. It bears the following inscription:

> *In memory of Oscar Taunton, Lieutenant, Royal Engineers, second son of Percy and Katherine Taunton of Redlynch. On the outbreak of war in 1914, he went with his regiment to Egypt and from there to Gallipoli. He was awarded a Military Cross for conspicuous gallantry on June 4th 1915, when he defended a trench for two hours almost single-handed against the enemy. He died of his wounds ten days later and was buried at Mudros in the Island of Lemnos. Fidelis Uaque Ad Mortem [Faithful Unto Death]*

The Memorial was the work of Mr Clement Osmond of St John Street, Salisbury and was placed in the Baptist Church in July 1916. Lieutenant Taunton had died on board the Hospital Ship *Clan Macgillivray* in the Dardanelles. He was born on 24th December 1893. Oscar was educated at Lindley Lodge and Charterhouse, where he joined the Officers' Training Corps and later enlisted in the Territorial Force in June 1913. He is also commemorated on the Morgan's Vale and Woodfalls War Memorial. Oscar's father Captain Henry Percy Taunton of The Ridge, Woodfalls, served in France during the Great War. He was a local magistrate and a member of Wiltshire County Council from 1895 until the mid-1930s.

The other individual Memorial in Downton Baptist Church reads:

> *In proud and loving memory of Taunton Elliott Viney DSO, Flight Lieutenant RN. Younger son of Arthur and Edith Viney and Grandson of William Taunton of Redlynch, who gave his life on 21st May 1916 aged 24. Laetus Sorte Mea [Happy at my fate]. He was buried with honour by the enemy in the Mariakeske Cemetery Ostende.*

Viney was the younger son of Arthur Elliott and Edith H. Viney. The Commonwealth War Graves Commission lists

Viney's address as c/o A C Jamieson, Esq., of *Bratton*, Second Avenue, Frinton-on-Sea, Essex. Viney's name appears on the Frinton War Memorial. Further details from the tome *Airmen Who Died in the Great War*, show that Viney of the Prince Alfred's Guards was a native of Johannesburg, South Africa and had been flying a Sopwith LCT 'Strutter' when he was killed in action.

The War Memorial in the Downton Parish Church was sculpted by a Mr Hoare of Boscombe. It cost in excess of £75, the majority of which was donated by forty-two subscribers,

Downton Parish Church War Memorial, 1920. Note the error in the initial of the final name 'C. Swanborough' which has since been corrected to 'E. J.' For Kieley v. Keeley, see p. 63.

many of whom were the next of kin of the fallen. The sum of £10 was granted from the balance remaining at the close of the war in the funds of the Red Cross Working Party. This Memorial lists the names in rank order, starting with Major Graves and also gives details of Regiment. The names of the ten Second World War dead have since been added, but these are listed alphabetically.

The Parish Church's Memorial was unveiled by Lord Radnor and dedicated by the Archdeacon of Sarum at a service on Sunday 4th July 1920. Before the ceremony members of the Downton Branch of the Comrades of the Great War marched in procession from the Cross to the Church, headed by the Downton Band.

The Memorial Gardens

Almost five months after the dedication of the Downton War Memorial, Mrs Emily Bonvalot of Wick House wrote to the Parish Council offering a piece of land – approximately two acres in area – immediately to the west of the Hall for use as a Memorial Garden. It is worth pointing out that the land had not belonged to Wick House, but had been purchased specifically for use as the Memorial Garden by Mrs Bonvalot. The text of the letter dated 16th September 1921 reads:

> *It is my desire to present to the village, as a memorial to my late son, the small field adjoining the Memorial Hall to be a public garden, a portion of which might be used as a play ground for children. If I have this field suitably laid out, would the Parish Council be willing to keep it in good order for the people for whom it is intended?*
>
> *I do not wish to saddle the Parish with any unnecessary expense and I shall endeavour to arrange the ground in such a manner that it might be kept tidy with a minimum amount of labour.*

Mrs Bonvalot's eldest son, Second Lieutenant Edward St. Laurent of the 2nd Battalion, Coldstream Guards had been killed in action at the Battle of Loos in October 1915. The Bonvalots were not an old Downton family. They had moved to Downton in August 1912 – a mere two years before the outbreak of the war. Wick House had previously been the residence of Dr George Penrose from about 1906. Mr Antoine St. Laurent Bonvalot was a French landowner of 'independent means.' He died at Wick House aged 81 on Sunday 17th September 1916.

Wick House was one of the most imposing country residences in Downton. Although the property has been sub-divided and much of its grounds have now disappeared under housing development, a 1952 Report of the HM Inspector of Schools gives an indication of the extent of the former estate. In the 1940s and '50s the house was used as a Preparatory School for girls and the report states that there were three classrooms and six dormitories catering for 37 pupils. The extensive grounds consisted of a playing field, hard tennis court, two net ball pitches, an archery range and a riding field.

The Parish Council unanimously accepted the generous offer

The hounds of the Wilton Hunt outside Wick House, c.1900 when the property was owned by Mr H. Curtis Gallup, see page 30.

at their meeting of 28th September. Mrs Bonvalot intended the land to be used primarily as a recreation ground for the adult inhabitants of Downton, with a portion of the ground set aside for children. She agreed as to the advisability of not allowing children in until after tea time because of the expense of keeping someone there to look after it.

It was decided to call the ground 'The Bonvalot Memorial Garden' and the Council came up with a list of provisional regulations:

(1) The Garden shall be open to the public from 10 o'clock in the morning until one hour before sunset.
(2) Children under 16 years of age unaccompanied by parents or guardians shall not be allowed in the ground until 5pm each day.
(3) Games such as cricket, football and the like shall be strictly forbidden.
(4) No dogs shall be admitted or allowed on the ground unless on a lead.
(5) Any boy or girl, or any person found carelessly, or maliciously damaging or destroying any flower, shrub, tree, seat etc. shall be liable to prosecution.

Footnote: As the Memorial Garden is a gift to the village for the benefit and enjoyment of the people, it is earnestly hoped that the public generally will co-operate with the Parish Council in every way to see that the flowers, shrubs, trees, seats etc are in no way damaged.

The official opening ceremony of the Memorial Garden was performed by Mrs Bonvalot and her youngest son Alfred Cecil at 6.30pm on Saturday 5th August 1922. At the ceremony Captain Cecil Bonvalot presented Mr Stevens (the Chairman of the Parish Council) with the deed of conveyance and key to the ground. Entertainment was provided by the Downton Band who played the National Anthem and a selection of other music. The *Salisbury Journal* of 11th August described the Bonvalot Memorial Garden as follows:

It has been attractively laid out by a well-known firm of Tunbridge-Wells landscape gardeners, and has a central avenue and side walks, including an excellent '8' path. There

are many flowerbeds, and the borders are planted with flower-
ing and other shrubs, whilst the avenue is planted alter-
natively with lime and beech trees. In the centre of the main
path a sundial has been erected on a circular crazy pavement
foundation, with four flowerbeds. Four tablets placed around
the top of the sun dial support the following inscription:

> *In honoured and loving memory of Edward St. Laurent*
> *Bonvalot, Second Lieutenant Coldstream Guards,*

> *Who fell in action at Loos in the Great War, October 8th*
> *1915.*

> *This Garden is presented to Downton by his mother Emily*
> *Bonvalot of Wick House.*

> *O valiant dead take comfort where you lie. So sweet to*
> *live? Magnificent to die!*

In September 1922, George Brown was appointed the first
caretaker of the Garden at a wage of 16 shillings a week for the
months April to September and 8 shillings a week October to
March. Mrs Bonvalot contributed towards the upkeep of
the grounds on an annual basis. Her generosity was recognised
by the Parish Council who presented Mrs Bonvalot with an
illuminated address.

The Memorial Gardens, 1922.

Despite slight early problems such as stray poultry from a neighbouring property, the Memorial Garden proved a big success with villagers. Children's swings were added in the spring of 1928, but by October of that year it was reported that 'the swings etc. in the Memorial Garden had been subjected to a considerable amount of rough use, with the result that they had been rendered useless.'

A fascinating attraction in the Memorial Garden was removed in June of the following year. This was an old German gun that had presumably been brought back to Downton as a war trophy in 1919. It was sold by the Parish Council to a Mr C. Saunders of Station Road Amesbury for 10 shillings.

Emily Bonvalot died in July 1933 at the age of 69. She is buried in Downton Churchyard, close to the grave of another particularly benevolent lady of early twentieth century Downton – Mrs Carver of The Moot. In her will Mrs Bonvalot bequeathed the sum of £70 to Downton Parish Council to be invested for the long-term upkeep of the memorial sundial in the Garden.

Since Mrs Bonvalot's death the Memorial Gardens have changed considerably, including the addition of a shelter in 1935 to commemorate the Silver Jubilee of George V. The greatest alterations took place in the 1960s. In 1963 the flower-beds and shrubs were cleared away. Several of the trees were removed three years later after being found unsafe. Additional land next to Long Close was purchased in 1967 and the extended area was laid out as a recreation ground. The sundial memorial was repaired and moved to a position close to the Memorial Hall. The three-tiered stone base of the Bonvalot Memorial – measuring 5 ft. square and just over 18 inches high – survives, but the column and sundial are missing.

The base of the Bonvalot Memorial, 2001.

What is our task?
To make Britain a fit country for heroes to live in.

David Lloyd George, November 1918

Boom and Slump

By the end of the war in November 1918, the people of Britain were in a state of exhaustion after four years of conflict. Following the cessation of hostilities the country entered a period of optimism about the future. The decade of the 1920s started promisingly. The Peace initially brought about a spell of prosperity. Wages and prices rose sharply as people bought many goods they had been unable to get during the war. This was, unfortunately, short lived, as by the summer of 1921 unemployment had risen sharply to a total of over 2,000,000. Britain had entered a slump, which preceded the Great Depression of the 1930s. Unemployment would not fall below 1,000,000 again until 1940.

This period of uneasy transition from war to peace has a strange parallel with the events of a century before, following the victory at Waterloo in 1815. The country went through a period of intense change and social unrest, which locally culminated in the Swing Riots when at least two Downtonians were transported to Australia. A century later the hardship was painful, but without the same degree of social unrest.

Nevertheless, life in Downton in the 1920's and '30s was not entirely bleak, even during the years of the depression. The sale of the Hale Estate in 1920 and a later sell off of a large number of properties by the Longford Estate meant that many villagers in Downton were able to buy their homes for the first time. Many improvements were made in basic local services too, including the provision of electric street lighting (1927), council housing (1921), a recreation ground (1922) and a free library which was opened by Mr Scott, the Headmaster of Downton Council School, in late 1926.

The Post-war Economic Boom

Although the 1920s and 1930s are associated with the economic decline and the Great Depression, there was initially a post-war economic boom. Over-production had taken place during the war and the peace brought an intense period of over-investment with a wave of mergers and buy-outs amongst established industries. Such corporate behaviour was carried out by Downton's largest employer, the Southern Tanning Company, and examples of excessive investment can be found in the surviving Directors' Minute Book preserved at the Wiltshire County Records Office.

A string of acquisitions took place between 1918 and 1920. On 3rd December 1918 an agreement was made to purchase the Downton Paper Mills and machinery for £5,250. One of these buildings was converted into a power station in the 1920s. Four cottages in Gravel Close were purchased in July 1919 and in May of the following year it was decided to buy the Downton Petrol Air Gas Company and land for £1,500.

Evidence of the immediate post-war prosperity remains permanently in Downton in the form of the handsome Tannery building. At a meeting of directors held on Tuesday 9th December 1918 it was decided to carry out an extension to the Tan Yard buildings and plans were drawn up by Mr Savage and Mr Bath. These plans for the new frontage were passed on 13th January 1919 and the old Tannery House a Georgian building which stood by the Mill Bridge was demolished to make way for the new scheme. After its construction the complex was known as the Tannery, rather than the Tan Yard.

The new, impressive 1919 building is particularly unusual in style, as it is reminiscent of the nineteenth century when industries conducted their processes on several storeys, such as the typical textile mill. From the 1920s however, the new industries that boomed in the '30s in the South East and Midlands were housed in bland single-storey buildings similar to the modern industrial buildings of the business parks and industrial estates of today. The Tannery closed in 1998 and the part of the

An aerial photograph of the 'top end' of Downton, c.1920-25, showing the massive Tannery complex.

Tannery built in the late nineteenth century was demolished in November 2000. The interesting 1919 main building – which dominates this part of Downton and is mentioned by Pevsner in his *Buildings of England* – was saved from destruction and will stand as a lasting legacy to this centuries-old industry.

As well as investing in new buildings in the anticipation of a lasting economic boom, the directors of the Southern Tanning Company recruited a large number of demobilised soldiers. Much to its credit the company also provided jobs for disabled former servicemen. At a dinner provided by the company for around 130 Downton servicemen in April 1919, the Managing Director spoke optimistically about the future.

The Slump and Industrial Action

It barely needs recording here that the immediate post First World War boom had, by 1922, turned into a slump for the staple industries of the nineteenth century British economy which contributed to the Great Depression of the '30s with its associated mass unemployment. The Southern Tanning Company itself failed in the early 1930s but was restarted on 17th January 1935 as the Downton Tanning Company Ltd. The 1920s is thought of as a period of industrial unrest and trade union militancy, culminating in the General Strike of 1926.

Anxieties about the future were present even in the spring of 1919, some nine weeks before Downton's day of peace celebrations. On the evening of Saturday 17th May the National Agricultural Labourers' and Rural Workers' Union held a demonstration in Downton. The event drew a large attendance. Between 300 and 400 workers gathered at the railway arch and marched in a procession to the Borough Cross, led by the Downton Band. At the Cross a political meeting was held, presided over by Mr N. Polden who was the Chairman of the local branch of the Agricultural Union. Polden mentioned that the branch now had a membership of nearly 200 as compared with 52 at its formation. Fellow agricultural workers were urged to join the union immediately, 'as the question of employment of non-union labour would be sure to crop up in the future.'

Another individual, 'cutting his political teeth' by speaking alongside the trade unionists at the meeting at the Borough

The Borough Cross, c.1925.

Cross was Alfred Ernest Brown MC, who had been the unsuccessful Liberal candidate for Salisbury at the 1918 Election. Brown was an interesting character whose political career continued until 1945. In the 1930s and '40s, the Rt. Hon Alfred Ernest Brown MP held a number of ministerial positions in the National and Coalition governments. These included being Minister of Health 1941-3 and Minister for Aircraft Production at the end of the Second World War. He led the Liberal National group in parliament from 1940-5.

On Friday 3rd October 1919 the uniform staff of Downton Station came out on strike as part of a national dispute. The Stationmaster Mr P. Rouledge and his assistant Miss Morris were the only two officials to remain on duty. There were no trains between Friday night and Monday, which caused considerable disruption, as most goods were transported by rail, including Saturday's milk, which had to be despatched to Kingston-on-Thames by motor lorry on the Sunday.

The local branch of the Comrades of the Great War were also involved in limited political activity. At their meeting held in their club room above the *Three Horse Shoes* on Saturday 21st June 1919, they passed the same resolutions that has been adopted by several other branches, namely:

(1) That the gratuity paid to ex-servicemen on their discharge is totally inadequate having regard to the services rendered in freeing the world from Prussian domination.
(2) That the scale of pensions awarded to those who had been disabled in their country's service must be immediately increased and is totally inadequate to meet the present cost of living.

Fund raising and assistance to disabled and unemployed ex-servicemen had been a key function of the Comrades organisation. On 'Warriors Day,' 31st March 1921 a sale had raised £17. 9s. 0d. for the relief of unemployed servicemen.

The term *positive discrimination* may be thought of as a modern phenomenon, but in 1920 in an attempt to counteract rising unemployment and recognise the valuable part played by the war's wounded the government launched the 'King's National Roll.' This was a register of firms who employed a certain proportion of disabled ex-servicemen. All local authorities were contacted to disclose their figures and Salisbury Rural

District Council's number of disabled employees was not quite sufficient for the council's name to be added to the Roll.

The Final Comrades Meeting

Less than a week after the dedication service of the Downton War Memorial in April 1921, the Downton branch of the Comrades of the Great War held their last meeting in their club room at the *Three Horse Shoes* Inn. After much discussion it was decided to close both the branch and the club, owing to lack of support. It was further resolved to sell the furniture to clear the club's debt, and to give any balance remaining to the Salisbury Infirmary. The pictures of the King and Queen presented to the Club by Colonel Ashley MP were placed in the Memorial Hall.

Fund raising and other valuable work was continued by the British Legion which was formed in 1921. Their first annual poppy appeal also took place in that year. Their well-known symbol of remembrance – the poppy – was chosen from a poem penned by John McCrae, a doctor serving with the Canadian Armed Forces. In northern France 1915, McCrae had noticed how, despite the slaughter and complete devastation, the poppy still flowered. The opening stanza begins:

> *In Flanders' fields the poppies blow*
> *Between the crosses, row on row*

The first Poppy Day in Downton took place the following year and was arranged by the Women's Institute and organised by Mrs Wrottesley of Wick Lane who was the wife of Commander Wrottesley RN. He had seen active war service in Mesopotamia during the war. A total of £12. 7s. 1d. was collected in Downton and £1. 5s. 9d. at Charlton.

The Old Order Changes

Between the years 1910 and 1920 Downton had gone through a period of intense change. In addition to the lost lives and casualties of the Great War and the social changes in the nature of village life, these ten years had also witnessed the departure of many of Downton's leading citizens. Community leaders of the late nineteenth century such as the Squareys and Lord Nelson died, others including the Vicar and the long standing village Doctor had decided to move on. Those who died or left Downton included:

Elias Pitts Squarey
owner of The Moot,
died February 1911

The Right Hon. 3rd Earl Nelson
of Trafalgar House
died 1913

George Charles Stretch
Downton Stationmaster since 1905
promoted to Lyndhurst Road Station, 1914

Mrs Lavinia Mary Squarey
of The Moot
died April 1915

Professor Wrightson
founder of the Agricultural College
left Downton 1911, died December 1916

Rev. Arthur H. Coombs
South Lane Baptist Minister
left Downton, September 1916

Rev. G. Lenthall Dickenson
Vicar of Downton
Resigned, February 1917

Colonel Marriott-Smith
of Fairfield House,
left Downton December 1919

Mr George William Whiteley
of Hamilton House
Downton's long-serving doctor
left the village in the autumn of 1919

Lord Nelson   George William Whiteley

Many of the names had been particularly long standing in the neighbourhood. The Squareys had lived at The Moot since 1872 when they moved to Downton from Odstock Manor. Dr Whiteley had been the local doctor for 35 years. This Yorkshire character was fondly remembered for decades after his retirement to Budleigh Salterton in the autumn of 1919. The early to mid-1920s were to witness continued upheaval with the premature death of the Vicar the Rev. George Salmon in November 1922, the tragic fire at The Moot in November of the following year and the sudden deaths of Mrs Carver in 1924 and Headmaster Mr Northover in 1925.

The Moot Fire

Mrs Carver's demise was surely hastened by the devastating fire which occurred at The Moot in the early hours of 1st November 1923. The fire was discovered by Mrs Carver who was awoken by the smell of smoke at 5.30am in her room on the south side of the house. She called for the butler Frederick William Nicholas who raised the alarm when it was clear that the room beneath the large drawing room was well ablaze. Mrs Carver phoned for the Salisbury Fire Brigade. There should have been no loss of life, but the terrified maid Gwendoline

The devastated Moot, following the dramatic fire, 1st November 1923.

Burnham panicked and jumped out of an upstairs window. Tragically the force of the fall was taken by the cook, Mrs Annie Wilson who was fatally injured. Neighbours were awoken at a quarter to six and soon the news 'Moot's afire!' had spread round the village. The blaze was so fierce that the house was completely gutted. Only the old laundry part of the building was saved.

Mrs Lavinia Mary Carver was born in March 1856, the daughter of Elias Pitts Squarey of The Moot. She married Sidney Henton Carver in September 1879 and for many years the couple lived in Alexandria, where there is still a property called Sidney Carver House. Carver, a native of Gibraltar, was a Director of the Egyptian firm Carver Brothers and Co. Ltd. He died at Liverpool in May 1907. For many years Mrs Carver lived at The Warren in the High Street, Downton. One of the couple's four daughters, Miriam was married to Lieutenant Arthur Amyot Steward of the Royal Flying Corps, who was killed in action in October 1917. The Stewards' three young children were living at The Moot at the time of the fire.

The Salisbury Fire Brigade pose for the camera outside the remains of The Moot. Would the outcome of the fire have been different had the Downton Fire Brigade still been in existence? Note the October date error on the postcard.

Another daughter, Christabell Margaret married Lieutenant Herbert Prinsep Somors Clogstoun also of the Royal Flying Corps in March 1915. A brass plaque in Downton Parish Church commemorates Christabel's death in January 1941, her husband in February 1955 and their son Anthony who was lost in HMS *Veteran* in September 1942 aged 21.

Mrs Carver was too ill to attend the inquest into Mrs Wilson's death in the Moot Fire. She died a few weeks later on 12th January 1924 at Highlands, Farnham. Thus the life of one of the most benevolent residents of early twentieth century Downton reached a particularly sad end. Her name and generous spirit lives on however, in the Carver Cottages, two semi-detached properties in Barford Lane, administered by the Carver Trust. The plaque on the wall of Carver Cottages reads:

To fulfil the work of
Lavinia Mary Carver
These cottages were
Built by her children
1925

212

Council Housing

The building of houses had virtually stopped during the war. In the months following the cessation of hostilities some progress was made in the provision of housing with the construction of Downton's first council houses by the old Salisbury Rural District Council. The dire need for 'state-aided housing' in Downton had been recognised by members of the Downton Women's Institute in the spring of 1918. The Institute's President Mrs Carver wrote to the Ministry of Reconstruction about the matter, but nothing could be done until the war was over and the demobilisation of troops had begun. In January 1919 the Institute wrote to the Parish Council, stressing the urgency for more homes to be provided and the Parish Council in turn contacted the Rural District Council. The Parish Council recommended the construction of at least twelve homes in Morgan's Vale and Woodfalls and at least twenty homes in Downton. Progress was slow, but by the autumn the first two plots of land had been purchased and in the summer of the following year the Council asked for tenders to build Downton's first council houses.

In October 1920 Salisbury Rural District Council accepted

Council houses in Wick Lane, 1923. Constructed by the same firm of builders who extended the Memorial Hall and were also a local firm of undertakers.

the tender from the Downton firm of builders Downer and Bailey to build four pairs of houses in Wick Lane, at a cost of £7,808. 11s. 0d. The land had been purchased from the Longford Estate, following a council meeting in October of the previous year. The houses were ready for occupation by the end November 1921, when No. 1 was let to W. R. Skeates. By February 1922 all of the properties had been let and it was reported that Mr Skeates was seeking permission from the Council to keep pigs in his back garden. Apart from Skeates, the Council records the following names as amongst the first tenants at these properties: W. V. Shergold, W. F. W. Fitch, G. Fulford, Gerald Sainsbury and E. Moody.

Tenders for council housing at Charlton had been accepted by Salisbury Rural District Council at the same meeting that approved the new houses in Wick Lane. These four houses were to be built in Church Road by Messrs. Wort and Way, who had put in a tender of £3,022. The Minutes of the old Standlynch with Charlton Parish Council show councillors' keenness for local men to be employed on the construction of the new homes. At their meeting in April 1921, Mr Hodges stated that the builders' foreman had been notified of three local men who were available for employment and he understood that they were to be taken on as soon as all the building materials were ready. These houses were completed and let by November of that year.

Elsewhere however, new council housing schemes were far from successful. Two other local sites had been earmarked for council housing – ten dwellings on a 2 acres site at Barford Lane and six dwellings on 1½ acres of land at Morgan's Vale. The Rural District Council had arranged for loans of £288 and £176 for the purchase of the respective sites from Lord Nelson and Mr J. W. Taunton by the end of 1919. Progress beyond that was slow and these schemes had not commenced by the time the 'Geddes Axe' on public sector spending had been wielded in 1921. Besides problems of central government spending cuts, the site at Morgan's Vale was dogged by legal arguments.

The Old and the New

Throughout the 1920s and '30s the period of intense change continued apace in Downton. One of the first local institutions to disappear was the old Downton Fire Engine which was last used to put out a fire at an implement shed at Wick Farm in 1920. The appliance proved hopelessly inadequate to deal with the task and onlookers resorted to the old chain of buckets method. There seems to have been no enthusiasm to revive the local fire brigade, not least because Captain William Barker had resigned and its Engineer Walter Durdle was seriously ill.

In April 1923 it was decided to sell the fire engine and use the proceeds to buy fire extinguishers which were to be kept at appropriate places in the village. Offers were sought for the old vehicle and the highest bid of £10 from Ernest G. Warren of Wick Farm was accepted. The appliance was converted to a light wagon and this recycled vehicle was used for many years to carry milk churns from the farm to Downton Station. Four *Minimax* fire extinguishers were purchased with the proceeds in early 1925 and these were fixed at:

- Richard Crisp's garden at The Headlands
- The Council School in Gravel Close
- East End Stores in the High Street
- Ernest Cove's house at Lode Hill

The village may have lost its own fire engine and been given a near useless replacement, but there were some improvements to basic services in the immediate years following the war. The gas street lighting was restored in the winter of 1919-20, but by the summer of 1920 the Parish Council was anxious to replace the system with electric lights. The old Downton Petrol Air Gas Company had been bought out by the Southern Tanning Company in May of that year and they offered the Parish Council free electricity for street lighting for a period of five years, providing the Council paid the costs of laying the cables. The scheme for 44 lights would have required the Council to borrow £650 from the County Council. It was estimated that after the five years of free supply the cost of electricity would be less than half of the cost of gas. Consent to borrow the money was given in March 1921, but in July of that year the Parish Council decided to hold the scheme in abeyance. So it was not until the winter of 1927-8 that Downton got its first electric street lighting – on the stretch of The Borough between the Iron Bridge and Mill Bridge.

A new service virtually unimaginable before the war was the

foundation of the Downton Radio Club, which was formed at the *Bull* on 9th October 1923. The British Broadcasting Company had been broadcasting for about a year, and it was resolved to commence the club's activities on the evening of the opening of the company's eighth radio station, in Bournemouth on Wednesday 17th October. The club's chairman was Richard Crisp and the advent of radio caused a great deal of excitement in Downton and Salisbury.

Technological advances may have been considerable, but some social attitudes remained firmly stuck in the past. Skimmingtons, skimmington rides or skimmity rides were a strange feature of local culture that had taken place throughout rural England for centuries. The effigies of those thought guilty of adultery were paraded through the streets accompanied by locals making a din, which also explains why in some parts of the country the spectacle was known as 'rough music.' Thomas Hardy famously wrote about the skimmington in *The Mayor of Casterbridge*. Footnotes frequently point out that the practice was made illegal by the 1882 Highway Act and had by then generally died out anyway. This was not the case. In about 1919 a skimmington took place on the East Green against a prominent member of the Unionist Club who had left his wife for another woman. The last skimmington in Downton took place in the early 1930s, outside a cottage on Lode Hill. The individual concerned had served in the army during the Great War. Locals gathered outside the residence banging saucepans and shouting. It was not however the last skimmington in the district – old traditions die hard – there was one in Redlynch shortly before the Second World War.

Downton's Roll of Honour

For all sad words of tongue or pen,
The saddest are these: 'It might have been!'

John Greenleaf Whittier (1807-1892), *Maud Muller*

Servicemen Who Died

The forty-four names that appear on Downton's War Memorial are listed below, with as much information about these individuals as it has been possible to find. Details of graves or memorials of the fallen registered with the Commonwealth War Grave Commission are also provided. Disturbingly, three of the servicemen have no memorial or grave registered with the Commonwealth War Graves Commission, so the War Memorials at Downton are the only places where these men are commemorated.

Village War Memorial lists were drawn up locally, mainly from bereaved families putting forward the names of their loved ones. It is therefore not uncommon to experience difficulties in trying to reconcile local lists with official sources, such as the records of the CWGC or the volumes of *Soldiers Who Died in the Great War*. These 'official' sources themselves are not short of occasional errors or omissions.

The three names on the Downton Memorial with no Memorial registered with the Commonwealth War Graves Commission are Private Frederick Batchelor, Private Reuben Batchelor and Gunner Arthur Jolliffe. The problems in finding information on the demise of Gunner Jolliffe have already been covered; locating information on the Batchelors has been even more frustrating.

Private Frederick Batchelor served in the Dorset Regiment in the early months of the War. His army service records do not survive, but his campaign medal index card filed at the Public

Record Office shows that he was a professional soldier, as he entered the War on 16th August 1914, less than two weeks after it was declared. Private Batchelor was discharged on 31st December 1914 and issued with a Silver War Badge. He therefore must have died from the effects of wounds when he was no longer in the Army which explains why he is not an 'official statistic', but he still should be recognised.

Private Reuben Batchelor was Frederick's elder brother. He was baptised 'Francis Reuben' at Downton Parish Church in May 1880. Reuben and Frederick were the sons of George and Jane Batchelor. George was the landlord successively of the *New Inn* (now the *Wooden Spoon*) and the *King's Arms*. He died of a heart attack at Bodenham, whilst driving his carriage home from Salisbury on 7th July 1891, leaving a widow and nine fatherless children. Despite what must have been a childhood of terrible hardship, the boys progressed well. In May 1894 Frederick and another brother Ernest received high attendance prizes from Downton National School.

Again there is no official information about the death of Private Reuben Batchelor. This is particularly curious as he was killed in action in the early months of the war. The *Western Gazette* of 12th March 1915 contains a photograph of him and states:

Our Roll of Honour contains a portrait of R. F. Batchelor a brother of Mrs W Barrow who was killed in action on 6th November. He was in the 3rd Dragoon Guards.

The records of the CWGC list no Batchelors with the initials R. or F. who served in the 3rd Dragoon Guards. Ironically, however, two brothers from another family called Batchelor served in the 3rd Dragoon Guards and were both killed on 31st October 1914. The Ernest Batchelor referred to above also served in the 3rd Dragon Guards. He was killed in action in France on 11th April 1917, having only joined the Dragoon Guards less than six weeks before his death.

The author has been in correspondence with Lieutenant Colonel R. J. Binks, the Regimental Secretary of the Royal Scots Dragoon Guards who is also anxious to resolve the matter. Lieutenant Colonel Binks cannot however find any reference to a Private R. F. Batchelor listed on either the Dragoon Guards' Roll of Honour or their First World War Casualty Register. Could this be because Private Batchelor served under a different name? This seems unlikely however, because he was clearly already a regular soldier before the start of the war, and at 34, he was obviously not too young to have joined up and so had to use a different name to lie about his age.

It is quite disturbing to think that three of the forty-four names listed on Downton's War Memorial died on active service for their country, yet their names are not amongst the records of the Commonwealth War Graves Commission. It would be very sad indeed if every village war memorial in England has a similar proportion of names that are not officially recognised.

AYLETT Percy John
L. Cpl   315037
32nd Battalion, Middlesex Regiment
Son of Mr and Mrs George Aylett of The Borough
Enlisted 30th May 1912
Discharged Sick, 23rd December 1918
Died 4th September 1919, aged 22
Buried in Downton Churchyard

BAILEY Frederick William
Private   44513
'B' Company, 8th Battalion, Gloucestershire Regiment
Formerly 2878 Hampshire Carabineers
Born 5th March 1898 (Bapt), Downton
Son of George and Alice Bailey, of Gravel Close
Enlisted Devizes
Died 30th May 1918, aged 19
Killed in Action
Memorial: Soissons Memorial, Aisne, France
Also commemorated in Downton Cemetery

BATCHELOR Ernest Samuel
Private   4685
3rd Dragoon Guards (Prince of Wales' Own)
Born 19th July 1885 (Bapt), Downton
Son of George Francis and Jane Batchelor of the 'New Inn',
High Street
Enlisted Londonderry
Died 11th April 1917
Memorial: Arras Memorial, Pas de Calais, France
Panel Number: Bay 1

BATCHELOR Frederick
Private   7533
Dorset Regiment
Born 29th March 1887 (Bapt), Downton
Brother of Ernest Samuel Batchelor
Entered the War 16th August 1914
Discharged 31st December 1914
Grave/ Memorial details not recorded with the CWGC

BATCHELOR Francis Reuben
Private
3rd Dragoon Guards
Born 25th May 1880 (Bapt), Downton
Brother of Frederick Batchelor
Died 6th November 1914
Killed in Action
Grave/ Memorial details not recorded with
the CWGC

Private Reuben
Batchelor

BENNETT Frederick James
Private   203229
6th Battalion, Wiltshire Regiment
Born 4th June 1893 (Bapt), Downton
Son of Alfred James and Ruth Ellen Amelia Bennett
Enlisted Salisbury
Died 22nd March 1918
Died of Wounds
Memorial: Pozieres Memorial, Somme, France
Panel Number: 61 to 64

BISHOP Charles
Private   44514
8th Service Battalion, Gloucestershire Regiment
Formerly 2879 Hampshire Carabineers
Born Downton
Son of Kate Bishop of The Borough
Occupation Apprentice Blacksmith
Enlisted Devizes
Died 30th May 1918, aged 19
Killed in Action
Memorial: Soissons Memorial, Aisne, France

BLAKE Edward James
Sergeant 8115
1st Battalion, Wiltshire Regiment
Born Downton
Enlisted Salisbury
Died 21st March 1918
Cemetery: Achiet-le-Grand Communal Cemetery Extension,
Pas de Calais, France
Grave Reference: II. G. 22.

BONVALOT Edward St. Laurent
2nd Lieutenant
2nd Battalion, Coldstream Guards
Born 5th July 1891 at 32 Onslow Square, London
Educated at Eton (1903-10) and Trinity College, Cambridge
Son of Antoine St. Laurent and Emily Bonvalot, of Wick House
Enlisted 7th October 1914
Died 9th October 1915
Died of Wounds at the Military Hospital, Rue Faidherbe,
Bethune
Cemetery: Bethune Town Cemetery, Pas de Calais, France
Grave Reference: II. K. 5.

BUNDY Bob
Private 9016
1st Battalion, Wiltshire Regiment
Born 2nd June 1895 (Bapt), Downton
Son of William and Susan Bundy
Died 20th September 1914, aged 19
Died of Wounds
Cemetery: Vailly British Cemetery, Aisne, France
Grave Reference: Sp. Mem. 13.

BUNDY Ralph
Private 18319
2nd Battalion, Wiltshire Regiment
Son of George and Martha Bundy, of Gravel Close
Born West Wellow, Hampshire
Enlisted Southampton
Died 8th July 1916, aged 23
Died of Wounds
Memorial: Thiepval Memorial, Somme, France

Panel Number: Pier and Face 13A
Also commemorated in Downton Cemetery

COOMBS Henry Whitaker
Lieutenant
18th Battalion, Northumberland Fusiliers
Born 7th January 1893
Son of Arthur Henry and Mary Sophie Coombs of The Manse,
South Lane
Educated at Keyford School, Frome, Somerset and Corpus
Christi College, Oxford
Junior House Master at Wellington College, Berkshire
Gazetted 23rd December 1914
Died 2nd July 1916
Died of Wounds
Cemetery: Corbie Communal Cemetery Extension, Somme,
France
Grave Reference: Plot I. Row B, Grave 8

DICKENSON Aubrey Greville Newton
2nd Lieutenant
2nd Battalion, King's Royal Rifle Corps
Born 25th October 1896
Son of Rev Lenthall Greville and Mrs Sybil Frances Dickenson
Educated at Twyford and Winchester College
Passed into Sandhurst, August 1914
Received his commission in the KRRC, January 1915
Died 1st July 1916, aged 19
Died of Wounds in hospital at Bethune
Cemetery: Bethune Town Cemetery, Pas de Calais, France
Grave Reference: III. K. 26.

EASTMAN Prince Leopold 'Leo'
Private   17798
3rd Battalion, Dorset Regiment Labour Corps
Born Downton, 16th February 1885
Son of Henry and Mary Eastman
Resided Waterside
Occupation Basket and Chair Maker
Husband of Alice Harris (formerly Eastman), of Regent Street,
Junee, New South Wales, Australia
Died 29th November 1918, aged 33

Cemetery: Beirut War Cemetery, Lebanese Republic
Grave Reference: 217.

ELLIOTT George
Private   3/326
5th Battalion, Wiltshire Regiment
Son of Mrs Duffett, of Lode Hill
Enlisted Monmouth
Died 10th August 1915, aged 39
Memorial: Helles Memorial, Gallipoli, Turkey
Panel Number: 156 to 158

FORDER George
Private   15283
7th Battalion, Royal Dublin Fusiliers
Formerly 703 Wiltshire Regiment
Born 1872
Son of Mrs Fanny Pretty of The Borough
Occupation Leather Tanner
Died 28th September 1915
Cemetery: East Mudros Military Cemetery, Greece
Grave Reference: III. A. 5.

GRAVES Evelyn Paget
Major
Royal Field Artillery
attached Royal Flying Corps
Squadron Commander of 60th Squadron, 1916-17
Born 5th June 1890 at Nagpur, Maharashtra, India
Son of Major the Hon. Adolphus Edward Paget and Katherine
Louisa Graves of The Headlands House, Downton and Queen
Anne's Mansions, London
Educated at Lancing College, West Sussex
Died 6th March 1917, aged 26
Killed in Action
Cemetery: Avesnes-le-Comte Communal Cemetery Extension,
Pas de Calais, France
Grave Reference: I. C. 10.

GUNSTONE William Alfred
Corporal   20633
2nd Battalion, Wiltshire Regiment

Son of Frank and Annie Gunstone, of The Headlands
Died 21st March 1918, aged 21
Memorial: Pozieres Memorial, Somme, France
Panel Number: 64

HAYDON Arthur Ellis MM
Sergeant   R/7434
12th Battalion, King's Royal Rifle Corps
Son of William Ellis and Emily Haydon of The Borough
Brother of Frank and John Vicent Haydon
Married Rose Spreadborough, January 1918
Taken Prisoner of War 21st March 1918
Died 31st March 1919, aged 26
Buried in Downton Churchyard

HAYDON William George
Private   3054
3rd/7th Battalion, Hampshire Regiment
Brother of Arthur Ellis Haydon
Enlisted Bournemouth
Died 23rd March 1916, aged 26
Died at Boscombe Military Hospital of bronchio-pneumonia
Buried in Downton Churchyard

HOBBS George Henry
Private   6949
1st Battalion, Hampshire Regiment
Born Fordingbridge
Enlisted Salisbury
Wounded and taken prisoner 26th August 1914
Died 28th August 1914
Memorial: La Ferte-Sous-Jouarre Memorial, Seine-et-Marne,
France

HUNT Geoffrey Thomas
Private   23638
1st Battalion, Wiltshire Regiment
Son of Amos and Emily Lawrence Hunt of The Borough
Brother of Archibald Hunt
Died at Salisbury Infirmary, 23rd February 1919, aged 22
Buried in Downton Churchyard

Gunner Arthur T. Jolliffe and Miss Julia May Witt on their wedding day at Fording-bridge, 4th March 1916.

JOLLIFFE Arthur Thomas
Gunner   11691
Royal Marine Artillery
Born 10th July 1887
Enlisted 6th March 1906
Died on Hospital Ship *Garth Castle*, 8th August 1917
Civilian Grave in Fordingbridge Cemetery
Also commemorated on Fordingbridge War Memorial
Grave/ Memorial details not recorded with the CWGC

KEELEY Arthur
Sergeant   4524
10th (Prince of Wales's Own Royal) Hussars
Brother of Mrs S. Downer, of *Yorks*, Totland Bay, Isle of Wight
Died 13th May 1915
Memorial: Ypres (Menin Gate) Memorial, Ieper, Belgium
Panel Number: 5

KEELEY Frederick Charles
Cy. Sgt. Major   31401
1st Battalion Wiltshire Regiment

Born Fovant, Wiltshire
Enlisted London
Brother of Arthur Keeley
Died 17th November 1914
Memorial: Ypres (Menin Gate) Memorial, Ieper, Belgium
Panel Number: 53

KINGSBURY William Ghazi
Private   18713
7th Battalion, King's Shropshire Light Infantry
Born 2nd April 1893 (Bapt), Downton
Son of William and Sarah Kingsbury of Barford Lane
Enlisted Shrewsbury
Died 25th April 1916, aged 23
Cemetery: Dickebusch New Military Cemetery, Ieper,
West-Vlaanderen, Belgium
Grave Reference: J. 15.

MITCHELL William
Able Seaman   187436
HMS Maidstone, Royal Navy
Son of George and Ellen Mitchell
Died 13th March 1915, aged 35
Died in accident at Parkestone Quay, Suffolk
Buried at St. Mary's Churchyard, Shotley, Suffolk
Grave Reference: R N Plot 31

MOODY Fred Penn
Private   10349
'D' Company, 2nd Battalion, Wiltshire Regiment
Born 25th December 1886 (Bapt), Downton
Son of John and Sarah Jane Moody of The Borough
Enlisted Salisbury August 1914
Died 26th September 1915
Cemetery: Cabaret-Rouge British Cemetery, Souchez, Pas de
Calais, France
Grave Reference: VIII. T. 12.

MOODY Percy
Gunner   701791
'A' Battery, 330th Brigade, Royal Field Artillery
Son of Mark and Emily Moody

Husband of Mrs L. I. Butcher (formerly Moody), of 73 Pearl
Farm, West Cholderton, Salisbury
Died 28th September 1917, aged 22
Cemetery: Zuydcoote Military Cemetery, Nord, France
Grave Reference: I. D. 14.

MORGAN Alfred Ernest
2nd Lieutenant
attached 12th Battalion, Middlesex Regiment
Formerly Lance Corporal in the Royal Dragoon Guards
Born West Kensington
Son of Mr and Mrs Richard Morgan of Meadowlands, The
Borough
Died 29th October 1916
Cemetery: Pozieres British Cemetery, Ovillers-La Boisselle,
Somme, France
Grave Reference: I. E. 32.

MOULAND Walter
Private   5420
2nd Battalion, Wiltshire Regiment
Enlisted Devizes
Died 24th October 1914
Killed in Action
Memorial: Ypres (Menin Gate) Memorial, Ieper, Belgium
Panel Number: 53

MUSSELWHITE Albert George Kimberley
Private   45930
8th Battalion, Royal Berkshire Regiment
Formerly 8/3757 Dorset Regiment
Son of Albert and Annie Musselwhite of Gravel Close
Enlisted Trowbridge
Married August 1918
Husband of Flora Ada Frampton (formerly Musselwhite), of
Long Close
Died 19th September 1918, aged 19
Memorial: Vis-En-Artois Memorial, Pas de Calais, France
Panel Number: 7

NEWMAN Fred
Private   241938
14th Battalion, Gloucestershire Regiment
Born 16th December 1888 (Bapt), Downton
Son of George and Ellen Newman of The Borough
Husband of Edith Mary Newman, of 48, Church Street, Lyme
Regis, Dorset
Enlisted Lyme Regis
Died 22nd October 1917, aged 29
Memorial: Tyne Cot Memorial, Zonnebeke, West-Vlaanderen,
Belgium
Panel Number: Panel 72 to 75

NICKLEN Reginald James
Able Seaman   J/45235(PO)
HMS *Caradoc*, Royal Navy
Born Downton
Son of Mr and Mrs James Nicklen of The Headlands
Died 22nd September 1919, aged 19
Memorial: Haidar Pasha Memorial, Turkey

NOBLE Harry William
Sergeant   19638
'J' Battery, Royal Horse Artillery
Born 12th February 1882 (Bapt), Downton
Son of Walter and Rosina Noble
Husband of Mary J. Noble of Lode Hill
Enlisted Poole, Dorset
Died 11th February 1916
Died of pneumonia
Cemetery: St. Sever Cemetery, Rouen, Seine-Maritime, France
Grave Reference: A. 17. 14.

PATIENCE Albert Edward
Private   203077
2nd Battalion, Wiltshire Regiment
Formerly 4485 Somerset Light Infantry
Enlisted Salisbury
Resided The Borough
Died 8th January 1919
Died whilst travelling home after the war
Cemetery: Copenhagen Western Cemetery, Denmark

SENIOR Henry
Sergeant   207335
3rd Battalion, Worcestershire Regiment
Born 2nd June 1895 (Bapt), Downton
Son of William and Edith Rose Senior, of 2 Natanbury,
Waterside
Enlisted Boscombe, Hampshire
Died 25th September 1918, aged 23
Cemetery: Le Touret Military Cemetery, Richebourg-L'Avoue,
Pas de Calais, France
Grave Reference: IV. C. 41.

SHEPPARD Albert Henry
Private   27604
7th Battalion, King's Shropshire Light Infantry
Formerly 34373 Wiltshire Regiment
Born Tidworth
Son of William and Mary J. Sheppard, of New Court Down
Buildings
Enlisted Salisbury
Died 1st October 1918, aged 21
Killed in action
Cemetery: Flesquieres Hill British Cemetery, Nord, France
Grave Reference: Sp. Mem. I.

SMITH Ernest
Sergeant   10584
1st Battalion, Wiltshire Regiment
Born 28th February 1887
Son of John and Rosa Smith, of The Borough
Died 8th June 1915 aged 28
Died of Wounds
Memorial: Ypres (Menin Gate) Memorial, Ieper, Belgium
Panel Number: 53
Also commemorated in Downton Churchyard

STEWARD Arthur Amyot
Lieutenant
Royal Field Artillery
attached 9th Section Balloon Company, Royal Flying Corps
Born 14th July 1882
Son of Edward and Margaret Steward

Educated at Wellington College, Berkshire and Magdalene
College, Oxford
Occupation Church of England Clergyman
Married 1912 to Miriam Agnes Carver
Son-in-law of Mr Sidney and Lavinia Carver of The Moot
Lieutenant with the 3rd Norfolk Regiment during the Boer War
Enlisted 6th October 1915
Died 6th October 1917
Killed in Action
Cemetery: Duhallow A.D.S. Cemetery, Ieper, Belgium
Grave Reference: I. D. 25.

Ernest Smith, c.1908

SWANBOROUGH Edwin John DCM
Lance Corporal   9769
2nd Battalion, Border Regiment
Born Figheldean
Brother of Charles Swanborough of Salisbury Road
Enlisted Devizes
Qualifying Date 5th October 1914
Died 1st July 1916, aged 24
Killed in action
Cemetery: Dantzig Alley British Cemetery, Mametz, Somme,
France
Grave Reference: VI. B. 4.

VINEY Arthur Ernest
Sergeant   9306
6th Battalion, Wiltshire Regiment
Born 13th June 1886 (Bapt), Downton
Son of Charles and Emily Viney
Enlisted Salisbury
Died 2nd July 1916, aged 30
Memorial: Thiepval Memorial, Somme,
France
Panel Number: Pier and Face 13A

Sergeant Arthur Viney

WINTON Harry M
Lance Corporal   9275
5th Battalion, Wiltshire Regiment
Born Upper Beeding, Sussex
Enlisted Salisbury
Died 13th August 1915.
Memorial: Helles Memorial, Gallipoli, Turkey
Panel Number: Panel 156 to 158

WYNDHAM George Heremon
2nd Lieutenant
3rd Battalion, Devonshire Regiment
attached, Northumberland Fusiliers
Born 25th October 1893
Son of Colonel Guy Percy and Edwina Virginia Wyndham of
Charford Manor, Downton and 44 Belgrave Square, London
Died 24th March 1915, aged 21
Killed in action

Cemetery: Dranouter Churchyard, Heuvelland, West-
Vlaanderen, Belgium
Grave Reference: II. B. 16 .
Also commemorated on the Memorial to Wyndhams killed in
the Great War in East Knoyle Church, Wiltshire.

The following three names are added to Downton's Roll of
Honour of those who paid the Supreme Sacrifice as a result of
physical and mental injuries sustained during the war. Although
Stretch's father was no longer Stationmaster at Downton when
his son died, Stretch had nevertheless lived in Downton longer
than anywhere else in his brief life. Both Stretch and Durdle
appear in the records of the Commonwealth War Graves
Commission. Haydon was buried on the same afternoon that the
Downton War Memorial was dedicated.

STRETCH Reginald Augustine
Private   204191
2nd Battalion, Wiltshire Regiment
Son of Charles George and Kate Stretch
Died 19th November 1918, aged 23
Cemetery: Etaples Military Cemetery, Pas de Calais, France
Grave Reference: L. E. 24.

HAYDON Frank
Gunner   129903
Royal Garrison Artillery
Born Redlynch, 11th May 1898
Brother of Arthur Ellis, John Vincent and William George
Haydon
Died 23rd March 1921, aged 22
Buried in Downton Churchyard (civilian grave)
Grave details not recorded with the CWGC

DURDLE Reginald Harry
Corporal   15940
Royal Marine Light Infantry
Born Downton, 8th July 1893
Son of Walter Andrew and Jane Durdle, of High Street
Died 13th April 1921
Buried in Downton Churchyard

In addition to the 47 names of Downton War dead listed above, even more soldiers of the First World War with Downton connections are to be located in *Soldiers Who Died in the Great War 1914-19* which was published by the War Office in 1921. The information in these eighty volumes has been recently made available on CD ROM.

The CD ROM database of *Soldiers Who died in the Great War* records the names of sixteen men who were born in Downton, Wiltshire and a further seven who resided here at the time they joined the forces. Cross-referencing these names with the CWGC Debt of Honour Register, information from local wartime newspapers and names recorded on other local War Memorials narrows this list down slightly.

Gunner Sidney Walter Hickman and Company Quartermaster Sergeant Bertram Warner can be excluded from the list of servicemen born in Downton as their names appear on the Morgan's Vale and Woodfalls Memorial. Private Ernest Brown can also be excluded as his name is recorded on the War Memorial at Redlynch. He served in the same Regiment as Private Reuben Batchelor and was killed on the same day, 6th November 1914. Yet unlike Batchelor his details are known to the CWGC and his name is commemorated on the Menin Gate at Ieper, Belgium.

Of the names recorded in *Soldiers Who Died* who resided in Downton, Privates Reginald Frank Arney, William J Frampton, Henry Mark Littlecott and Henry James Wort are commemorated at Morgan's Vale. Private Alfred Charles Wilkins is commemorated on Redlynch War Memorial and Private Charles Edward King in St Mary's Church, Redlynch.

This leaves the additional names of thirteen servicemen who were born in Downton and killed in the War but not commemorated on a local War Memorial and one serviceman who lived in Downton at the time of his enlistment. The details of these men are recorded below. If these names are added to Downton's Roll of Honour the number climbs to more than sixty.

Servicemen from *Soldiers Who Died in the Great War*, who were born in Downton

FULLER Mornington
Private   G/11089
10th Battalion, Queen's Own Royal West Kent Regiment
Born Downton
Son of Roland Lacy and Alice Fuller, of St. Ines, Hoo,
Rochester, Kent
Enlisted Chatham, Kent
Resided Rochester, Kent
Died 29th June 1916, aged 20
Died of Wounds
Cemetery: Dartmoor Cemetery, Becordel-Becourt, Somme,
France
Grave Reference: II. C. 89.

GOODRIDGE George Thomas
Private   8301
6th Dragoon Guards (The Carabiniers)
Born Downton
Son of Harry and Annie Ellen Goodridge, of 2, Shelley Rd.,
Horsham, Sussex.
Died 1st November 1914, aged 21
Killed in Action
Memorial: Ypres (Menin Gate) Memorial, Ieper, Belgium
Panel Number: 5

HARRISON Lewis Charles
Private   32366
1st Battalion, Somerset Light Infantry
Formerly 26069 Hampshire Regiment
Born Downton
Husband of Winifred Harrison, of Cadnam, Hampshire
Enlisted Winchester
Resided Southampton
Died 12th May 1917, aged 32
Died of wounds
Cemetery: Aubigny Communal Cemetery Extension, Pas de
Calais, France
Grave Reference: II. H. 77.

HAYTER Henry
Rifleman   8717
2nd Battalion, Rifle Brigade
Born Downton
Husband of Mrs H Hayter, High Street, Wheatley, Oxfordshire
Enlisted Reading
Resided Basildon
Died 31st March 1918, aged 33
Died of Wounds
Cemetery: Moreuil Communal Cemetery Allied Extension,
Somme, France
Grave Reference: Y. 4.

HOOKEY William George
Rifleman   372909
8th Battalion, London Regiment (Post Office Rifles)
Born Downton
Son of G. and M. Hookey of Downton
Husband of Eliza Ann Hookey, of Gladstone Villa, Eastern
Road, Rayleigh, Essex
Enlisted Southend
Resided Thundersley, Essex
Died 5th December 1917, aged 28
Died of Wounds
Cemetery: Grevillers British Cemetery, Pas de Calais, France
Grave Reference: IX. C. 11.

KNIGHT Charles James
Private   6909
5th Battalion, Wiltshire Regiment
Born Downton
Husband of E E Bricknell (formerly Knight), of Nether Compton,
Dorset
Enlisted Salisbury
Resided Sherborne, Dorset
Theatre of War Mesopotamia
Died 23rd April 1916, aged 32
Died of Wounds
Memorial: Kirkee 1914-1918 Memorial, Bombay, India
Panel Number: Face E.

NEWHAM Harry
Private   G/21678
Royal West Surrey Regiment
Born Downton
Enlisted Brighton
Resided Downton
Died 24th February 1917
Killed in Action
Theatre of War France and Flanders
Formerly 1998, Sussex Yeomanry
Grave/ Memorial details not recorded with the CWGC

NEWMAN Frank
Sergeant   G/8473
Queen's Own Royal West Kent Regiment, Depot
Born Downton
Son of George and Harriet Newman
Served in the Egyptian Campaign (1882-85)
Husband of A R Newman, Terrace Cottage, London Road,
Stroud
Enlisted Stroud, Gloucestershire
Resided Stroud, Gloucestershire
Died 29th April 1916, aged 54
Cemetery: Maidstone Cemetery, Kent
Grave Reference: 1. OO. 251.

NOBLE William Henry
Private   6876
23rd Battalion, London Regiment
Formerly 25356 Somerset Light Infantry
Enlisted Winchester
Born Downton
Died 2nd October 1916
Killed in Action
Memorial: Thiepval Memorial, Somme, France
Panel Number: Pier and Face 9D 9C 13C and 12C

READ Charles William
Private   20093
1/4th Battalion, Wiltshire Regiment
Born Downton

Son of George N Read, Golden Cross Hotel, Havlock Road,
Hastings
Enlisted Durrington
Resided Wilton
Died 21st November 1917, aged 20
Killed in Action, Egypt
Cemetery: Jerusalem War Cemetery, Israel
Grave Reference: P. 14.

READ Ralph
Corporal   14940
9th Battalion, Royal Dublin Fusiliers
Formerly 12140 Wiltshire Regiment
Born Downton
Enlisted Salisbury
Killed in Action 9th September 1916
Cemetery: Delville Wood Cemetery, Longueval, Somme, France
Grave Reference: II. F. 7.

SANSON Eric
Private   15492
11th Battalion, Welsh Regiment
Born Downton
Enlisted Cardiff
Resided Llandaff, Glamorgan
Died at home, 26th October 1914

WHATLEY James
Private   24210
5th Battalion, Royal Berkshire Regiment
Formerly 20911 Somerset Light Infantry
Born Downton
Son of Arthur and Fanny Whatley, of Higher Lawn, Tisbury
Husband of Mabel F Whatley, of Higher Lawn, Tisbury
Enlisted Salisbury
Resided Tisbury
Died of Wounds 18th March 1917, aged 23
Cemetery: Avesnes-le-Comte Communal Cemetery Extension,
Pas de Calais, France
Grave Reference: I. C. 26.

Servicemen from *Soldiers Who Died in the Great War*, who resided at Downton

CHOULES Albert Henry
Private   33495
2nd Battalion, Wiltshire Regiment
Born Marlborough
Son of John Choules, of Marlborough
Husband of S. A. Collins (formerly Choules), of Rose Cottage, Littleton Panell, Devizes
Enlisted Marlborough
Resided Downton
Killed in Action 21st March 1918, aged 36
Memorial: Pozieres Memorial, Somme, France
Panel Number: Panel 64

The exact number of First World War dead with Downton connections will never be known. The names recorded in the Roll of Honour are the most the author has been able to find and the length of the list demonstrates the sheer enormity of the loss of life.

There is also a local story that a soldier from Downton was amongst the 227 people killed in Britain's worst railway accident at Quintinshill near Gretna Green in May 1915. No information can be found to authenticate this.

In conclusion, the son of a family temporarily living in Wick Lane was also one of the war dead. Prior to his enlistment he was employed at the Downton Tan Yard. Regrettably, he was accidentally omitted from the Downton War Memorial, because his family had left the area before the names for the Memorial were put forward. It is unlikely that he is commemorated anywhere in England.

Who was he? It is possible that he was one of those located in the pages of *Soldiers Who Died in the Great War* and has, therefore, been unwittingly included here. Today, many decades after the Armistice, his former work colleagues long dead, his name may never be ascertained. It is therefore perhaps fitting that he poignantly remains Downton's Unknown Soldier.

They are all gone into a world of light,
And I alone sit lingering here.

Henry Vaughan (1622-1695), *They are All Gone*

Servicemen Who Survived

The following list of servicemen who survived combines the names listed inside the Memorial Hall with those recorded on the Roll of Honour in Downton Parish Church, plus a few other local individuals mentioned in the local press during the course of the war. Additional information on the individuals has been found at the Public Record Office, in local Trade Directories, on memorial and grave stone inscriptions, in old Parish Magazines, Downton Parish Registers and in the pages of the *Salisbury Journal* and the *Western Gazette* newspapers. The criteria used for inclusion on this list is that the men were either born in, or lived in Downton before the War. As this book was going to press, Gordon Bishop pointed out another omission from the list, his grandfather Reginald Paddock, whose family moved away from Downton during the war and did not return until the early 1920s.

The list below is not without its problems. It is rather unfortunate that the second and third names are identical. One of these is undoubtedly pictured in the 1902 photograph of the Church choir. Their names are taken from the Roll of Honour in Downton Parish Church. One is Reginald Horace, the son of Andrew and Alice Alford who was baptised on 6th March 1892. His father was a local blacksmith. Similarly confusing are the entries with the surname Jones, of whom it is impossible to ascertain further details without family knowledge.

A group of individuals who served in the Great War, but whose names are not recorded in the lists of servicemen either in the Church or the Memorial Hall were members of local Gypsy communities. Avoiding military service was more easy for Gypsy men than for other members of the population, as they had the ability to evade the authorities if they so wished. For those who did enlist there may have been some pressure to keep their roots private, to avoid the sort of isolation and victimisation that was generally a part of life outside the armed forces.

More research has to be carried out into the part played by Romanies in the First World War, but amongst the local Gypsies who served was Robert Cooper. With bright blue eyes and flaxen hair in tight curls, Cooper was well known in Downton. He lived in a camp at a disused chalk pit near the Lions at Charford. His elder brother Nehemiah was a former king of the Hampshire gypsies. His sister was the wonderfully named Cinderella, which begs the question was her name given in humour or given wistfully?

Robert Cooper was deaf and mute, a disability apparently caused by an injury to his palate sustained in the Great War. He died in the early evening 4th January 1956, whilst walking along the Bournemouth Road. In atrocious weather conditions of thick fog, Cooper was hit by a Wilts and Dorset double-decker bus. The accident took place on the county bridge between Wiltshire and Hampshire. In Cooper's pocket was a piece of Christmas cake given to him by Mrs Annie Lydford.

ALDIS Arthur
Driver   54543
Royal Engineers
Entered the War 24th December 1914

ALFORD R H
Sergeant   Royal Naval Division

ALFORD R H
Sergeant   53rd Queens Own West Surrey

AYLETT Ernest G
L. Cpl.   14590
6th Dragoon Guards
Enlisted 12th December 1915
Discharged 2nd September 1918

BATCHELOR Arthur James
Private   4th Royal Fusiliers
Born 22nd February 1884 (Bapt), Downton
Son of George and Jane Batchelor
Brother of Ernest, Frederick and Reuben Batchelor

BATTEN Walter
Gunner   Royal Horse Artillery

BENNETT Alexander
Private   Hampshire Regiment
Born 10th June 1883 (Bapt), Downton
Lived at Lode Hill and worked as a gardener at The Moot

BENNETT Horam C
Bombadier   Royal Field Artillery

BENNETT Percy
Corporal   2nd Wiltshire Regiment
Wounded Prisoner

BENNETT Percy
Private   Dorset Regiment

BENNETT Walter
Able Seaman   Royal Navy
Born 25th December 1889 (Bapt), Downton
Son of Harry Edward and Emmeline Bennett

BISHOP Arthur 'Sunny'
Private   Wiltshire Regiment
Born Downton, 10th February 1894
Enlisted 1918
Married Mary Penny
Foreman at Downton Tannery for many years
Died 9th November 1979

BISHOP Albert
Private   Army Service Corps
Born 13th January 1881
Married Mabel Ella Gurd
Resided The Borough
Died 15th April 1959

BLAKE A G
Private   Wiltshire Regiment

BLAKE A G
Private   Army Service Corps

BLAKE Frank
Gunner   Royal Field Artillery

BLAKE Frederick William
Private   1st Wiltshire Regiment
Son of Edward James and Betsy Blake of The Borough
Born 15th September 1889 (Bapt), Downton
Enlisted 1905
Brother of Edward Blake, (killed March 1918)

BLAKE George
Private   Army Service Corps, Mechanical Transport

BLAKE H Charles
Sapper   Royal Engineers
Son of Mr and Mrs A Blake of Salisbury Road

BLAKE William John 'Buff'
Corporal   Royal Garrison Artillery
Born 7th May 1893 (Bapt),
Downton
Son of Henry and Sarah Blake
Lived at *Elmsleigh*, Lode Hill

BLAKE Willie
Private   Tank Corps

BONVALOT Alfred Cecil
Captain   2nd Coldstream Guards
Born 16th August 1896 at
Tunbridge Wells
Brother Edward St. Laurent
Bonvalot (killed October 1915)
Educated at Eton
Enlisted to 7th Battalion Wiltshire
Regiment, 20th September 1914

Corporal William John Blake

Applied for Commission with Coldstream Guards 2nd
November 1914
Captain 28th January 1921

BOULTER Edward
Private   2nd Wiltshire Regiment
Enlisted 1904
Resided The Borough

BOULTER George
Private   1st Wiltshire Regiment

BOWERMAN A
Artificer   Royal Navy

BOXALL William
Private   27878
Royal Berkshire Regiment

BRAND Ernest George
Able Seaman
Royal Naval Division
Son of George Brand of The Borough

BRAND Harold B
Sergeant   5th Bedford Regiment

BROWN George
Private   3rd Wiltshire Regiment

BUNDY Bert
Private   Dublin Fusiliers

BUNDY Edwin Frank
Private   10408
2nd Wiltshire Regiment
Brother of Ralph Bundy, (killed July 1916)
Qualifying Date 11th December 1914
Prisoner of War March-November 1918
Resided Barford Lane

BUNDY Fred W
Private   Royal Marine Light Infantry

BUNDY Henry Frank
Private   19232
3rd Wiltshire Regiment
Formerly 30983 Somerset Light Infantry
Born 18th April 1897 (Bapt), Downton
Son of Henry and Eva Bundy

BUNDY John
Chief Stoker   Royal Navy

BUNDY Reginald Philip
Corporal   234294
Army Service Corps
Born 25th December 1893 (Bapt), Downton
Grandson of Peter and Mary Bundy
Enlisted 21st January 1916
Discharged 27th February 1919
Married Lilian Rosa Bailey, 24th June 1916
Resided Alma Cottages, Salisbury Road

BUNDY Walter
Private   Wiltshire Regiment
Born 25th December 1888 (Bapt), Downton
Brother of Bob Bundy, (killed September 1914)

BUNDY William
Private   5417
Somerset Light Infantry

BUNDY William
Sapper   108919
Royal Engineers
Born London, 1892
Attested 11th December 1915
Enlisted at Devizes, 21st January 1916
Resided Lode Hill

BUNDY William Charles 'Churby' DCM
Sergeant   22250

1st Wiltshire Regiment
Son of Mrs Mary Elliott
Born 17th May 1891 (Bapt), Downton
Awarded DCM in April 1919

BURDOCK Walter
Gunner   Royal Field Artillery

CARVER Felix Edward OBE
Captain   1/4th Dorset Regiment
Born 1896
Son of Mr and Mrs S Carver of The Moot
Captain 1st June 1916
Temporary Major January 1919
Released to civil employment, 1st March 1921

CHALK Charles
Private   Labour Corps

CHALK Charles
Private   3rd Hampshire Regiment

CHALK Charlie
Private   Army Ordnance Corps

CHALK Frederick James
Corporal   5371
Army Service Corps
Born 22nd April 1888 (Bapt),
Downton
Son of Frank and Harriet Chalk
Entered the War 28th March 1915
Died 4th November 1970, aged 82
Buried at Downton Cemetery

CHALK Joseph F
Sergeant   13416
Animal Veterinary Corps

CHALK S F
Private   2nd Devonshire Regiment

Private Frederick James
Chalk

CLARKE Sidney
Private   2nd Devonshire Regiment
Mons Star

CLOGSTOUN Herbert Prinsep Sommers MBE
Captain   Royal Flying Corps
Born 19th September 1886
Married Christabell Margaret Carver of The Moot,
March 1915
Died 21st February 1955

COLLIER John Howard
Captain   RD Corps
Son of the Rev. John Collier of Downton Baptist Chapel
Enlisted 1914
Resided Long Close House
Former prospective Liberal Candidate for South Wiltshire
Died 14th July 1921, aged 57
Buried in South Lane Baptist Burial Ground

COOMBES Charles
Private   Devonshire Regiment

COOMBES Frank
Private   5th Wiltshire Regiment

COOMBES George
Private   5th Wiltshire Regiment

COOMBES William
Private   11th Hampshire Regiment

COOPER Edward
Private   Royal Marine Light Infantry

COOPER George
Private

COPPOCK Oswald J
Corporal   Royal Army Medical Corps
Resided Avon House, The High Street
Occupation Ironmonger

COSENS Edwin Thomas 'Tom'
Private   270878
Army Service Corps
Born Wield, Hampshire, 6th October 1879
Died 14th November 1920

COVE Ernest L
Corporal   Animal Veterinary Corps
Lived next to the Railway Bridge, Lode Hill

CRISP Richard
Petty Officer   Royal Naval Air Service
Ran Headlands Garage

DALY John William
Carptr.   Mercantile Marines
Born London, 1882
Resided Green Cottage, The Borough

DICKENSON Lenthall Greville DSO
Major   Senior Chaplain to the Forces
Born 1864
Vicar of Downton 1910-17
Father of Aubrey Greville Newton Dickenson, (killed July 1916)

DICKENSON Edward Newton MC
Captain   King's Royal Rifle Corps
Son of the Rev L G Dickenson
Born Burnley, 25th September 1895
Educated at Winchester College
Occupation Teacher
Enlisted Darlington

DOMMETT F
Private   Duke of Cornwall's Light
Infantry

DOWNER Albert Bailey
L. Cpl.   2nd Wiltshire Regiment
Born 2nd June 1889 (Bapt), Charlton
Son of Isaac and Alice Downer

Private Albert Downer

DOWNER Arthur
Sapper   108634
Royal Engineers

DOWNER George E
Private   8752
Animal Veterinary Corps
Entered the War 5th June 1915

DOWNER John F
Sapper   Royal Engineers

DREDGE Bert
Private   2nd Worcester Regiment

DREDGE Bert
Private   29434
Oxfordshire & Buckinghamshire Light Infantry
Son of Walter and Agnes Dredge
Died 9th June 1924, aged 26
Buried in Downton Churchyard

DREDGE Charlie
L. Cpl.   306836
1/8th Royal Warwickshire Regiment

DUFFETT Arthur
Private   87090
Army Service Corps
Son of Henry and Fanny Duffett
Born 8th November 1896 (Bapt), Downton

DUFFETT Charles
Driver   69995
Royal Horse Artillery
Resided Lode Hill

DUFFETT John
L. Cpl.   47022
Machine Gun Corps
Formerly 1st Dragoon Guards 904
Entered the War 11th November 1914

DURDLE Ambrose Samuel
2nd Lieut.   6th Rifle Brigade
Son of Walter Andrew and Jane Durdle
Born 27th September 1896 (Bapt), Downton
Enlisted Wiltshire Regiment, 9th May 1915
Gazetted 20th March 1917

DURDLE Arthur A
Corporal   290782
Middlesex Regiment
Discharged 4th March 1919

EALES A S
Private   12th Gloucester Regiment

EALES A V
Private   Hampshire Regiment

EALES E F
Corporal   Army Service Corps

ELLIOTT Harry
Private   Coldstream Guards
Born 9th April 1899 (Bapt), Downton
Son of James Albert and Mary Elliott
Half brother of William Charles Bundy

FANSTONE Percy
Sapper   66371
Royal Engineers
Entered the War 26th July 1915

FRANCIS Owen Lyall
Major   The Carabiniers
Lived at Hill House, Lode Hill

FULFORD Bertram Henry
Private   10608
Army Cyclist Corps
Born 7th October 1889 (Bapt), Downton
Son of George and Emily Fulford

FULFORD E
Driver   Royal Field Artillery

FULFORD Ernest J
Driver   476
Royal Horse Artillery
Born 30th September 1894 (Bapt), Downton
Brother of Bertram Henry Fulford
Entered the War 25th April 1915

FULFORD Frederick John
Driver   59401
Royal Horse Artillery
Born 16th August 1891 (Bapt), Downton
Son of George and Emily Fulford of The Borough
Qualifying Date 21st May 1915

FUTCHER Albert George 'Bert'
Air Mechanic   Royal Naval Air Service
Born 8th July 1894 (Bapt), Downton
Son of George and Mary Waterman Futcher of Gravel Close

FUTCHER Charles
Private   Duke of Cornwall's Light Infantry

FUTCHER William C
Sergeant   28488
Royal Engineers
Qualifying Date 21st February 1915

FUTCHER William C
Private   30344
7th Somerset Light Infantry
Formerly 29562 Dorset Regiment

GALLUP Henry Curtis
Captain   56th (Wessex) Brigade, Royal Field Artillery (TF)
Born London, 24th October 1874
Mobilised at Salisbury Plain, August 1914
Educated at Eton and Oxford
Married January 1903 to Mary Margaret Whitfield
Resided Wick House until 1906

GILBERT William J
Gunner   RMC

GOWLAND Geoffrey
Captain   Royal Engineers
Son-in-law of Colonel Marriett-Smith of Fairfield House

GRAVES Hon Adolphus Edward Paget
Major   GSO
Born 11th January 1855
Father of Evelyn Paget Graves (killed March 1917)
Died 5th August 1931

GRIFFEN Victor
Sergeant   6th Wiltshire Regiment

GUNSTONE Cecil H MM
Sergeant   10311
1st Wiltshire Regiment

GUNSTONE Percy E
Private   43817
4th Worcestershire Regiment

GWYER Albert Victor
L. Cpl.   16th Royal Welsh Fusiliers
Son of Charles Gwyer
Resided The High Street
Killed in a motorbike accident near Tidworth, 7th December
1927, aged 30
Buried in Downton Churchyard

HARRINGTON A G
Private   East Kent Regiment

HARRINGTON Victor J
Driver   Royal Garrison Artillery

HARRINGTON William H
Bandsman   1/4th Wiltshire Regiment
Son of Mr and Mrs George Harrington of Wick

HARRIS Francis J
2nd Lieut.   Royal Welsh Fusiliers
Resided The Headlands

HARRIS William K
Private   Hampshire Regiment
Prisoner

HART Ernest Harry Iden
Chaplain to the Forces 1917-19
Curate of Downton, 1914-17
Vicar of Wilsford with Woodford 1919-26

HASKELL Henry
Private   7666
1st Dorset Regiment
Entered the War 16th August 1914
Prisoner of War

HATCHER Leonard
1st Driver   56768
25th Brigade, Royal Field Artillery

HATCHER William
L. Cpl.   Army Service Corps

HATTON Charles F
Gunner   Royal Garrison Artillery
Resided The Borough
Father of Aileen Middleton, who helped compile the Downton
book *Reflections*.

HATTON Percy Frank
Private   22253
2nd Wiltshire Regiment
Born 15th August 1897 (Bapt), Downton
Son of Police Sergeant George and Charlotte Elizabeth Hatton
of The Borough
Enlisted October 1915
Wounded and Discharged, 1917

HATTON William T
Sergeant   Royal Marine Artillery

HAYDON John Vincent 'Jack'
L. Cpl.   10505
2nd Wiltshire Regiment
Born 3rd November 1894
Brother of Frank, George and Arthur Ellis Haydon MM
Qualifying Date 4th January 1915
Prisoner of War March–November 1918
Died 17th July 1981

HAYTER Percy W
Private   1st Wiltshire Regiment
Resided The Borough

HAYTER Wilfred Tom
Sergeant   Wiltshire Regiment
Born 24th February 1895 (Bapt),
Downton
Son of Joseph and Rose Jane Hayter

HENDERSON James
Ldg Stoker   Royal Navy

HENNING Bereford DSO
Lieut. Col.   Royal Field Artillery

HOLDEN Walter G
Private   Army Service Corps

HORTON A S J
Sergeant   Royal Flying Corps

HUNT Archibald J W
Private   Canadian F F

IRELAND John D
Private   1st London Scottish Regiment

JACOBS Bertram A
L. Cpl.   7th Worcestershire Regiment

Private Percy Hayter

JONES Alec
CF, RA

JONES C
Tpr   Royal Wiltshire Yeomanary

JONES G E M
Private   Army Service Corps

JONES L
Private   3rd Wiltshire Regiment

JONES Percy M
Sapper   Royal Engineers

JONES Ralph
Air Mechanic   Royal Air Force

JONES S C
Engineer   Royal Navy

JONES Sidney
Electrician

JONES T
Captain   Remount

JONES V A
CERA.   Royal Navy

KENCHINGTON William George
Private   228386
Royal Engineers
Born 23rd June 1889 (Bapt), Downton
Son of Charles and Elizabeth Kenchington
Resided The Borough

KIMBER Ernest W
Private   40th Canadian Regiment
Family home Wick

KING Frank
Private   2nd Wiltshire Regiment

KING James
Sergeant   Royal Marines

KING Tom
Sergeant

KINGSBURY James
Sergeant   Royal Marines

KINGSBURY Nelson Frederick
Gunner   87876
Royal Horse Artillery
Born 12th January 1895 (Bapt), Downton
Son of William and Sarah Bruce Kingsbury of Barford Lane
Entered the War 15th March 1915

LAWES William G
Sergeant   2nd Wiltshire Regiment

LIGHT Reginald Francis
2nd Lieut.   Royal West Surrey Regiment
Formerly 281762 Hampshire Regiment
Born 14th October 1886

LITTLECOTT Bertram L
Gunner   87817
Royal Horse Artillery
Son of Mr and Mrs Littlecott of Long Close
Entered the War 27th April 1915

LYDFORD Frederick Hugh
2nd Lieut.   1st Somerset Light Infantry
Born Sherborne, 14th February 1892
Demobilised 24th October 1919
Killed in motor cycle accident, 19th December 1927
Buried in Downton Churchyard

MAIN Douglas E
Private   520909

Royal Engineers
Formerly 792, 320157 Royal Wiltshire Yeomanry
And 203311 Wiltshire Regiment

MARKS Leonard James
Private   1st Wiltshire Regiment
Born 1st October 1893 (Bapt), Downton
Son of William and Ellen Mary Marks

MARRIOTT SMITH Harry Reginald Walter DSO
Lieut. Col.   Royal Field Artillery
Born 1875
Son of Colonel Marriott-Smith

MARRIOTT SMITH Walter William DSO, CBE
Colonel   7th Wessex Brigade, Royal Field Artillery
Resided Fairfield House
Awarded the CBE for war duties in 1918

MASTERS Bernard
Private   Army Veterinary Corps

MASTERS B G
Corporal   Devon Regiment

MASTERS Herbert W
Sergeant   Royal Flying Corps

MATTHEWS Arthur Bruce
Born 6th July 1879 (Bapt), Downton
Son of Charles and Elizabeth Bruce
Private   Army Ordnance Corps

MATTHEWS Kenneth G
Corporal   1/7th Hampshire Regiment

MIDDLETON Archibald
Sergeant   Royal Engineers

MITCHELL Charles
Private   Army Service Corps

MOODY Edward
Private   2nd Wiltshire Regiment
Resided The Borough

MOODY G A
Private   1st Wiltshire Regiment

MOODY William J
1st Air Mech.   Royal Air Force

MORRIS Samuel Howard
Private   King's Royal Rifle Corps
Born 28ht November 1887 (Bapt), Downton
Died 4th February 1960
Buried at Downton Cemetery

MORRIS Harry Dorin
Corporal   10th Middlesex Regiment
Born 4th June 1893 (Bapt), Downton

MORGAN Robert W
Corporal   Royal Army Medical Corps
Brother of Alfred Ernest Morgan, (killed October 1916)

MOULAND Walter Frank
Driver   Royal Horse Artillery
Enlisted 1917

MUSSELL Archibald John
Private   Leicestershire Regiment
Born 27th December 1891 (Bapt), Downton
Son of John and Elizabeth Mussell

MUSSELL Albert Frank
L. Cpl.   5th Wiltshire Regiment
Son of Mr and Mrs Mark Mussell of Gravel Close

MUSSELL Archie
3rd Air Mech.   Royal Air Force

MUSSELL Henry
Private   2nd Wiltshire Regiment
Brother of Frank Mussell

MUSSELL William
Private   Wiltshire Regiment
Brother of Frank and Harry Mussell

MUSSELWHITE George
Corporal   Army Service Corps

NEWMAN Albert 'Bert'
Private   Army Ordnance Corps
Born 21st June 1896 (Bapt), Downton
Son of George and Fanny (Ellen) Newman of The Borough
Brother of Fred Newman, (killed October 1917)

NEWMAN Charles
Sapper   Royal Engineers
Born 18th September 1898 (Bapt), Downton
Brother of Bert and Will Newman
Invalided out 1917

NEWMAN Frank
Driver   Army Service Corps
Resided The Headlands

NEWMAN Frederick
Private   2/4th Dorset Regiment

NEWMAN L
Private   Army Service Corps

NEWMAN Leonard
Private   14th Worcestershire Regiment

NEWMAN S
Private   Australian Imperial Force

NEWMAN Sidney
Private   Wiltshire Regiment
Invalided out

NEWMAN William DCM, MM
Serg. Major   56744
C/177 Bde, Royal Field Artillery

Private Albert Newman

Born 22nd March 1891 (Bapt), Downton
Brother of Bert and Charlie Newman

NICHOLAS Fred William
Private   5th Wiltshire Regiment
Born 7th March 1897 (Bapt), Downton
Son of Alfred and Emma Jane Nicholas of The Borough
Discharged, wounded

NICHOLAS Philip A
Private   Army Service Corps

NICKLEN Henry A
Private   Wiltshire Regiment

OLIPHANT J R
Private   Devon Regiment

PADDOCK Reginald
Private   Army Service Corps, Mechanical Transport
Born East Dean, 5th March 1887
Attested 10th December 1915
Discharged 30th November 1919
Married Evelyn Light, December 1912
Died 5th October 1971 at Vine Cottage, Lode Hill

PALMER Bertram T
Private   Duke of Cornwall's Light Infantry

PALMER Clement G
Sergeant   Royal Garrison Artillery
Son of George Palmer of Lode Hill

PALMER George Ewart
Private   Royal Garrison Artillery
Brother of Clem Palmer

PALMER O
Private   Royal Wiltshire Yeomanry

PALMER Sidney H
Private   1/4th Wiltshire Regiment

PARBERY Edward
2nd Air Mech.   Royal Flying Corps
Died 27th August 1939 aged 62
Buried in Downton Churchyard

PENNY Stanley
Stoker   Royal Navy

PENNY S G
Private   2/4th Wiltshire Regiment

PHILLIPS A E L
Private   Wiltshire Regiment

PHILLIPS P H V
Gunner   Royal Field Artillery

PHILLIPS W L
Private   Animal Veterinary Corps

PHILPOTT Reginald
Private   Army Service Corps, Mechanical Transport

PIKE A Charles MM
Sgt. Major   44338
75th Field Company, Royal Engineers
Resided Wick

PIKE William A
Private   2nd Wiltshire Regiment

PLASKET Walter Harold
Private   36555
Machine Gun Corps
Born 11th June 1896
Son of Edward and Sarah Rebecca Plaskett
of High Street
Enlisted Hampshire Regiment, 5th
November 1915
Transferred to Machine Gun Corps, 12th May 1916
Arrived in France 12th August 1916
Transferred to Royal Engineers 1st May 1918
Died 14th November 1964
Buried at Downton Cemetery

Private W. H. Plaskett

POPE William
Baker   Merchant Service

PORTER Frank J G
Private   2nd Dorset Regiment

PRATER Charles
Private   2/5th Gloucestershire Regiment
Resided Barford Park

PRATER William
Private   V Dragoon Guards

PRICE George H
Serg. Major   Army Service Corps

Lance Corporal
Charlie Senior

READ Cecil J
Corporal   Signal Section, Royal Engineers

READ W G
Corporal   Oxford and Bucks Light Infantry

RIDOUT Sidney
Private   204080
6th Wiltshire Regiment
Prisoner of War March-November 1918
Resided The Borough

ROSE Charles J
Sergeant   FAC

ROSE Ernest W
Signaller   Royal Garrison Artillery

SALMON George Edward
Chaplain to the Forces
Born 14th April 1878
Son of the Rev Prebendary R I Salmon
Educated at Winchester and Keeble College, Oxford
Vicar of Downton 1917-1922
Served in France and Germany 1918-19

Died 4th November 1922
Buried in Downton Churchyard

SENIOR Charles
L. Cpl.   1/4th Wiltshire Regiment

SENIOR William
L. Cpl.   1/4th Dorset Regiment
Born 6th December 1891 (Bapt),
Downton

SHERGOLD V
1st Air Mech.   Royal Air Force

Lance Corporal
William Senior

SHORTT Sansmare Dobree
Major   1st Norfolk Regiment
Resided The Warren

SKILBECK John T
L. Cpl.   West Yorkshire Regiment

SMITH Alfred
Co. QM Sgt.   12th East Surrey
Regiment

SMITH Bertram
Private   21104
Animal Veterinary Corps
Born 3rd April 1894, at Waterside
Son of John and Rosa Smith
Brother of Ernest Smith, (killed June
1915)
Died 22nd October 1969
The grandfather of this book's author.

SMITH Robert
Private   3446
19th London Regiment
Born Downton, 28th December 1891
Brother of Ernest and Bert Smith
Entered the War 10th March 1915
Died at Portsmouth, 6th October 1972

Private Bertram Smith

SMITH Walker
2nd Air Mech.   Royal Air Force

SMITH William
Corporal   Royal Air Force

SNOOK Frank
Leading Seaman Signaller, Royal Navy

SPREADBURY E F
Private   Wiltshire Regiment

STRETCH Lewis George MC
2nd Lieut.   Machine Gun Corps
Formerly Private 104801 Machine Gun Corps
and 1292 Wiltshire Yeomanry
Son of Mr C. G. Stretch Stationmaster at Downton, 1905-14
Born 17th June 1891
Educated at Bishop Wordsworth's School, Salisbury
Entered the War 3rd December 1915

STONE Charles J
Private   4th Wiltshire Regiment

STREET Bertram T
Private   24088, 202011
2/4th Wiltshire Regiment

STREET Ernest
Gunner   193420
Royal Garrison Artillery

SWANBOROUGH Charles
Private   Army Ordnance Corps
Brother of John Edwin Swanborough DCM,
(killed July 1916)
Resided Salisbury Road

TAYLOR Bertram F
Gunner   Royal Garrison Artillery

TAYLOR John
Store Keeper   Mercantile Marines
Born Southampton, 1885
Resided Barford Lane

TAYLOR William E
Private   1st Wiltshire Regiment
Prisoner of War

THWAITES E B
Private   1/7th Hampshire Regiment

THUGOLD Vincent
Air Mechanic   Royal Air Force

TRAPNEL L
Private   Royal Marine Light Infantry

VIVIAN Charles
Co. Sergt.   1st Dorset Regiment

VIVIAN Frederick W DCM
Co. Sergt. Major   4858
1st Dorset Regiment
Brother of Charles Vivian
Entered the War 16th August 1914

WARNER Edward
Able Seaman   Royal Naval Division

WARNER James
Private   Canadian Expeditionary Force

WEEKS Charles
Private   Warwickshire Regiment
Resided The Borough

WHATLEY W G
Private   Wiltshire Regiment

WHITCHER Charles H
Private   2nd Wiltshire Regiment

WHITCHER George J
Sergeant   3rd Dorset Regiment

WHITCHER Harry T
Private   Australian Imperial Force

WHITE Bernard
Stoker   Royal Navy

WILLIAMS G
Private   5th Wiltshire Regiment

WILLIS George
Private   Hampshire Regiment

WINTON James
Private   Canadians

WITT Arthur H
Private   Labour Batt.

WITT Charles
Sapper   Royal Engineers

WOODFORD Andrew J
Gunner   Royal Garrison Artillery
Resided Lode Hill

WRIGHTSON Archibald Ingram 'Archie' MC
Lieutenant   7th Canadian Infantry Battalion
Born Downton, 1882
Son of Professor John Wrightson of Downton Agricultural
College
Died 1953

WRIGHTSON Edmund Gilchrist 'Eddie' DSO
Lt. Cmmnder   Royal Navy
Born 1879
Brother of Archie Wrightson MC
Died 1953

WROTTESLEY Francis Robert DSO
Commander   Royal Navy
Born 1877
Son of the Rev F J Wrottesley
Married Lelia Staveley
Joined the Navy in 1893; Sub-Lieutenant 1897; Lieutenant
1899; Commander 1909.
Invalided out with rank of Captain, 1919
Saw service in the North Sea, Egypt and Mesopotamia in the
Great War
Three times mentioned in despatches.
Resided Wick Lane

WYNDHAM Guy Richard 'Dick' MC
Captain   King's Royal Rifle Corps
Born 1896
Brother of George Heremon Wydham (killed March 1915)
Died 1948

WYNDHAM Guy Percy CBE
Colonel   GSO
Born 1865
Son of George Wyndham
Father of George Heremon and Guy Richard Wyndham
Married Minnie Brooke, 1892
Resided at Charford Manor
Died 1941

One owes respect to the living;
But to the dead one owes nothing but the truth.

Voltaire (1694-1778)

Counting the Cost

Having recorded Downton's Roll of Honour comprising the names of servicemen who survived and those who died in the Great War, it becomes painfully clear that a high proportion of local men paid the ultimate price of war. The chilling figure of one in five killed is reached by counting the forty-four names of the fallen on the War Memorial and comparing this total with the names recorded on the commemorative boards inside the Memorial Hall, which is headed:

Below are the names of the men of Downton who went forth to fight, 1914–19

The boards list 227 men who served in the war, including those who died and from this comparison the disturbing ratio of one in five becomes evident. Yet is it really that straightforward? The commemorative boards in the Memorial Hall were added in 1922 being generously donated to the village by Mrs Carver of The Moot. By then the war had been over for four years. Several families had moved away, so it is inevitable that there are omissions and mistakes. Noticeably, among the several omissions there is no record of Company Sergeant Major Frederick W. Vivian DCM of the Dorset Regiment.

Another Roll of Honour survives in Downton – the two framed lists penned in neat copperplate handwriting and displayed on either side of the War Memorial in Downton Parish Church. This Roll was drawn up by the Downton

Women's Institute in 1918, following a house-to-house canvass. It is a snapshot of Downton men fighting in the war at that particular time, whereas Mrs Carver's commemorative boards were intended as a permanent historic record.

A comparison of the two lists has been used as the basis of the Roll of Honour recorded in this book, together with other names found in the Downton news sections of the *Salisbury and Winchester Journal* and the *Western Gazette*. This combined list amounts to over 240 names, excluding those who died, which in turn produces a similar figure of two in eleven killed.

The figure of one in five does not include the additional names to be found in the volumes of *Soldiers Who Died*. If these men are taken into account, the calculations produce the ratio of one in four. In truth the precise figure can never be ascertained. On the one hand, the proportion killed is increased by names from *Soldiers Who Died* who might have only had tenuous connections with Downton. On the other it is decreased by the inclusion of the names of men who served in this country and never saw action abroad. Therefore, perhaps the best approximation as to the proportion of Downton's men and officers who were killed in the First World War is that for every nine who served in the armed forces two of them died an untimely death.

Epilogue

On Tuesday 5th February 1918, 2nd Air Mechanic Edward Parbery of the Royal Flying Corps was seriously injured whilst starting the propeller of an aeroplane at Tidworth. The accident caused severe head injuries and laceration to the brain. Before joining the armed services Parbery had been the Verger at Downton Parish church.

For over 21 years Parbery was a patient at the old Roundway Hospital, Devizes. He never once recognised any of those dear to him, although he was frequently visited by his family.

The tragic misery of his injuries bridged the gap between the two major conflicts of the twentieth century. Parbery died on Sunday 27th August 1939 and was buried in Downton Church-yard on the following Wednesday. By the time his funeral was reported in the *Salisbury Journal*, Britain was again at war with Germany.

2nd Air Mechanic Edward Parbery
of the Royal Flying Corps, 1916

Appendix I: Chronology of the Fallen

28 August 1914	George Henry Hobbs
20 September 1914	Bob Bundy
24 October 1914	Walter Mouland
6 November 1914	Reuben Batchelor
17 November 1914	Frederick Charles Keeley
13 March 1915	William Mitchell
24 March 1915	George Heremon Wyndham
13 May 1915	Arthur Keeley
8 June 1915	Ernest Smith
10 August 1915	George Elliott
13 August 1915	Harry M Winton
26 September 1915	Fred Penn Moody
28 September 1915	George Forder
8 October 1915	Edward St. Laurent Bonvalot
11 February 1916	Harry William Noble
23 March 1916	William George Haydon
25 April 1916	William Ghazi Kingsbury
1 July 1916	Aubrey Greville Newton Dickenson
1 July 1916	Edwin John Swanborough DCM
2 July 1916	Henry Whittaker Coombs
2 July 1916	Arthur Ernest Viney
8 July 1916	Ralph Bundy
29 October 1916	Alfred Ernest Morgan
6 March 1917	Evelyn Paget Graves
11 April 1917	Ernest James Batchelor
8 August 1917	Arthur Thomas Jolliffe
28 September 1917	Percy Moody
6 October 1917	Arthur Amyot Steward
22 October 1917	Fred Newman
21 March 1918	Edward James Blake
21 March 1918	William Alfred Gunstone

22 March 1918	Frederick James Bennett
30 May 1918	Frederick William Bailey
30 May 1918	Charles Bishop
19 September 1918	Albert George Kimberley Musselwhite
25 September 1918	Henry Senior
1 October 1918	Albert Henry Sheppard
11 November 1918	Armistice
29 November 1918	Prince Leopold Eastman
8 January 1919	Albert Edward Patience
23 February 1919	Geoffrey Thomas Hunt
31 March 1919	Arthur Ellis Haydon MM
4 September 1919	Percy John Aylett
22 September 1919	Reginald James Nicklen
Not yet known	Frederick Batchelor

Remembrance Sunday, 12th November 2000. The Downton Band leads the procession from the Memorial Hall to St Laurence's Church. The thatched cottage was the family home of one of the victims of the war, Fred Newman. Two members of the Band – Ralph Bundy and Harry Winton – were also killed in the war.

Appendix II: Gallantry Awards

The Downton Servicemen listed below were awarded Honours for Gallantry during the First World War.

DCM   BUNDY William Charles
Sergeant, 1st Wiltshire Regiment

NEWMAN William
Battery Sergeant Major, Royal Field Artillery

SWANBOROUGH Edwin John
Lance Corporal, 2nd Border Regiment

VIVIAN Frederick W
Company Sergeant Major, 1st Dorset Regiment

DSO   DICKENSON Lenthall Greville
Major, Senior Chaplain to the Forces

HENNING Beresford
Lieutenant Colonel, Royal Field Artillery

MARRIOTT SMITH Harry Reginald Walter
Lieutenant Colonel, Royal Field Artillery

WRIGHTSON Edmund Gilchrist
Lieutenant Commander, Royal Navy

WROTTESLEY Francis Robert
Commander, Royal Navy

MM   GUNSTONE Cecil H
Private, 1st Wiltshire Regiment

HAYDON Arthur Ellis
Sergeant, 12th Battalion, King's Royal Rifle Corps

NEWMAN William
Battery Sergeant Major, Royal Field Artillery

PIKE A Charles
Sergeant, 75th Field Company, Royal Engineers

MC   DICKENSON Edward Newton
Captain, King's Royal Rifle Corps

STRETCH Lewis George
2nd Lieutenant, Machine Gun Corps

WRIGHTSON Archibald Ingram
Lieutenant, 7th Canadian Infantry Battalion

WYNDHAM Guy Richard
Captain, King's Royal Rifle Corps

DCM   Distinguished Conduct Medal

For non-commissioned officers and men for 'individual acts of conduct in the field'

DSO   Distinguished Service Order

British military order awarded to officers. Officers could be nominated only after their names have appeared in despatches 'for meritorious or distinguished service in the field or before the enemy.'

MC   Military Cross

Instituted in 1915 to reward meritorious service, such as may not be deemed the same standard necessary for the DSO.

MM   Military Medal

Instituted in April 1916 for non-commissioned officers, men (and women) for 'individual or associated acts of bravery on the recommendation of a commander-in-chief in the field.'

Appendix III: Graves and Memorials to the Fallen in Downton

The following seven military graves in Downton Churchyard are of local servicemen who were in the forces during the Great War.

Names on the Downton War Memorial:

315037 Lance Cpl.
P.J. Aylett
Middlesex Regiment
4th September 1919
Age 22

Till the Day Breaks

R3434 Sergeant
A.E. Haydon MM
Kings Royal Rifle Corps
31st March 1919
Age 26

He Rose Responsive
To the Call
He Left His Task
His Gains His All

5054 Private
W.G. Haydon
Hampshire Regiment
23rd March 1916
Age 26

Peace Perfect Peace

23638 Private
G.T. Hunt
Wiltshire Regiment
23rd February 1919
Age 22

The Path of Glory
Was the Way of Glory

Names on the Morgan's Vale and Woodfalls War Memorial:

S12218 Private
F.J. Bettridge
Argyll & Sutherland Highrs.
27th March 1916
Age 31

Rest In Peace

L. Green
Stoker 2nd Class R.N. K52679
HMS Victory
12th September 1918
Age 18

Private Frank John Bettridge of the Argyll and Sutherland Highlanders was the son of John Thomas and Harriet Bettridge of 'Argyle', Morgan's Vale.

Stoker Leonard Green was the son of Frank and Elizabeth Green of Slab Lane. He died at Haslar Hospital of double pneumonia, having joined the Royal Navy only six weeks before his death. Leonard's elder brother Gunner 87818 Frank Green of the Royal Horse Artillery had died of wounds in France in March 1917.

The Military Grave of a Downton Great War Serviceman who died post 1919:

PO/15940 Corporal
R.H. Durdle
Royal Marine Light Infantry
13th April 1921
Age 27

Till the Day Breaks

Apart from the commemorative plaques in the Baptist Church, there are at least three other Memorials to Downton servicemen who were killed overseas during the War. Each appears as part of an inscription to relatives of the deceased serviceman.

Downton Churchyard:

In
Ever Loving Memory of
William Charles Smith
Who Died 13th February 1944, aged 55
And Sergeant Ernest Smith 1st Wilts Regt.
Killed in Action B.E.F. France June 1915, aged 28
Beloved sons of John and Rosa Smith
Free from Sorrow, Grief and Pain
In God's Own Time We Shall Meet Again

Downton Cemetery:

In	In
Loving Memory of	Loving Memory of
Alice Bailey	Martha Beloved Wife of
Who Passed Away	George Bundy
Aug 3rd 1946	Died June 11 1943
Aged 73 Years	Aged 80 Years
Also	At Rest
Her Beloved Husband	And of Their Son
George,	Ralph Bundy
Who Passed Away	Pte. 2nd Wilts Regt.
April 8th 1954	Died of Wounds in France
Aged 86 Years	July 1916
And Their Beloved Son	Aged 23 Years
Pte. Frederick William	Also of the Above
Gloucester Regt.	George Bundy
Killed in Action 1918	Died Sept 13 1948
Aged 19 Years	Aged 85 Years
	Reunited

Private F. W. Bailey.

Appendix IV: Other Local War Memorials

It is interesting to record the names on the War Memorials of the Wiltshire villages neighbouring Downton.

CHARLTON ALL SAINTS

The War Memorial at Charlton takes the form of a lych gate entrance to the churchyard. The names of the fallen for Standlynch and Charlton are carved in wood beneath a crucifix in the gable of the gate. The other side of the gable on the church side of the lych gate carries the names of six service personnel who died in the Second World War.

'Greater Love Hath No Man Than This'

In Memory of those fallen in the
Great War 1914-19

I Elliott	C Palmer	C S Street
S Elliott	F Perry	J L Street
A Ellis	H H Phillips	G Tanner
W J Frampton	V C Sheppard	L J Wort
P R Gould	E J Street	A Wort
W Litten	C G Street	

MORGAN'S VALE & WOODFALLS

This prominent local landmark stands at the junction of Bowers Hill, Kiln Lane and The Ridge at Morgan's Vale. It takes the form of a typical village War Memorial in the shape of a cross and commemorates the nineteen servicemen who died. The memorial stands next to a flag pole, in the centre of a grassed area planted with trees. It also includes the names of the fallen from the Slab Lane area of Downton. There are the names of nine Second World War dead and an officer killed in Palestine in 1946.

In Memory of Our Glorious Dead
Who fell in the Great War 1914-18

Arney R F	Green F	Taunton O H
Browne L	Green L	Warner B
Beauchamp W	Hickman S W	Wort H J
Bettridge F J	Littlecott H	Green G
Cave A	Parrott F H	Blandford A E
Elkins G	Parsons F J	
Frampton W J	Sharp F G	

Private Frank Green and Stoker Leonard Green were from Slab Lane, their details have been given in Appendix III. Sergeant PO/15611 William Beauchamp was also from Slab Lane, the son of William and Elizabeth Beauchamp. Sergeant Beauchamp served in the Royal Marine Light Infantry and was killed in action during the Gallipoli campaign on 6th May 1915. He was 21. Beauchamp is commemorated on the Helles Memorial, Turkey, Panel Reference No. 2 to 7.

REDLYNCH WAR MEMORIAL

The Redlynch War Memorial is situated in Quavey Road, almost opposite the junction of Chapel Road and takes the form of a Shrine. It contains the names of nineteen servicemen from the village who died in the Great War, together with a roll of honour of 167 men who served in the war. The Memorial also lists those who died in the Second World War.

This Shrine was erected to the
GLORY OF GOD
and in Memory of those
who died for
and served their country in
The Great War

Presented to the Parish of Redlynch by
George and William Eyre-Matcham 19.7.1919

FOR KING & COUNTRY
THE HERIOC DEAD

Greater Love Hath No Man than this

Brown A E
Card D
Fowler G
Frampton N W J
Hand W
Hiscock A
Lane N W

Long B
Marsh D
Marsh W
Moody W
Mouland W
Newman W C
Pilgrim C

Ransom R H
Shelly E G
Shergold A B
Wilkins A C
Withers E

Redlynch Roll of Honour

Adcock E
Adcock H
Adcock H
Adlam C W
Atkey B
Bailey H
Bailey B
Barter F
Beauchamp L G
Bell F
Blake G F
Blake F W
Blake W
Brewer H
Brown G E J
Brown C P
Brown H C
Brown H W
Brown L F
Bryant W F
Bryant W C
Bryant W E
Bryant H P
Bunday A W
Chandler C F
Chandler D C

Chandler H F
Coles H F
Cook W J
Crook A H
Crouch E E W
Deacon E
Deacon C
Dear A G
Downer J F
Dunn C
Emms
Emms W
Elkins G
Faithful W F
Fiford
Ford C
Forder F
Forder W
Fry W C
Fulford A
Fowler R
Genge L
Gray E S
Gray R G
Gray L S
Green H A

Green R H
Hand F S
Hand H G
Hand H J
Hand H B
Hand H W
Hand H C
Harris F
Harris R
Harris S C
Harrison W L
Harwood W F
Hiscock T J
Hiscock K H
Hobbs J
Ings R C
Ings F G
Jones W H
Jones F
Keats J
Kerley C
King A M
King W G
Lane A
Lane E W
Lane F

Lane E
Lane W G
Lane A C
Lane R L
Long S
Long C
Marsh E
Matcham G Eyre
Matcham J
Matcham W
Mitchell F
Mitchell B W
Mitchell S F
Moody J
Moody W
Moody F
Moody W
Moody L F
Mowland H
Mowland
Nation L J
Newman A F
Newman B S
Newman H W
Newman A J
Newman H W
Newman C J
Newman F
Newman L F
Newman P F

Newman S G
Newman B
Newman J
Newman P
Newman P G
Newman I
Noble R I
Noble A E
Payne H D
Phillimore E
Phillimore A E
Phillimore T
Pickett W H H
Plaskett W G
Plaskett J
Plaskett E F
Plaskett P J
Pressey F
Prince B
Quinton E C
Roberts W A
Scovell C F
Scutt A F
Shelley F F
Shelley W C
Sheppeard J F
Shergold F J
Skeates R
Snelgar J T
Snelgar E E

Snelgrove C
Snelgrove L M
Snelgrove V
Snelgrove W J
Stacey C F N
Stanley F
Stanley H
Stanley R
Stevens A
Stone B G
Swanton H F
Tanner G
Targett E H
Terry B
Vivian H C
Warner E
Warner S
Warner K C
Warner S W
Webb B G
Weeks A
Willis W E
Wilkins B W
Wilkins T G
Wilkins C
Wilkins W
Wilkins B
Wilkins A J
Wort W

Select Bibliography

A list of the main primary source material used to compile this book is given below.

Local Studies Department, Salisbury Central Library
Trade Directories: Brown's 1912; Kelly's 1911, 1915, 1923.
Downton news in the *Salisbury and Winchester Journal* 1900-1925

Wiltshire County Records Office, Trowbridge
Bratton Baptist Church: Pastorate Correspondence, 1900-70.
Downton Baptist Church: Deacon's Meeting Minute Book.
Downton Parish Church: Baptism Records 1870-901; Parish Magazines 1885-97; Vestry Minute Book 1901-78; Papers relating to Church House, Downton, 1903-55; Register of Services 1910-20; Correspondence relating to Downton Churchyard.
Downton Parish Council: Minute Books, 1894-1972; Parish Meetings Minute Book, 1894-1933; Parish Lighting, Allotments and Public Hall Minute Book; Letters relating to Downton Memorial Hall, 1915-33.
Downton Women's Institute: Minute Books, 1916-27; Downton W.I. Scrapbook, 1956.
Salisbury Rural District Council: Minute Books, 1914-20; Housing Committee Minutes, 1920-22.
Southern Tanning Company Ltd: Correspondence 1901-17; Directors' Minute Book 1913-20.
Standlynch-with-Charlton Parish Council: Minute Books 1897-1928; Parish Meetings Minute Book, 1897-1928.

British Newspaper Library, Colindale, London NW9
The War Illustrated
Western Gazette (Berks, Wilts and Hants edition) 1914-1921

Family Records Centre, London EC1
Census Returns 1881, 1891
Indexes of Births, Marriages and Deaths
Index of Marine Deaths

Imperial War Museum Archive, London SE1
Airmen Who Died in the Great War
Officers Who Died in the Great War
Soldiers Who Died in the Great War
Various Regimental Histories and War Diaries

Public Record Office, Kew
Gallantry Award Index; *London Gazette* Index; Medal Rolls
   Indexes; Merchant Navy Medal Index; Royal Marine Attesta-
   tion and Service Records.
Surviving Army and RFC Service Records – Officers: A C
   Bonvalot WO339 21042; E St. L Bonvalot WO339 26358; F
   E Carver WO374 12749; H W Coombs WO339 22304; A G
   N Dickenson WO339 4353; E N Dickenson WO339 30695; H
   C Gallup WO339 26283; The Hon. A E P Graves WO339
   4000; E P Graves WO339 7780; R F Light WO374 42124; F
   H Lydford WO339 121035; A A Steward WO339 44387; L G
   Stretch WO339 89455; O Taunton WO374 67082; Rev L G
   Trotman-Dickenson WO374 69555; G H Wyndham WO339
   22790.
Surviving Army and FRC Service Records – Men: Various
   papers to be found amongst the 'burnt documents' WO363
   and servicemen discharged to pension WO364.

Approximately 72,000 Indian soldiers were killed in the Great War.

INDEX

The index excludes the pages of the Downton Roll of Honour.

**Your silent tents of green
We deck with fragrant flowers;
Yours has the suffering been,
The memory shall be ours.**

Henry Wadsworth Longfellow (1807–1882), *Decoration Day*